Confederation, Constitution, and Early National Period, 1781-1815

E. James Ferguson

Goldentree Bibliographies
in American History

Confederation, Constitution, and Early National Period, 1781-1815

GOLDENTREE BIBLIOGRAPHIES
In American History
under the series editorship of
Arthur S. Link

WASHINGTON

Confederation, Constitution, and Early National Period, 1781-1815

compiled by

E. James Ferguson

Queens College
City University of New York

WITHDRAWN

AHM Publishing Corporation
Northbrook, Illinois 60062

Copyright © 1975

AHM PUBLISHING CORPORATION

All rights reserved

This book, or parts thereof, must not be
used or reproduced in any manner without
written permission. For information address
the publisher, AHM PUBLISHING
CORPORATION, 1500 Skokie Boulevard,
Northbrook, Illinois 60062.

ISBN: 0-88295-534-9

Library of Congress Card Number: 74-76969

Burgess

Z

1238
.F46
c. 2

PRINTED IN THE UNITED STATES OF AMERICA

715

Contents

CONTENTS

CONTENTS

CONTENTS

Editor's Foreword

GOLDENTREE BIBLIOGRAPHIES IN AMERICAN HISTORY are designed to provide students, teachers, and librarians with ready and reliable guides to the literature of American History in all its remarkable scope and variety. Volumes in the series cover comprehensively the major periods in American history, while additional volumes are devoted to all important subjects.

Goldentree Bibliographies attempt to steer a middle course between the brief list of references provided in the average textbook and the long bibliography in which significant items are often lost in the sheer number of titles listed. Each bibliography is, therefore, selective, with the sole criterion for choice being the significance—and not the age—of any particular work. The result is bibliographies of all works, including journal articles and doctoral dissertations, that are still useful, without bias in favor of any particular historiographical school.

Each compiler is a scholar long associated, both in research and teaching, with the period or subject of his volume. All compilers have not only striven to accomplish the objective of this series but have also cheerfully adhered to a general style and format. However, each compiler has been free to define his field, make his own selections, and work out internal organization as the unique demands of his period or subject have seemed to dictate.

The single great objective of *Goldentree Bibliographies in American History* will have been achieved if these volumes help researchers and students to find their way to the significant literature of American history.

Arthur S. Link

Preface

A bibliography reflects current interpretation and new research.
This one also tries to express the expanded range of history, as now
conceived, and the interests of contemporary students. Many of the
works cited are relevant to more than one topic; but, to avoid
endless repetition, cross-references have been held to a minimum in
the expectation that subjects will be approached under a variety of
headings. One principle of selection has been availability—the
choice in most instances of works issued or reprinted in the last few
decades. For this reason, too, unpublished dissertations have been
omitted. Anthologies and "problems" books have not been in-
cluded unless they contain material that is unusual or hard to find.

E. James Ferguson

Abbreviations

Ag Hist	Agricultural History
Ala Hist Q	Alabama Historical Quarterly
Ala Rev	Alabama Review
Am Anthro	American Anthropologist
Amer	Americana
Am Hist Rev	American Historical Review
Am J Int Law	American Journal of International Law
Am J Leg Hist	American Journal of Legal History
Am Jew Archiv	American Jewish Archives
Am Neptune	American Neptune
Am Poli Sci Rev	American Political Science Review
Am Q	American Quarterly
Am Sch	American Scholar
Ann Assn Am Geog	Annals, Association of American Geographers
Ann Med Hist	Annals of Medical History
Ann Rep Am Hist Assn	American Historical Association, Annual Report
Antioch Rev	Antioch Review
Ark Hist Q	Arkansas Historical Quarterly
Atl Mo	Atlantic Monthly
Bull Bus Hist Soc	Bulletin, Business Historical Society
Bull Hist Med	Bulletin of the History of Medicine. (Title varies.)
Bull NY Publ Lib	Bulletin, New York Public Library
Bur Am Ethno Bull	Bureau of American Ethnology, Bulletin
Bus Hist Rev	Business History Review. (Title varies.)
Calif Hist Soc Q	California Historical Society Quarterly
Can J Econ Pol Sci	Canadian Journal of Economic and Political Science
Cent Rev	Centennial Review
Chron Okla	Chronicles of Oklahoma
Church Hist	Church History
Chym	Chymia
Coll Mass Hist Soc	Collections, Massachusetts Historical Society
C W Hist	Civil War History
Col Law Rev	Columbia Law Review
Comp Stud Soc Hist	Comparative Studies in History and Society
Conn Hist Soc Bull	Connecticut Historical Society Bulletin
Cotton Hist Rev	Cotton History Review
Daed	Daedalus
Del Hist	Delaware History
Early Am Lit	Early American Literature
Econ	Economica
Econ Hist Rev	Economic History Review
Essex Inst Hist Coll	Essex Institute Historical Collections

ABBREVIATIONS

Eth	Ethics. (Title varies.)
Ethnohist	Ethnohistory
Explo Entrep Hist	Explorations in Entrepreneurial History
Filson Club Hist Q	Filson Club Historical Quarterly
Fla Hist Q	Florida Historical Quarterly
Ga Hist Q	Georgia Historical Quarterly
Ga Rev	Georgia Review
Geog Rev	Geographical Review
Great Plains J	Great Plains Journal
Har Bus Rev	Harvard Business Review
Har Law Rev	Harvard Law Review
His-Am Hist Rev	Hispanic-American Historical Review
Hist	Historian
Hist Bull	Historical Bulletin. (Title varies.)
Hist Educ Q	History of Education Quarterly
Hist Mag P E Ch	Historical Magazine of the Protestant Episcopal Church
Hist N H	Historical New Hampshire
Hist Today	History Today
Huntington Lib Q	Huntington Library Quarterly
Ind Mag Hist	Indiana Magazine of History
Ind U Stud Am Hist	Indiana University Studies in American History
Inter-Am Econ Affairs	Inter-American Economic Affairs
Int Rev Soc Hist	International Review of Social History
Iowa J Hist Pol	Iowa Journal of History and Politics
J Abnormal Soc Psych	Journal of Abnormal and Social Psychology
J Amer Hist	Journal of American History
J Am Stud	Journal of American Studies
J Econ Bus Hist	Journal of Economic and Business History
J Econ Hist	Journal of Economic History
J Heredity	Journal of Heredity
J Hist Ideas	Journal of the History of Ideas
J Ill State Hist Soc	Journal of the Illinois State Historical Society
J Lancaster Co Hist Soc	Journal of the Lancaster County Historical Society
J L I Hist	Journal of Long Island History
J Miss Hist	Journal of Mississippi History
J Mod Hist	Journal of Modern History
J Neg Hist	Journal of Negro History
J Pol	Journal of Politics
J Pol Econ	Journal of Political Economy
J Presby Hist Soc	Journal of the Presbyterian Historical Society
J Pub Law	Journal of Public Law
J S Hist	Journal of Southern History
J Soc Hist	Journal of Social History
Labor Hist	Labor History
La Hist	Louisiana History
La Hist Q	Louisiana Historical Quarterly
La Stud	Louisiana Studies
Mar Mirror	Mariner's Mirror
Md Hist Mag	Maryland Historical Magazine
Mich Hist	Michigan History

ABBREVIATIONS

Mid-Am	Mid-America
Midcont Am Stud J	Midcontinental American Studies Journal
Mid W J	Midwest Journal
Mid W J Pol Sci	Midwest Journal of Political Science
Mil Affairs	Military Affairs
Mil Hist Econ	Military Historian and Economist
Miss Val Hist Rev	Mississippi Valley Historical Review
Mo Hist Rev	Missouri Historical Review
N C Hist Rev	North Carolina Historical Review
Neb Hist	Nebraska History
Negro Hist Bull	Negro History Bulletin
N Eng Q	New England Quarterly
N Eng Soc Stud Bull	New England Social Studies Bulletin
N J Hist	New Jersey History
N M Hist Rev	New Mexico Historical Review
N Y Hist	New York History
N Y Hist Soc Q	New York Historical Society Quarterly
Ohio Arch Hist Q	Ohio Archaeological and Historical Quarterly
Ohio Hist	Ohio History
Ohio Hist Q	Ohio Historical Quarterly
Pac Hist Rev	Pacific Historical Review
Pac N W Q	Pacific Northwest Quarterly
Pa Hist	Pennsylvania History
Pa Mag Hist Biog	Pennsylvania Magazine of History and Biography
Paps Am Hist Assn	Papers, American Historical Association
Perspectives Am Hist	Perspectives in American History
Pol Sci Q	Political Science Quarterly
Proc Am Ant Soc	Proceedings, American Antiquarian Society
Proc Am Phil Soc	Proceedings, American Philosophical Society
Proc Mass Hist Soc	Proceedings, Massachusetts Historical Society
Proc Miss Val Hist Assn	Proceedings, Mississippi Valley Historical Association
Proc N J Hist Soc	Proceedings, New Jersey Historical Society
Proc U S Nav Inst	Proceedings, United States Naval Institute
Pub Am Econ Assn	Publications, American Economic Association
Pub Am Jew Hist Soc	Publications, American Jewish Historical Society
Publ Col Soc Mass	Publications, Colonial Socety of Massachusetts
Pub S Hist Assn	Publications, Southern Historical Association
Q J Econ	Quarterly Journal of Economics
Q J N Y Hist Assn	Quarterly Journal, New York Historical Association
Rec Am Cath Hist Soc Phil	Records, American Catholic Historical Society of Philadelphia
Reg Ky Hist Soc	Register of the Kentucky Historical Society
Rev Pol	Review of Politics
R I Hist	Rhode Island History
S Atl Q	South Atlantic Quarterly
S C Hist Mag	South Carolina Historical Magazine. (Title varies.)
Sci Mo	Scientific Monthly

ABBREVIATIONS

S Econ J	Southern Economic Journal
Smith Col Stud Hist	Smith College Studies in History
Smithsonian J Hist	Smithsonian Journal of History
Soc Res	Social Research
Soc Serv Rev	Social Service Review
Soc Stud	Social Studies
S Q	Southern Quarterly
Stud Soc Sci (Ill)	Studies in the Social Sciences, University of Illinois
S W Hist Q	Southwestern Historical Quarterly
Tasks Econ Hist	Tasks of Economic History
Tech Cult	Technology and Culture
Tech Rev	Technology Review
Tenn Hist Q	Tennessee Historical Quarterly
Texas Law Rev	Texas Law Review
Trans Conn Acad Art Sci	Transactions, Connecticut Academy of Arts and Sciences
U S Cath Hist Soc Rec Stud	U. S. Catholic Historical Society, Historical Records and Studies
Va Law Rev	Virginia Law Review
Va Mag Hist Biog	Virginia Magazine of History and Biography
Va Q Rev	Virginia Quarterly Review
Vt Hist	Vermont History
Vt Q	Vermont Quarterly
Wel Rev	Welfare in Review
W Hist Q	Western Historical Quarterly
Wis Mag Hist	Wisconsin Magazine of History
Wm Mar Q	William and Mary Quarterly
Worc Hist Soc Pub	Worcester Historical Society Publications
W Pa Hist Mag	Western Pennsylvania Historical Magazine
W Pol Q	Western Political Quarterly
W Va Hist	West Virginia History
Yale Law J	Yale Law Journal
Yale Law Rev	Yale Law Review
Yale Rev	Yale Review

NOTE: Cross-references are to item numbers. Items marked by a dagger (†) are available in paperback edition at the time this bibliography goes to press. The publisher and compiler invite suggestions for additions to future editions of the bibliography.

I. Guides and General Sources

1. Bibliographical Guides

1 American Historical Association. *Writings on American History.* 46 vols. Washington, D.C., 1902-1964.

2 American Historical Association. Service Center for Teachers, Washington, D.C. The Association has published a pamphlet series of guides, several of which are relevant to the period covered by this volume, including *American Foreign Policy, The American Frontier, The Federal Age, 1789-1829,* and *The Founding Fathers: Young Men of the Revolution.*

3 BEMIS, Samuel Flagg, and Grace Gardner GRIFFIN, eds. *Guide to the Diplomatic History of the United States, 1775-1921.* Washington, D.C., 1935.

4 *Dissertation Abstracts: A Guide to Dissertations and Monographs Available in Microfilm.* Ann Arbor, Mich., 1938-   . (Early volumes entitled *Microfilm Abstracts.*)

5 EVANS, Charles, Clifford K. SHIPTON, and Roger P. BRISTOL, comps. *American Bibliography: A Chronological Dictionary of All Books, Pamphlets and Periodical Publications Printed in the United States from . . . 1639 to . . . 1820.* 14 vols. Chicago and Worcester, Mass., 1903-1959. Vol. 14 is index. Roger P. BRISTOL, comp. *Supplement to Charles Evans' American Bibliography.* Charlottesville, Va., 1970. Clifford K. SHIPTON and James E. MOONEY, comps. *National Index of American Imprints Through 1800: The Short Title Evans.* Worcester and Barre, Mass., 1969.

6 GOODRICH, Carter. "Recent Contributions to Economic History: The United States, 1789-1860." *J Econ Hist,* XIX (1959), 25-43.

7 HALE, Richard W., Jr., ed. *Guide to Photocopied Historical Materials in the United States and Canada.* Ithaca, N.Y., 1961.

8 HAMER, Philip M., ed. *A Guide to Archives and Manuscripts in the United States.* New Haven, Conn., 1961.

9 HANDLIN, Oscar, et al., eds. *The Harvard Guide to American History.* Cambridge, Mass., 1954.†

10 HARPER, Lawrence A. "Recent Contributions to American Economic History. American History to 1789." *J Econ Hist,* XIX (1959), 1-24.

11 HASSE, A. R., comp. *Index of Economic Material in Documents of the United States.* 13 vols. Washington, D.C., 1907-1922.

12 HOWE, George F., et al., eds. *The American Historical Association's Guide to Historical Literature.* New York, 1961.

13 HUTCHINS, John G. B. "Recent Contributions to Business History: The United States." *J Econ Hist,* XIX (1959), 103-121.

14 KUEHL, Warren F. *Dissertations in History: An Index to Dissertations Completed in History Departments of United States and Canadian Universities, 1873-1960*. Lexington, Ky., 1972. Reprint of 1965 ed.

15 Library of Congress. *National Union Catalog of Manuscript Collections*. 6 vols. to date. Washington, D.C., 1959-

16 MILLER, Elizabeth W., ed. *The Negro in America: A Bibliography*. Cambridge, Mass., 1966.†

17 NEUFELD, Maurice F. *A Representative Bibliography of American Labor History*. Ithaca, N.Y., 1964.

18 POORE, Benjamin P. *A Descriptive Catalogue of Government Publications of the United States, September 5, 1774-March 4, 1881*. Washington, D.C., 1885.

19 SABIN, Joseph A. *Bibliotheca Americana. A Dictionary of Books Relating to America from Its Discovery to the Present Time*. 29 vols. New York, 1868-1936.

20 SHAW, Ralph R., and Richard H. SHOEMAKER, comps. *American Bibliography: A Preliminary Checklist for 1801-1819*. 22 vols. New York, 1958-1966.

21 SPILLER, Robert E., et al., eds. *Literary History of the United States*. Volume III: *Bibliography*. 3d ed. New York, 1963.

2. Reference Works and Documentary Collections

22 ADAMS, James T., ed. *Dictionary of American History*. 7 vols. New York, 1940-1963.

23 *American State Papers: Documents, Legislative and Executive of the Congress of the United States*. 38 vols. Washington, D.C., 1832-1834.

24. [Annals of Congress] *Debates and Proceedings in the Congress of the United States, 1789-1824*. 42 vols. Washington, D.C., 1834-1856.

25 CARTER, Clarence E., ed. *The Territorial Papers of the United States*. 26 vols. to date. Washington, D.C., 1934-

26 COMMAGER, Henry Steele. *Documents of American History*. 6th ed. New York, 1958.

27 HALL, E. F., et al., eds. *Official Opinions of the Attorneys-General of the United States, 1791-1948*. 40 vols. Washington, D.C., 1852-1949.

28 HART, Albert Bushnell, ed. *American History Told by Contemporaries*. 5 vols. New York, 1897-1929.

29 JOHNSTON, Alexander, and J. A. WOODBURN, eds. *American Orations: Studies in American Political History*. 4 vols. Rev. ed. New York, 1896-1897.

30 LORD, Clifford Lee, and Elizabeth H. LORD. *Historical Atlas of the United States*. Rev. ed. New York, 1969.

31 MALONE, Dumas, and Allen JOHNSON, eds. *Dictionary of American Biography.* 22 vols. New York, 1969.

32 MILLER, Hunter. *Treaties and Other International Acts of the United States of America, 1776-1863.* 8 vols. Washington, D.C., 1931-1948.

33 MILLER, Marion Mills. *American Debate: A History of Political and Economic Controversy in the United States, with Critical Digests of Leading Debates.* Part I: *Colonial, State and National Rights, 1761-1861.* New York, 1916.

34 MORRIS, Richard B., ed. *Encyclopedia of American History.* Rev. ed. New York, 1961.

35 PAULLIN, Charles O. *Atlas of the Historical Geography of the United States.* Washington, D.C., 1932.

36 PETERS, Richard, ed. *The Public Statutes at Large of the United States from . . . 1789 to March 3, 1845.* 8 vols. Boston, 1848-1850.

37 RICHARDSON, James D., ed. *A Compilation of the Messages and Papers of the Presidents, 1789-1897.* 10 vols. Washington, D.C., 1896-1899.

38 TANSILL, Charles C., comp. *The Making of the American Republic: The Great Documents, 1774-1789.* 1927. New Rochelle, N.Y., 1972.

39 THORPE, Francis Newton, ed. *The Federal and State Constitutions, Colonial Charters, and Other Organic Laws of the States, Territories, and Colonies.* 7 vols. Washington, D.C., 1909.

40 United States Bureau of the Census. *Historical Statistics of the United States, Colonial Times to 1957.* Washington, D.C., 1960.

41 United States Congress. *Biographical Directory of the American Congress, 1774-1961.* Rev. ed. Washington, D.C., 1961.

3. General Works

United States History

42 BANCROFT, George. *History of the United States from the Discovery of the American Continent.* 10 vols. Boston, 1834-1874. Rev. and extended in 6 vols. New York, 1883-1885. Abr. and ed. Russel B. Nye. Chicago, 1966.†

43 BEARD, Charles A., and Mary R. BEARD. *The Rise of American Civilization.* 2 vols. 4th ed. New York, 1956.

44 BERWICK, Keith B. *The Federal Age, 1789-1829.* Washington, D.C., 1961.†

45 BOORSTIN, Daniel Joseph. *The Americans: The National Experience.* New York, 1965.†

46 CHANNING, Edward. *A History of the United States.* 6 vols. New York, 1905-1925. Separate index vol. New York, 1932.

47 CUNLIFFE, Marcus. *The Nation Takes Shape, 1789-1837.* Chicago, 1959.†

48 HILDRETH, Richard. *The History of the United States.* 6 vols. Rev. ed. New York, 1880-1882.

49 KROUT, John A., and Dixon Ryan FOX. *The Completion of Independence, 1790-1830.* New York, 1944.

50 LIPSET, Seymour Martin. *The First New Nation: The United States in Historical and Comparative Perspective.* New York, 1963.†

51 McMASTER, John Bach. *A History of the People of the United States from the Revolution to the Civil War.* 8 vols. 1883-1913. Rev. ed. New York, 1931-1938.

52 MILLER, John C. *The Young Republic, 1789-1815.* New York, 1970.†

53 PALMER, R. R. *The Age of the Democratic Revolution: A Political History of Europe and America, 1760-1800.* 2 vols. Princeton, N.J., 1959, 1964.†

54 ROSSITER, Clinton. *The American Quest, 1790-1860: An Emerging Nation in Search of Identity, Unity, and Modernity.* New York, 1971.

55 SCHOULER, James. *History of the United States under the Constitution.* 6 vols. New York, 1880-1899. Rev. and extended in 7 vols. New York, 1894-1913.

56 WINSOR, Justin, ed. *Narrative and Critical History of America.* 8 vols. Boston, 1884-1889.

57 WRIGHT, Esmond. *Fabric of Freedom, 1763-1800.* New York, 1961.†

Foreign Relations

58 BAILEY, Thomas A. *A Diplomatic History of the American People.* 7th ed. New York, 1964.

59 BANNON, John Francis. *The Spanish Borderlands Frontier, 1513-1821.* New York, 1970.

60 BEMIS, Samuel Flagg, ed. *The American Secretaries of State and Their Diplomacy.* 10 vols. New York, 1927-1929.

61 BEMIS, Samuel Flagg. *John Quincy Adams and the Foundations of American Foreign Policy.* 2d ed. New York, 1969.

62 BEMIS, Samuel Flagg. *The Latin American Policy of the United States.* New York, 1943.

63 BERNSTEIN, Harry. *Origins of Inter-American Interest, 1700-1812.* 2d ed. New York, 1965.

64 BOLTON, Herbert Eugene. *The Spanish Borderlands: A Chronicle of Old Florida and the Southwest.* New Haven, Conn., 1921.

65 BREBNER, John Bartlet. *North Atlantic Triangle: The Interplay of Canada, the United States and Great Britain.* New Haven, Conn., 1945.

66 BURT, A. L. *The United States, Great Britain and British North America, from the Revolution to the Establishment of Peace after the War of 1812.* New Haven, Conn., 1940.

67 CARLSON, Knute Emil. *Relations of the United States with Sweden.* Allentown, Pa., 1921.

68 GRABER, Doris A. *Public Opinion, the President, and Foreign Policy: Four Case Studies from the Formative Years.* New York, 1968.

69 GRAHAM, Gerald S. *Seapower and British North America, 1783-1829.* Cambridge, Mass., 1941.

70 HILDT, J. C. *Early Diplomatic Relations of the United States with Russia.* Baltimore, Md., 1906.

71 HYNEMAN, Charles S. *The First American Neutrality: A Study of the American Understanding of Neutral Obligations during the Years 1792 to 1815.* Urbana, Ill., 1934.

72 IRWIN, Roy Watkins. *The Diplomatic Relations of the United States with the Barbary Pirates, 1776-1816.* Chapel Hill, N.C. 1931.

73 LOGAN, Rayford Whittingham. *The Diplomatic Relations of United States with Haiti, 1776-1891.* Chapel Hill, N.C., 1941.

74 LYON, Elijah Wilson. *Louisiana in French Diplomacy, 1759-1804.* Norman, Okla., 1934.

75 MALLORY, W. M., C. F. REDMOND, and E. J. TREWORTH, eds. *Treaties, Conventions, International Acts, Protocols, and Agreements between the United States of America and Other Powers, 1776-1904.* 4 vols. Washington, D.C., 1910-1938.

76 MANNING, W. R., ed. *Diplomatic Correspondence of the United States-Canadian Relations 1784-1860.* 4 vols. Washington, D.C., 1940-1945.

77 MANNING, W. R. *Early Diplomatic Relations between the United States and Mexico.* Baltimore, Md., 1916.

78 MAYO, Bernard, ed. "Instructions to the British Ministers to the United States 1791-1812." *Ann Rep Am Hist Assn*, 1936. Washington, D.C., 1941. Repub. New York, 1971.

79 MOORE, John B., ed. *Digest of International Law, as Embodied in Diplomatic Discussions, Treaties, and Other International Agreements* . . . 8 vols. Washington, D.C., 1906.

80 MOORE, John B., ed. *History and Digest of the International Arbitrations to Which the United States Has Been a Party.* 6 vols. Washington, D.C., 1898.

81 MOORE, John B. *The United States and International Arbitration.* Boston, 1896.

82 NASATIR, Abraham P., and Gary Elwyn MONELL. *French Consuls in the United States: A Calendar of Their Correspondence in the Archives Nationales.* Washington, D.C., 1967.

83 NICHOLS, Roy F. "Trade Relations and the Establishment of the United States Consulates in Spanish America, 1779-1809." *His-Am Hist Rev*, XIII (1933), 291-313.

84 PAULLIN, Charles O. *Diplomatic Negotiations of American Naval Officers, 1778-1883.* Baltimore, Md., 1912.

85 PRATT, Julius W. *A History of United States Foreign Policy.* Englewood Cliffs, N.J., 1955.

86 RITCHESON, Charles R. *Aftermath of Revolution: British Policy toward the United States 1783-1795.* Dallas, Tex., 1969.

87 SETSER, Vernon G. *The Commercial Reciprocity Policy of the United States, 1774-1829.* Philadelphia, 1937.

88 TANSILL, Charles C. *The United States and Santo Domingo, 1798-1873: A Chapter in Caribbean Diplomacy.* Baltimore, Md., 1938.

89 THISTLETHWAITE, Frank. *The Anglo-American Connection in the Early Nineteenth Century.* Philadelphia, 1959.

90 VAN ALSTYNE, R. W. *The Rising American Empire.* Cambridge, Mass., 1960.†

91 WHITAKER, Arthur P. *The Mississippi Question, 1795-1803: A Study in Trade, Politics, and Diplomacy.* New York, 1934.

92 WHITAKER, Arthur P. *The Spanish American Frontier 1783-1795: The Westward Movement and the Spanish Retreat in the Mississippi Valley.* Boston, 1927.†

States and Regions

93 ABERNETHY, Thomas Perkins. *The South in the New Nation, 1789-1819.* Baton Rouge, La., 1961.

94 ADAMS, James Truslow. *New England in the Republic, 1776-1850.* Boston, 1926.

95 AMBLER, Charles Henry. *Sectionalism in Virginia from 1776 to 1861.* Chicago, 1910.

96 BANKS, Ronald F. *Maine Becomes a State: The Movement to Separate Maine from Massachusetts, 1785-1820.* Middletown, Conn., 1970.

97 BICKNELL, Thomas Williams. *The History of the State of Rhode Island and Providence Plantations.* 4 vols. New York, 1920.

98 COLE, Donald B. *Jacksonian Democracy in New Hampshire, 1800-1851.* Cambridge, Mass., 1970.

99 COLEMAN, Peter J. *The Transformation of Rhode Island, 1790-1860.* Providence, R.I., 1963.

100 CROCKET, Walter Hill. *Vermont, the Green Mountain State.* 5 vols. New York, 1921-1923.

101 DANIELL, Jere R. *Experiment in Republicanism: New Hampshire Politics and the American Revolution, 1741-1794.* Cambridge, Mass., 1970.

102 DUNAWAY, Wayland Fuller. *A History of Pennsylvania.* 2d ed. New York, 1948.

103 EATON, Clement. *The Growth of Southern Civilization, 1790-1860.* New York, 1961.†

104 FLICK, Alexander C., ed. *History of the State of New York.* 10 vols. New York, 1933-1937.

105 HART, Albert Bushnell, ed. *Commonwealth History of Massachusetts Colony, Province and State.* 5 vols. New York, 1927-1930.

106 HATCH, Louis Clinton. *Maine: A History.* 5 vols. New York, 1919.

107 LEFLER, Hugh Talmage, and Albert Ray NEWSOME. *North Carolina: The History of a Southern State*. Rev. ed. Chapel Hill, N.C., 1963.

108 LUDLUM, David McWilliams. *Social Ferment in Vermont, 1791-1850*. Montpelier, Vt., 1939.

109 PHILLIPS, Ulrich B. "Georgia and States Rights. A Study of the Political History of Georgia from the Revolution to the Civil War, with Particular Regard to Federal Relations." *Ann Rep Am Hist Assn*, 1901. Washington, D.C., 1902, pp. 3-224.

110 POLISHOOK, Irwin H. *1774-1795: Rhode Island and the Union*. Evanston, Ill., 1969.

111 PURCELL, Richard J. *Connecticut in Transition, 1775-1818*. Washington, D.C., 1918. Reprinted Middletown, Conn., 1963.

112 SCHARF, John Thomas. *History of Delaware, 1609-1888*. 2 vols. Philadelphia, 1888.

113 SCHARF, John Thomas. *History of Maryland from the Earliest Period to the Present Day*. 2 vols. Hatboro, Md., 1967. Facsimile repr. of 1867 ed.

114 STACKPOLE, Everett Schermerhorn. *History of New Hampshire*. 5 vols. New York, 1916-1918.

115 WAGSTAFF, Henry M. *States Rights and Political Parties in North Carolina, 1776-1861*. Baltimore, Md., 1906.

116 WALLACE, David D. *The History of South Carolina*. 4 vols. New York, 1934-1935.

117 WILLIAMSON, Chilton. *Vermont in Quandary: 1763-1825*. Montpelier, Vt., 1949.

118 WILSON, Harold F. *The Hill Country of Northern New England: Its Social and Economic History, 1790-1930*. New York, 1936.

II. National Public Affairs

1. The Confederation Period

Effects of the American Revolution

119 GENTZ, Frederick von. *The French and American Revolutions Compared*. Trans. John Quincy Adams. 1800. Chicago, 1955.

120 HEIMERT, Alan. *Religion and the American Mind from the Great Awakening to the Revolution*. Cambridge, Mass. 1966.

121 HOOKER, Richard J. *The American Revolution: The Search for Meaning.* New York, 1970.†

122 JACOBSON, Norman. "Class and Ideology in the American Revolution." *Class, Status and Power.* Eds. Reinhard Bendix and Seymour Martin Lipset. Glencoe, Ill., 1953.

123 JAMESON, J. Franklin. *The American Revolution Considered as a Social Movement.* New ed. Boston, 1964.†

124 JENSEN, Merrill. "The American People and the American Revolution." *J Amer Hist,* LVII (1970), 5-35.

125 JENSEN, Merrill. "Democracy and the American Revolution." *Huntington Lib Q,* XX (1957), 321-341.

126 JENSEN, Merrill. "The Idea of a National Government during the American Revolution." *Pol Sci Q,* LVIII (1943), 356-379.

127 KENYON, Cecelia M. "Republicanism and Radicalism in the American Revolution: An Old-Fashioned Interpretation." *Wm Mar Q,* XIX, 3d ser. (1962), 153-182.

128 KLEIN, Milton M. "The American Revolution in the Twentieth Century." *Hist,* XXXIV (1972), 213-229.

129 LYND, Staughton. "Who Should Rule at Home; Dutchess County, New York, in the American Revolution." *Wm Mar Q,* XVIII, 3d ser. (1961), 330-359.

130 LYND, Staughton, and Alfred YOUNG. " After Carl Becker: The Mechanics and New York Politics, 1774-1801." *Labor Hist,* V (1964), 215-224.

131 MAIN, Jackson Turner. "The American Revolution and the Democratization of the Legislatures." *Wm Mar Q,* XXIII, 3d ser. (1966), 391-407.

132 MAIN, Jackson Turner. "The Results of the American Revolution Reconsidered." *Hist,* XXXI (1969), 539-554.

133 MAIN, Jackson Turner. *The Upper House in Revolutionary America, 1763-1788.* Madison, Wis., 1967.

134 MORGAN, Edmund S. "The American Revolution Considered as an Intellectual Movement." *Paths of American Thought.* Eds. Arthur M. Schlesinger, Jr., and Morton White. Boston, 1963.

135 MORRIS, Richard B. *The American Revolution Reconsidered.* New York, 1967.†

136 MORRIS, Richard B. "Class Struggle and the American Revolution." *Wm Mar Q,* XIX, 3d ser. (1962), 3-29.

137 MORRIS, Richard B. "The Confederation Period and the American Historian." *Wm Mar Q,* XIII, 3d ser. (1956), 139-156.

138 NELSON, William H. "The Revolutionary Character of the American Revolution." *Am Hist Rev,* LXX (1965), 998-1014.

139 POLE, Jack R. "Historians and the Problem of Early American Democracy." *Am Hist Rev,* LXVII (1961), 626-646.

140 POLE, Jack R. *Political Representation in England and the Origins of the American Republic.* New York, 1966.

141 TOLLES, Frederick B. "The American Revolution Considered as a Social Movement: A Re-Evaluation." *Am Hist Rev*, LX (1954), 1-12.

142 VER STEEG, Clarence L. "The American Revolution Considered as an Economic Movement." *Huntington Lib Q*, XX (1957), 361-372.

Government and Politics

143 BURNETT, Edmund C. *The Continental Congress*. New York, 1941.†

144 BURNETT, Edmund C., ed. *Letters of the Members of the Continental Congress*. 8 vols. Washington, 1921-1936. Reprint. Gloucester, Mass., 1963.

145 COLEMAN, John M. "How 'Continental' Was the Continental Congress?" *Hist Today*, XVIII (1968), 540-550.

146 COMETTI, Elizabeth. "Civil Servants of the Revolutionary Period." *Pa Mag Hist Biog*, LXXV (1951), 159-169.

147 CRANE, Verner W. "Franklin's 'The Internal State of America' (1786)." *Wm Mar Q*, XV, 3d ser. (1958), 214-227.

148 DeCONDE, Alexander. "William Vans Murray's *Political Sketches:* A Defense of the American Experiment." *Miss Val Hist Rev*, XLI (1955), 623-640.

149 FERGUSON, E. James. "The Nationalists of 1781-1783 and the Economic Interpretation of the Constitution." *J Amer Hist*, LVI (1969), 241-261.

150 FORD, Worthington C., et al., eds. *Journals of the Continental Congress, 1774-1789*. 34 vols. Washington, D.C., 1904-1937.

151 GREENE, Evarts Boutell. *The Revolutionary Generation, 1763-1790*. New York, 1950.

152 HENDERSON, H. James. "Constitutionalists and Republicans in the Continental Congress, 1778-1786." *Pa Hist*, XXXVI (1969), 119-144.

153 JEFFERSON, Thomas. *Notes on the State of Virginia*. Ed. William Peden. New York, 1972.

154 JENSEN, Merrill. *The New Nation: A History of the United States during the Confederation, 1781-1789*. New York, 1950.†

155 JOHNSON, Herbert A. "Toward a Reappraisal of the 'Federal' Government: 1783-1789." *Am J Legal Hist*, VIII (1964), 314-325.

156 KELLEY, Darwin. "Jefferson and the Separation of Powers in the States, 1776-1787." *Ind Mag Hist*, LIV (1958), 25-40.

157 McDONALD, Forrest. *E Pluribus Unum: The Formation of the American Republic, 1776-1790*. Boston, 1965.† Paperback ed. title *The Formation of the American Republic*.

158 McLAUGHLIN, Andrew Cunningham. *The Confederation and the Constitution, 1783-1789*. New York, 1905.†

159 MAIN, Jackson T. *The Antifederalists: Critics of the Constitution, 1781-1788*. Chapel Hill, N.C., 1961.†

160 MONTROSS, Lynn. *The Reluctant Rebels: The Story of the Continental Congress, 1774-1789*. New York, 1950.

161 MORGAN, Edmund S. *The Birth of the Republic: 1763-1789.* Chicago, 1956.†

162 OLSON, Gary D. "The Soderstrom Incident: A Reflection upon Federal-State Relations under the Articles of Confederation." *N Y Hist Soc Q,* LV (1971), 109-118.

163 SANDERS, Jennings B. *The Presidency of the Continental Congress, 1774-1789: A Study of American Institutional History.* Chicago, 1930.

164 TATE, Thad W. "The Social Contract in America, 1774-1787: Revolutionary Theory as a Conservative Instrument." *Wm Mar Q,* XXII, 3d ser. (1965), 375-391.

165 THACH, Charles C., Jr. *The Creation of the Presidency, 1775-1789: A Study in Constitutional History.* 1922. Baltimore, Md., 1969.

166 WOOD, Gordon S. *The Creation of the American Republic, 1776-1787.* Chapel Hill, N.C., 1969.†

167 WOOD, Gordon S. "A Note on Mobs in the American Revolution." *Wm Mar Q,* XXIII, 3d ser. (1966), 635-642.

168 WRIGHT, Benjamin Fletcher. *Consensus and Continuity, 1776-1787.* Boston, 1958.†

The States

169 ABBOT, William W. "The Structure of Politics in Georgia: 1782-1789." *Wm Mar Q,* XIV, 3d ser. (1957), 47-65.

170 ALDEN, John Richard. *The First South.* Baton Rouge, La., 1961.

171 BATES, Frank Greene. *Rhode Island and the Formation of the Union.* New York, 1898.

172 BREWSTER, William. *The Fourteen Commonwealths, Vermont and the States That Failed.* Philadelphia, 1960.

173 BROWN, Dorothy M. "Politics of Crisis. The Maryland Elections of 1788-1789." *Md Hist Mag,* LVII (1962), 195-209.

174 BRUNHOUSE, Robert L. *The Counter-Revolution in Pennsylvania, 1776-1790.* Harrisburg, Pa., 1942.

175 COCHRAN, Thomas C. *New York in the Confederation: An Economic Study.* Philadelphia, 1932.

176 COLEMAN, Kenneth. *The American Revolution in Georgia, 1763-1789.* Athens, Ga., 1958.

177 CROWL, Philip A. *Maryland during and after the Revolution.* Baltimore, Md., 1943.

178 DAVIES, Wallace Evans. "The Society of the Cincinnati in New England 1783-1800." *Wm Mary Q,* V, 3d ser. (1948), 3-25.

179 EAST, Robert A. 'The Massachusetts Conservatives in the Critical Period." *The Era of the American Revolution: Studies Inscribed to Evarts Boutell Greene.* Ed. Richard B. Morris. New York, 1939.

180 GERLACH, Larry R. "A Delegation of Steady Habits: The Connecticut Representatives to the Continental Congress, 1774-1789." *Conn Hist Soc Bull*, XXXII (1967), 33-39.

181 HALL, Van Beck. *Politics without Parties: Massachusetts, 1780-1791.* Pittsburgh, Pa., 1972.

182 HART, Freeman H. *The Valley of Virginia in the American Revolution.* Chapel Hill, N.C., 1942.

183 HUME, Edgar Erskine. "Early Opposition to the Cincinnati." *Amer*, XXX (1936), 597-638.

184 KAPLAN, Sidney. "Veteran Officers and Politics in Massachusetts, 1783-1787." *Wm Mar Q*, IX, 3d ser. (1952), 29-57.

185 LAMPLUGH, George R. "Farewell to the Revolution: Georgia in 1785." *Ga Hist Q*, LVI (1972), 387-403.

186 LYND, Staughton. *Anti-Federalism in Dutchess County, New York: A Study of Democracy and Class Conflict in the Revolutionary Era.* Chicago, 1962.

187 LYND, Staughton. "The Mechanics in New York Politics, 1774-1788." *Labor Hist*, V (1964), 225-246.

188 McCORMICK, Richard P. *Experiment in Independence: New Jersey in the Critical Period, 1781-1789.* New Brunswick, N.J., 1950.

189 MAIN, Jackson T. "The One Hundred." *Wm Mar Q*, XI, 3d ser. (1954), 354-384.

190 MAIN, Jackson T. "Political Parties in Revolutionary Maryland, 1780-1787." *Md Hist Mag*, LXII (1967), 1-27.

191 MAIN, Jackson T. "Sections and Politics in Virginia, 1781-1787." *Wm Mar Q*, XII, 3d ser. (1955), 96-112.

192 MORRILL, James R. *The Practice and Politics of Fiat Finance: North Carolina in the Confederation, 1783-1789.* Chapel Hill, N.C., 1969.

193. NEVINS, Allan. *The American States during and after the Revolution, 1775-1789.* New York, 1924.

194 NEWCOMER, Lee Nathaniel. *The Embattled Farmers: A Massachusetts Countryside in the American Revolution.* New York, 1953.

195 SCHAFFER, Allan. "Virginia's 'Critical Period.' " *The Old Dominion: Essays for Thomas Perkins Abernethy.* Ed. Darrett B. Rutman. Charlottesville, Va., 1964.

196 SINGER, Charles G. *South Carolina in the Confederation.* Philadelphia, 1941.

197 SPAULDING, E. Wilder. *New York in the Critical Period, 1783-1789.* New York, 1932.

198 SYRETT, David. "Town Meeting Politics in Massachusetts, 1776-1786." *Wm Mar Q*, XXI, 3d ser. (1964), 352-366.

199 TAYLOR, Robert J. *Western Massachusetts in the Revolution.* Providence, R.I., 1954.

200 THOMAS, Earl Bruce. *Political Tendencies in Pennsylvania, 1783-1794.* Philadelphia, 1939.

201 UPTON, Richard Francis. *Revolutionary New Hampshire*. Hanover, N.H., 1936.

202 WALSH, Richard. *Charleston's Sons of Liberty: A Study of the Artisans, 1763-1789*. Columbia, S.C., 1959.

203 WATLINGTON, Patricia. *The Partisan Spirit: Kentucky Politics, 1779-1792*. New York, 1972.

204 WEBSTER, William C. "Comparative Study of the State Constitutions of the American Revolution." *Annals*, IX (1897), 64-104.

205 WILSON, Janet. "The Bank of North America and Pennsylvania Politics, 1781-1787." *Pa Mag Hist Biog*, LXVI (1942), 3-28.

Foreign Affairs

206 BARBÉ-MARBOIS, François, Marquis de. *Our Revolutionary Forefathers: The Letters of François, Marquis de Barbé-Marbois during His Residence in the United States as Secretary of the French Legation, 1779-1785*. Ed. Eugene Parker Chase. New York, 1929.

207 BOYD, Julian P. "Two Diplomats between Revolutions: John Jay and Thomas Jefferson." *Va Mag Hist Biog*, LXVI (1958), 131-146.

208 CLARK, Dora Mae. "British Opinion of Franco-American Relations, 1775-1795." *Wm Mar Q*, IV, 3d ser. (1947), 305-316.

209 DIN, Gilbert C. "The Immigration Policy of Governor Esteban Miró in Spanish Louisiana [1785-1791]." *S W Hist Q*, LXXXIII (1969), 155-175.

210 *The Diplomatic Correspondence of the United States of America from . . . 10th September, 1783 to . . . March 4, 1789*. 7 vols. Washington, D.C., 1833-1834.

211 JAMESON, J. Franklin, ed. "Letters of Phineas Bond, British Consul at Philadelphia, to the Foreign Office of Great Britain, 1787, 1788, 1789." *Ann Rep Am Hist Assn*, 1896. Washington, D.C., 1897, pp. 513-659.

212 KETCHAM, Ralph L. "France and American Politics, 1763-1793." *Pol Sci Q*, LXXVIII (1963), 198-223.

213 KINNAIRD, Lawrence, ed. "Spain in the Mississippi Valley, 1765-1794." *Ann Rep Am Hist Assn*, 1945. Washington, D.C., 1946-1949.

214 LAWSON, Murray G. "Canada and the Articles of Confederation." *Am Hist Rev*, LVIII (1952), 39-54.

215 NUSSBAUM, Frederick L. "American Tobacco and French Politics, 1783-1789. *Pol Sci Q*, XL (1925), 497-516.

216 NUSSBAUM, Frederick L. "The French Colonial Arrêt of 1784." *S Atl Q*, XXVII (1928), 62-78.

217 O'DONNELL, William Emmett. *The Chevalier de La Luzerne, French Minister to the United States, 1779-1784*. Bruges, Belgium, 1936.

218 REID, David S. "An Analysis of British Parliamentary Opinion on American Affairs at the Close of the War of Independence." *J Mod Hist*, XVIII (1946), 202-221.

219 SHACKELFORD, George Greene. "William Short: Diplomat in Revolutionary France, 1785-1793." *Proc Am Phil Soc*, CII (1958), 596-612.

220 SULLIVAN, Kathryn. *Maryland and France, 1774-1789.* Philadelphia, 1936.

221 TAILBY, Donald G. "Foreign Interest Remittances by the United States, 1785-1787: A Story of Malfeasance." *Bus Hist Rev*, XLI (1967), 161-176.

222 WHARTON, Francis, ed. *The Revolutionary Diplomatic Correspondence of the United States.* 6 vols. Washington, D.C., 1889.

Economic Aspects

223 BAMFORD, Paul W. "France and the American Market in Naval Timber and Masts, 1776-1786." *J Econ Hist*, XII (1952), 21-34.

224 BURNETT, Edmund C., ed. "Observations of London Merchants on American Trade, 1783." *Am Hist Rev*, XVII (1913), 769-780.

225 CONLEY, Patrick T. "Rhode Island's Paper Money Issues and Trevett v. Weeden (1786)." *R I Hist*, XXX (1971), 95-108.

226 CRITTENDEN, Charles C. *The Commerce of North Carolina, 1763-1789.* New Haven, Conn., 1936.

227 CRITTENDEN, Charles C. "Ships and Shipping in North Carolina, 1763-1789." *N C Hist Rev*, VIII (1931), 1-13.

228 DORSEY, Rhoda M. "The Pattern of Baltimore Commerce during the Confederation Period." *Md Hist Mag*, LXII (1967), 119-134.

229 EVANS, Emory G. "Private Indebtedness and the Revolution in Virginia, 1776 to 1796." *Wm Mar Q*, XXVIII, 3d ser. (1971), 349-374.

230 FERGUSON, E. James. "State Assumption of the Federal Debt during the Confederation." *Miss Val Hist Rev*, XXXVIII (1951), 403-424.

231 GIESECKE, Albert A. *American Commercial Legislation before 1789.* New York, 1910.

232 HIGGINS, W. Robert. "The South Carolina Revolutionary Debt and Its Holders, 1776-1780." *S C Hist Mag*, LXXII (1971), 15-29.

233 HUNTER, William C. *The Commercial Policy of New Jersey under the Confederation, 1783-1789.* Princeton, N.J., 1922.

234 KOHLMEIER, Albert Ludwig. "The Commerce Between the United States and the Netherlands, 1783-1789." *Ind U Stud Am Hist*, XII, nos. 66-68 (1926), 3-47.

235 LOSSE, Winifred. "The Foreign Trade of Virginia, 1789-1809." *Wm Mar Q*, I, 3d ser. (1944), 161-178.

236 LOW, W. A. "The Farmer in Post-Revolutionary Virginia, 1783-1789." *Ag Hist*, XXV (1951), 122-127.

237 LOW, W. A. "Merchant and Planter Relations in Post-Revolutionary Virginia, 1783-1789." *Va Mag Hist Biog*, LXI (1953), 308-318.

238 RICH, Myra L. "Speculations on the Significance of Debt: Virginia, 1781-1789." *Va Mag Hist Biog*, LXXVI (1968), 301-317.

239 SEE, Henry, ed. "Commerce between France and the United States, 1783-1784." *Am Hist Rev,* XXXI (1926), 732-752.

240 SHARRER, G. Terry. "Indigo in South Carolina, 1671-1796." *S C Hist Mag,* LXXII (1971), 94-103.

241 STOVER, John F. "French-American Trade during the Confederation, 1781-1789." *N C Hist Rev,* XXXV (1958), 399-414.

242 TYLER, Bruce. "The Mississippi River Trade, 1784-1788." *La Hist,* XII (1971), 255-267.

243 ZORNOW, William F. "Massachusetts Tariff Policies, 1775-1789." *Essex Inst Hist Coll,* XC (1954), 194-216.

244 ZORNOW, William F. "New Hampshire Tariff Policies, 1775-1789." *Soc Stud,* XLV (1954), 252-256.

245 ZORNOW, William F. "New York Tariff Policies, 1775-1789." *N Y Hist,* XXXVII (1956), 40-63.

246 ZORNOW, William F. "North Carolina Tariff Policies, 1775-1789." *N C Hist Rev,* XXXII (1955), 151-164.

247 ZORNOW, William F. "Tariff Policies in South Carolina, 1775-1789." *S C Hist Mag,* LVI (1955), 31-44.

248 ZORNOW, William F. "The Tariff Policies of Virginia, 1775-1789." *Va Mag Hist Biog,* LXII (1954), 306-319.

Indians and the West

249 BARRETT, Jay Amos. *Evolution of Ordinance of 1787: With an Account of the Earlier Plans for the Government of the Northwest Territory.* New York, 1891.

250 BERKHOFER, Robert F., Jr. "Jefferson, the Ordinance of 1784, and the Origins of the American Territorial System." *Wm Mar Q,* XXIX, 3d ser. (1972), 231-262.

251 COLEMAN, Kenneth. "Federal Indian Relations in the South, 1781-1789." *Chron Okla,* XXXV (1957), 435-458.

252 EBLEN, Jack E. "Origins of the United States Colonial System: The Ordinance of 1787." *Wis Mag Hist,* LI (1968), 294-314.

253 FREUND, Rudolf. "Military Bounty Land and the Origin of the Public Domain." *Ag Hist,* XX (1946), 8-18.

254 HORSMAN, Reginald. "American Indian Policy in the Old Northwest, 1783-1812." *Wm Mar Q,* XVIII, 3d ser. (1961), 35-53.

255 JAMES, James Alton. "Some Phases of the History of the Northwest, 1783-1786." *Proc Miss Val Hist Assn,* VII (1913-1914), 168-195.

256 JENSEN, Merrill. "The Cession of the Old Northwest." *Miss Val Hist Rev,* XXIII (1936), 27-48.

257 JENSEN, Merrill. "The Creation of the National Domain, 1781-1784." *Miss Val Hist Rev,* XXVI (1939), 323-342.

258 LUTZ, Paul V. "Land Grants for Service in the Revolution." *N Y Hist Soc Q,* XLVIII (1964), 221-236.

259 TATTER, Henry. "State and Federal Land Policy during Confederation Period." *Ag Hist,* IX (1935), 176-186.

Loyalists and Their Property

260 BRADLEY, Arthur Granville. *Colonial Americans in Exile: Founders of British Canada.* New York, 1932.

261 BROWN, Richard D. "The Confiscation and Disposition of Loyalist Estates in Suffolk County, Massachusetts." *Wm Mar Q,* XXI, 3d ser. (1964), 534-550.

262 BROWN, Wallace. *The King's Friends: The Composition and Motives of the American Loyalist Claimants.* Providence, R.I., 1966.

263 CARELESS, J. M. S., ed. *Colonists and Canadiens 1760-1867.* Toronto, 1971.

264 DAVIS, Andrew M. *The Confiscation of John Chandler's Estate.* Boston, 1903.

265 EGERTON, Hugh Edward ed. *The Royal Commission on the Losses and Service of the American Loyalists, 1783-1785.* Oxford, England, 1915.

266 FINGERHUT, Eugene R. "Uses and Abuses of the American Loyalists' Claims: A Critique of Quantitative Analyses." *Wm Mar Q,* XXV, 3d ser. (1968), 245-258.

267 LAMBERT, Robert S. "The Confiscation of Loyalist Property in Georgia, 1782-1786." *Wm Mar Q,* XX, 3d ser. (1963), 80-94.

268 MORISON, S. E. "The Property of Harrison Gray, Loyalist." *Pub Col Soc Mass,* XIV (1912), 320-350.

269 NORTON, Mary Beth. *The British Americans: The Loyalist Exiles in England, 1775-1789.* Boston, 1972.

270 PETERS, Thelma. "The American Loyalists in the Bahama Islands: Who They Were." *Fla Hist Q,* XL (1962), 226-240.

271 REUBENS, Beatrice G. "Pre-Emptive Rights in the Disposition of a Confiscated Estate: Philipsburg Manor, New York." *Wm Mar Q,* XXII, 3d ser. (1965), 435-456.

272 RICCARDS, Michael P. "Patriots and Plunderers: Confiscation of Loyalists' Lands in New Jersey, 1776-1786." *N J Hist,* LXXXVI (1968), 14-28.

273 SIEBERT, Wilbur H. "Dispersion of American Tories." *Miss Val Hist Rev,* I (1914), 185-197.

274 SIEBERT, Wilbur H. "East Florida as a Refuge of Southern Loyalists, 1774-1785." *Proc Am Ant Soc,* XXXVII, New Ser. (1927), 226-246.

275 SIEBERT, Wilbur H. *Flight of American Loyalists to the British Isles.* Columbus, Ohio, 1911.

276 SIEBERT, Wilbur H. "Kentucky's Struggle with Its Loyalist Proprietors." *Miss Val Hist Rev,* VII (1920), 113-126.

277   SIEBERT, Wilbur H. *The Legacy of the American Revolution to the British West Indies and Bahamas.* Columbus, Ohio, 1913.

278   SIEBERT, Wilbur H. "The Loyalists in West Florida and the Natchez District." *Miss Val Hist Rev,* II (1916), 465-483.

279   WALLACE, William Stewart. *The United Empire Loyalists: A Chronicle of the Great Migration.* Toronto, 1914.

280   WRIGHT, Esther C. *The Loyalists of New Brunswick.* Ottawa, 1955.

281   YOSHPE, Harry Beller. *The Disposition of Loyalist Estates in the Southern District of the State of New York.* New York, 1939.

282   ZEICHNER, Oscar. "Loyalist Problem in New York after the Revolution." *N Y Hist,* XXI (1940), 284-302.

283   ZEICHNER, Oscar. "The Rehabilitation of Loyalists in Connecticut." *N Eng Q,* XI (1938), 308-330.

Shays Rebellion

284   DAVIS, Andrew M. "The Shays Rebellion: A Political Aftermath." *Proc Am Ant Soc,* XXI, New Ser. (1911), 57-79.

285   DYER, Walter A. "Embattled Farmers." *N Eng Q,* IV (1931), 460-481.

286   FEER, Robert A. "George Richard Minot's History of the Insurrections: History, Propaganda, and Autobiography." *N Eng Q,* XXV (1962), 203-228.

287   FEER, Robert A. "Shays's Rebellion and the Constitution: A Study in Causation." *N Eng Q,* XLII (1969), 388-410.

288   MINOT, George Richards. *The History of the Insurrections in Massachusetts . . .* 2d ed. Boston, 1810.

289   MOODY, R. E. "Samuel Ely: Forerunner of Shays." *N Eng Q,* V (1932), 105-134.

290   MORRIS, Richard B. "Insurrection in Massachusetts." *America in Crisis.* Ed. Daniel Aaron. New York, 1952.

291   SMITH, Jonathan. "The Depression of 1785 and Daniel Shays' Rebellion." *Wm Mar Q,* V, 3d ser. (1948), 77-94.

292   STARKEY, Marion L. *A Little Rebellion.* New York, 1955.

293   TAYLOR, Robert J. *Western Massachusetts in the Revolution.* See 199.

294   WARREN, Joseph Parker. "The Confederation and Shays Rebellion." *Am Hist Rev,* XI (1905), 42-67.

2. Formation of the National Government

The Constitution

General

295 BANCROFT, George. *History of the Formation of the Constitution of the United States of America.* 2 vols. New York, 1893.

296 CHIDSEY, Donald Barr. *The Birth of the Constitution: An Informal History.* New York, 1964.

297 *Documentary History of the Constitution of the United States of America.* 5 vols. Washington, D.C., 1894-1905.

298 JAMESON, J. Franklin, ed. *Essays in the Constitutional History of the United States in the Formative Period, 1775-1789.* Boston, 1889.

299 McLAUGHLIN, Andrew C. *The Foundations of American Constitutionalism.* New York, 1932.

300 MITCHELL, Broadus, and Louise Pearson MITCHELL. *A Biography of the Constitution of the United States: Its Origin, Formation, Adoption, Interpretation.* New York, 1964.

301 MURPHY, William P. *The Triumph of Nationalism: State Sovereignty, the Founding Fathers, and the Making of the Constitution.* Chicago, 1967.

302 SCHUYLER, Robert L. *The Constitution of the United States.* New York, 1923.

303 VAN DOREN, Carl. *The Great Rehearsal: The Story of the Making and Ratifying of the Constitution of the United States.* New York, 1948.†

304 WARREN, Charles. *The Making of the Constitution.* Cambridge, Mass., 1937.†

Interpretation

305 ANDERSON, William. "The Intention of the Framers: A Note on Constitutional Interpretation." *Am Poli Sci Rev,* XLIX (1955), 340-352.

306 BARKER, Eugene C. "Economic Interpretation of Constitution." *Texas Law Rev,* XXII (1944), 373-391.

307 BEARD, Charles A. *An Economic Interpretation of the Constitution of the United States.* New York, 1913. Reissued 1935.†

308 BENSON, Lee. *Turner and Beard: American Historical Writing Reconsidered.* Glencoe, Ill., 1960.†

309 BROGAN, D. W. "The Quarrel over Charles Austin Beard and the American Constitution." *Econ Hist Rev,* XVIII, 2d ser. (1965), 199-223.

310 BROWN, Robert E. *Charles Beard and the Constitution: A Critical Analysis of "An Economic Interpretation of the Constitution."* Princeton, N.J., 1956.†

311   BROWN, Robert E. "Economic Democracy before the Constitution." *Am Q*, VII (1955), 257-274.

312   BROWN, Robert E. *Reinterpretation of the Formation of the American Constitution*. Boston, 1963.

313   BRUCHEY, Stuart. "The Forces behind the Constitution: A Critical View of the Framework of E. James Ferguson's *The Power of the Purse*." *Wm Mar Q*, XIX, 3d ser. (1962), 429-438.

314   DEAN, Howard E. "J. Allen Smith: Jeffersonian Critic of the Federalist State." *Am Poli Sci Rev*, L (1956), 1093-1104.

315   DEWEY, Donald O. "James Madison Helps Clio Interpret the Constitution." *Am J Legal Hist*, XV (1971), 38-55.

316   DIAMOND, Martin. "Democracy and the Federalist: A Reconsideration of the Framers' Intent." *Am Poli Sci Rev*, LIII (1959), 52-68.

317   DUNBAR, Louise. *A Study of "Monarchical" Tendencies in the United States from 1776 to 1801*. Urbana, Ill., 1922.

318   EIDELBERG, Paul. *The Philosophy of the American Constitution: A Reinterpretation of the Intentions of the Founding Fathers*. New York, 1968.

319   ELKINS, Stanley, and Eric McKITRICK. "The Founding Fathers: Young Men of the Revolution." *Poli Sci Q*, LXXVI (1961), 181-216.

320   FERGUSON, E. James. "The Nationalists of 1781-1783 and the Economic Interpretation of the Constitution." See 149.

321   HOFSTADTER, Richard. "Beard and the Constitution: The History of an Idea." *Am Q*, II (1950), 195-213.

322   HUME, Edgar E. "The Role of the Cincinnati in the Birth of the Constitution of the United States." *Pa Hist*, V (1938), 101-107.

323   KENYON, Cecilia M. "An Economic Interpretation of the Constitution After Fifty Years." *Cent Rev*, VII (1936), 327-352.

324   KENYON, Cecilia M. "Men of Little Faith: The Anti-Federalists on the Nature of Representative Government." *Wm Mar Q*, XII, 3d ser. (1955), 3-43.

325   LYND, Staughton. "Abraham Yates's History of the Movement for the United States Constitution." *Wm Mar Q*, XX, 3d ser. (1963), 223-245.

326   LYND, Staughton. *Class Conflict, Slavery, and the United States Constitution: Ten Essays*. Indianapolis, 1968.

327   McDONALD, Forrest. *We the People: The Economic Origins of the Constitution*. Chicago, 1958.†

328   MAIN, Jackson T. *The Antifederalists: Critics of the Constitution, 1781-1788*. See 159.

329   MARKS, Frederick W., III. "American Pride, European Prejudice, and the Constitution." *Hist*, XXXIV (1972), 579-597.

330   NETTELS, Curtis P. "The American Merchant and the Constitution." *Col Soc Mass*, XXXIV (1938), 26-37.

331   NETTELS, Curtis. "The Mississippi Valley and the Constitution." *Miss Val Hist Rev*, XI (1924), 332-357.

332 POOL, William C. "An Economic Interpretation of the Ratification of the Federal Constitution in North Carolina." *N C Hist Rev,* XXVII (1950), 119-141, 289-313, 437-461.

333 ROCHE, John P. "The Founding Fathers: A Reform Caucus in Action." *Am Poli Sci Rev,* LV (1961), 799-816.

334 SCHUYLER, Robert L. "Forrest McDonald's Critique of the Beard Thesis." *J S Hist,* XXVIII (1961), 73-80.

335 SMITH, J. Allen. *The Spirit of American Government.* 1907. Ed. Cushing Strout. Cambridge, Mass., 1965.

336 SODERBERGH, Peter A. "Charles Beard, the Quaker Spirit, and North Carolina." *N C Hist Rev,* XLVI (1969), 19-32.

337 THOMAS, Robert E. "A Re-Appraisal of Charles A. Beard's 'An Economic Interpretation of the Constitution of the United States.' " *Am Hist Rev,* LVII (1952), 370-375.

338 THOMAS, Robert E. "The Virginia Convention of 1788: A Criticism of Beard's 'An Economic Interpretation of the Constitution.' " *J S Hist,* XIX (1953), 63-72.

339 TRASK, David F. "Historians, the Constitution and Objectivity: A Case Study." *Antioch Rev,* XX (1960), 65-78.

340 WOOD, Gordon S. *The Creation of the American Republic, 1776-1787.* See 166.

Political Analysis

341 ADAIR, Douglass. "Experience Must Be Our Only Guide: History, Democratic Theory, and the United States Constitution." *The Reinterpretation of Early American History: Essays in Honor of John Edwin Pomfret.* Ed. Ray A. Billington. San Marino, Cal., 1966.

342 CHINARD, Gilbert. "Polybius and the American Constitution." *J Hist Ideas,* I (1940), 38-58.

343 CORWIN, Edward S. "The Progress of Constitutional Theory between the Declaration of Independence and the Meeting of the Philadelphia Convention." *Am Hist Rev,* XXX (1925), 511-536.

344 GUNMERE, Richard M. "The Classical Ancestry of the United States Constitution." *Am Q,* XIV (1962), 3-18.

345 KATZ, Stanley N. "The Origins of American Constitutional Thought." *Perspectives Am Hist,* III (1969), 474-490.

346 KAUPER, Paul G. *Constitutionalism in America–Origin and Evolution of Its Fundamental Ideas.* New York, 1965.

347 McKEON, Richard. "The Development of the Concept of Property in Political Philosophy: A Study of the Background of the Constitution." *Ethics,* XLVIII (1938), 297-366.

348 MOREY, William C. "The Genesis of a Written Constitution." *Annals,* I (1891), 529-557.

349 PARGELLIS, Stanley. "The Theory of Balanced Government." *The Constitution Reconsidered*. Ed. Conyers Read. New York, 1938.

350 RANNEY, John C. "The Bases of American Federalism." *Wm Mar Q*, III, 3d ser. (1946), 1-35.

351 ROBINSON, Harvey. "The Original and Derived Features of the Constitution." *Annals*, I (1890), 203-243.

352 WRIGHT, Benjamin F. *Consensus and Continuity, 1776-1787*. See 168.

353 WRIGHT, Benjamin F. "The Origins of the Separation of Powers in America. *Econ*, XIII (1933), 169-185.

The Convention

354 ADAIR, Douglass. "Fame and the Founding Fathers." *Fame and the Founding Fathers*. Ed. Edmund P. Willis. Bethlehem, Pa., 1967.

355 BANKS, Margaret A. "Drafting the American Constitution—Attitudes in the Philadelphia Convention Towards the British System of Government." *Am J Leg Hist*, X (1966), 15-33.

356 BOWEN, Catherine D. *Miracle at Philadelphia*. Boston, 1966.†

357 BUTZNER, Jane. *Constitutional Chaff: Rejected Suggestions of the Constitutional Convention of 1787*. New York, 1941.

358 CRAVEN, Wesley Frank. *The Legend of the Founding Fathers*. New York, 1956.

359 FARRAND, Max. *The Fathers of the Constitution: A Chronicle of the Establishment of the Union*. New Haven, Conn., 1921.

360 FARRAND, Max, ed. *The Records of the Federal Convention of 1787*. 4 vols. New Haven, Conn., 1966. Reprint.

361 GERLACH, Larry R. "Toward 'a more perfect Union': Connecticut, the Continental Congress, and the Constitutional Convention." *Conn Hist Soc Bull*, XXXIV (1969), 65-78.

362 GOVAN, Thomas P. "The Rich, the Well-Born, and Alexander Hamilton." *Miss Val Hist Rev*, XXXVI (1950), 675-680.

363 HOFFER, Peter C. "The Constitutional Crisis and the Rise of a Nationalistic View of History in America, 1786-1788." *N Y Hist*, LII (1971), 305-323.

364 JENSEN, Merrill. *The Making of the American Constitution*. Princeton, N.J., 1964.†

365 KROUT, John A. "Alexander Hamilton's Place in the Founding of the Nation." *Proc Am Phil Soc*, CII (1958), 124-128.

366 LYON, [Walter] Hastings. *The Constitution and the Men Who Made It: The Story of the Constitutional Convention, 1787*. Boston and New York, 1936.

367 MADISON, James. *Notes of Debates in the Federal Convention of 1787*. New York, 1969.†

368 OHLINE, Howard A. "Republicanism and Slavery: Origins of the Three-Fifths Clause in the United States Constitution." *Wm Mar Q*, XXVIII, 3d ser. (1971), 563-584.

369 PADOVER, Saul K. *To Secure These Blessings.* New York, 1962.

370 PARSONS, Lynn Hudson. "Federalism, the British Empire, and Alexander Hamilton." *N Y Hist Soc Q,* LII (1968), 62-80.

371 PRESCOTT, Arthur Taylor. *Drafting the Federal Constitution.* Baton Rouge, La., 1941.

372 ROGOW, Arnold A. "The Federal Convention: Madison and Yates." *Am Hist Rev,* LX (1955), 323-335.

373 ROSSITER, Clinton. *1787: The Grand Convention.* New York, 1936.†

374 SCHACHNER, Nathan. *The Founding Fathers.* New York, 1954.

375 SMITH, David G. *The Convention and the Constitution: The Political Ideas of the Founding Fathers.* New York, 1965.†

376 STRAYER, J. R., ed. *The Delegate from New York, or Proceedings of the Federal Convention of 1787 from the Notes of John Lansing, Jr.* Princeton, N.J., 1939.

377 TANSILL, Charles C., ed. *Documents Illustrative of the Formation of the Union.* Washington, 1927.

Ratification

The Federalist Papers

378 ADAIR, Douglass. "The Federalist Papers." *Wm Mar Q,* XXII, 3d ser. (1965), 131-139.

379 ADAIR, Douglass. 'The Tenth Federalist Revisited." *Wm Mar Q,* VIII, 3d ser. (1951), 48-67.

380 ADAIR, Douglass. " 'That Politics May Be Reduced to a Science': David Hume, James Madison, and the Tenth *Federalist.*" *Huntington Lib Q,* XX (1957), 343-360.

381 COOKE, Jacob E., ed. *The Federalist.* Middletown, Conn., 1961.†

382 CRANE, Elaine F. "Publius in the Provinces: Where Was The Federalist Reprinted Outside New York City?" *Wm Mar Q,* XXI, 3d ser. (1964), 589-592.

383 DIETZE, Gottfried. *The Federalist: A Classic on Federalism and Free Government.* Baltimore, Md., 1960.

384 KETCHAM, Ralph L. "Notes on James Madison's Sources for the Tenth Federalist Paper." *Mid W J Pol Sci,* I (1957), 20-25.

385 SCANLAN, James P. "The Federalist and Human Nature." *Rev Pol,* XXI (1959), 657-677.

386 SMITH, Maynard. "Reason, Passion and Political Freedom in *The Federalist.*" *J Pol,* XXII (1960), 525-544.

387 WRIGHT, Benjamin F. "The Federalist on the Nature of Political Man." *Ethics,* LIX, Part II (1949), 1-31.

Antifederalists

388 BISHOP, Hillman Metcalf. "Why Rhode Island Opposed the Federal Constitution." *R I Hist,* VIII (1949), 1-10, 33-44, 85-95, 115-126.

389 BORDEN, Morton, ed. *The Antifederalist Papers.* 3 vols. Ann Arbor, Mich., 1965.

390 CROWL, Philip A. "Anti-Federalism in Maryland, 1787-1788." *Wm Mar Q,* IV, 3d ser. (1947), 446-469.

391 KENYON, Cecilia M., ed. *The Antifederalists.* Indianapolis, Ind., 1966.†

392 KENYON, Cecilia M. "Men of Little Faith: The Anti-Federalists on the Nature of Representative Government." See 324.

393 McDONALD, Forrest. "The Anti-Federalists, 1781-1789." *Wis Mag Hist,* XLVI (1963), 206-214.

394 MAIN, Jackson Turner. *The Antifederalists: Critics of the Constitution, 1781-1788.* See 159.

395 MASON, Alpheus Thomas. *The States Rights Debate: Antifederalism and the Constitution.* Englewood Cliffs, N.J., 1964.†

396 MUSMANNO, Michael Angelo. *Proposed Amendments to the Constitution: A Monograph on the Resolutions Introduced in Congress Proposing Amendments to the Constitution of the United States of America.* Washington, D.C., 1929.

397 SMITH, E. P. "The Movement toward a Second Constitutional Convention." *Essays in the Constitutional History of the United States.* Ed. J. Franklin Jameson. See 298.

Adoption of the Constitution

398 BATES, Frank Greene. *Rhode Island and the Formation of the Union.* See 171.

399 BELL, Whitfield J., Jr. "The Federal Processions of 1788." *N Y Hist Soc Q,* XLVI (1962), 5-40.

400 BENTON, William A. "Pennsylvania Revolutionary Officers and the Federal Constitution." *Pa Hist,* XXXI (1964), 419-435.

401 BROOKS, Robin. "Alexander Hamilton, Melancton Smith, and the Ratification of the Constitution in New York." *Wm Mar Q,* XXIV, 3d ser. (1967), 339-358.

402 COTNER, Robert C., ed. *Theodore Foster's Minutes of the Convention Held at South Kingstown, Rhode Island, in March, 1790, Which Failed to Adopt the Constitution of the United States.* Providence, R.I., 1929.

403 DePAUW, Linda Grant. *The Eleventh Pillar: New York State and the Federal Constitution.* Ithaca, N.Y., 1966.

404 ELLIOTT, Jonathan, ed. *The Debates in the Several State Conventions on the Adoption of the Federal Constitution.* 5 vols. 2d ed. Philadelphia, 1876.

405 FORD, Paul Leicester, ed. *Essays on the Constitution of the United States, Published during Its Discussion by the People, 1787-1788.* New York, 1892.

406 FORD, Paul Leicester, ed. *Pamphlets on the Constitution of the United States, Published during Its Discussion by the People, 1787-1788.* 1888. New York, 1968.

407 FORD, Worthington C., ed. "The Federal Constitution in Virginia, 1787-1788." *Proc Mass Hist Soc*, XVII, 2d ser. (1903), 449-510.

408 GRIGSBY, Hugh Blair. *The History of the Virginia Federal Convention of 1788 with Some Account of the Eminent Virginians of That Era Who Were Members of the Body.* Ed. R. A. Brock. 2 vols. 1890-1891. New York, 1969.

409 HARDING, Samuel Bannister. *The Contest over the Ratification of the Federal Constitution in the State of Massachusetts.* New York, 1896.

410 KATZ, Judith M. "Connecticut Newspapers and the Constitution, 1786-1788." *Conn Hist Soc Bull*, XXX (1965), 33-44.

411 LIBBY, Orin Grant. *The Geographical Distribution of the Vote of the Thirteen States on the Federal Constitution, 1787-1788.* 1894. Grand Forks, N.D., 1969.

412 McMASTER, John Bach, and Frederick D. STONE. *Pennsylvania and the Federal Constitution, 1787-1788.* 1888. Philadelphia, 1942.

413 MARKS, Frederick W., III. "Foreign Affairs: A Winning Issue in the Campaign for Ratification of the United States Constitution." *Pol Sci Q*, LXXXVI (1971), 444-469.

414 MINER, Clarence Eugene. *The Ratification of the Federal Constitution by the State of New York.* New York, 1921.

415 NEWSOME, Albert Ray. "North Carolina's Ratification of the Federal Constitution." *N C Hist Rev*, XVII (1940), 287-301.

416 PITTMAN, R. Carter. "Jasper Yeate's Notes on the Pennsylvania Ratifying Convention, 1787." *Wm Mar Q*, XXII, 3d ser. (1965), 301-318.

417 POLISHOOK, Irwin W. *1774-1795: Rhode Island and the Union.* See 110.

418 POOL, William C. "An Economic Interpretation of the Ratification of the Federal Constitution in North Carolina." See 332.

419 ROLL, Charles W., HJr. "We, Some of the People: Apportionment in the Thirteen State Conventions Ratifying the Constitution." *J Am Hist*, LVI (1969), 21-40.

420 RUTLAND, Robert A. *The Ordeal of the Constitution: The Antifederalists and the Ratification Struggle of 1787-1788.* Norman, Okla., 1966.

421 STEINER, Bernard C. "Connecticut's Ratification of the Federal Constitution." *Proc Am Ant Soc*, XXV (1915), 70-127.

422 STEINER, Bernard C. "Maryland's Adoption of the Federal Constitution." *Am Hist Rev*, V (1899)1900), 22-44, 207-224.

423 TALBERT, Charles Gano. "Kentuckians in the Virginia Convention of 1788." *Reg Ky Hist Soc*, LVIII (1960), 187-193.

424 THOMAS, Robert E. "The Virginia Convention of 1788: A Criticism of Beard's 'An Economic Interpretation of the Constitution.' " See 338.

425 TRENHOLME, Louise. *The Ratification of the Federal Constitution in North Carolina.* New York, 1932.

426 WALKER, Joseph Burbeen. *Birth of the Federal Constitution: A History of the New Hampshire Convention.* Boston, 1888.

427 WARREN, Charles. "Elbridge Gerry, James Warren, Mercy Warren and the Ratification of the Federal Constitution in Massachusetts." *Proc Mass Hist Soc*, LXIV (1930-1932), 143-164.

The Bill of Rights

428 CHAFEE, Zechariah, Jr. *How Human Rights Got into the Constitution.* Boston, 1952.

429 DUMBAULD, Edward. "State Precedents for the Bill of Rights." *J Pub Law,* VII (1958), 323-344.

430 HENDERSON, Edith Guild. "The Background of the Seventh Amendment." *Har Law Rev,* LXXX (1966), 289-337.

431 LEVY, Leonard W. *Legacy of Suppression: Freedom of Speech and Press in Early American History.* Cambridge, Mass., 1960.†

432 LEVY, Leonard W. *Origins of the Fifth Amendment: The Right against Self-Incrimination.* New York, 1968.

433 PITTMAN, R. Carter. "The Colonial and Constitutional History of the Privilege against Self-Incrimination in America." *Va Law Rev,* XXI (1935), 763-789.

434 RUTLAND, Robert Allen. *The Birth of the Bill of Rights, 1776-1791.* Chapel Hill, N.C., 1955.†

435 WILLIAMSON, René de Visme. "Political Process of Judicial Process: The Bill of Rights and the Framers of the Constitution." *J Pol,* XXIII (1961), 199-211.

The Funding Program

436 BATES, Whitney K. "Northern Speculators and Southern State Debts: 1790." *Wm Mar Q,* XIX, 3d ser. (1962), 30-48.

437 BOWLING, Kennth R. "Dinner at Jefferson's: A Note on Jacob E. Cooke's 'The Compromise of 1790,' with a Rebuttal by Jacob E. Cooke." *Wm Mar Q,* XXVIII, 3d ser. (1971), 629-648.

438 BRUCHEY, Stuart. "Alexander Hamilton and the State Banks, 1789 to 1795." *Wm Mar Q,* XXVII, 3d ser. (1970), 347-378.

439 COLLIER, Christopher. "Continental Bonds in Connecticut on the Eve of the Funding Measure." *Wm Mar Q,* XXII, 3d ser. (1965), 646-651.

440 COOKE, Jacob E. "The Compromise of 1790." *Wm Mar Q,* XXVII, 3d ser. (1970), 523-545.

441 COSTELLO, Frank B. "James Madison and the Hamilton Funding Plan: A Charge of Inconsistency Investigated." *Hist Bull,* XXXII (1953), 12-26.

442 DODD, Walter F. "Effect of Adoption of Constitution on Finances of Virginia." *Va Mag Hist Biog,* X (1903), 360-370.

443 FERGUSON, E. James. "Public Finance and the Origins of Southern Sectionalism." *J S Hist*, XXVIII (1962), 450-461.

444 MEYER, Freeman W. "A Note on the Origins of the 'Hamiltonian System.' " *Wm Mary Q*, XXI, 3d ser. (1964), 579-588.

445 MITCHELL, Broadus. "Alexander Hamilton as Finance Minister." *Proc Am Phil Soc*, CII (1958), 117-123.

446 SWANSON, Donald F. *The Origins of Hamilton's Fiscal Policies*. Gainesville, Fla., 1963.

447 WETTEREAU, James O. "Letters from Two Business Men to Alexander Hamtilton on Federal Fiscal Policy, November, 1789." *J Econ Bus Hist*, III (1931), 667-686.

3. The Federalist Decade

General

448 AGAR, Herbert. *The Price of Union*. Boston, 1950.†

449 BASSETT, John Spencer. *The Federalist System, 1789-1801*. New York, 1906.

450 BEARD, Charles A. *Economic Origins of Jeffersonian Democracy*. 2d ed. New York, 1952.†

451 BOWERS, Claude G. *Jefferson and Hamilton: The Struggle for Democracy in America*. Boston, 1925.†

452 DAUER, Manning J. *The Adams Federalists*. Baltimore, Md., 1953.†

453 FORD, Henry Jones. *Washington and His Colleagues: A Chronicle of the Rise and Fall of Federalism*. New Haven, Conn., 1921.

454 GIBBS, George. *Memoirs of the Administrations of George Washington and John Adams, edited from the papers of Oliver Wolcott, Secretary of the Treasury*. 2 vols. New York, 1846.

455 KURTZ, Stephen G. *The Presidency of John Adams: The Collapse of Federalism, 1795-1800*. New York, 1957.†

456 MILLER, John C. *The Federalist Era: 1789-1801*. New York, 1960.†

457 WHITE, Leonard D. *The Federalists: A Study in Administrative History*. New York, 1948.

Rise of National Political Parties

Formation and Development

458 BINKLEY, Wilfred E. *American Political Parties: Their Natural History*. 4th ed. New York, 1962.

459 BOORSTIN, Daniel. *The Genius of American Politics.* Chicago, 1953.†

460 BORDEN, Morton. *Parties and Politics in the Early Republic, 1789-1815.* New York, 1967.†

461 BROWN, Stuart Gerry. *The First Republicans: Political Philosophy and Public Policy in the Party of Jefferson and Madison.* Syracuse, N.Y., 1954.

462 BUEHL, Richard. *Securing the Revolution: Ideology in American Politics, 1789-1815.* Ithaca, N.Y., 1972.

463 CHAMBERS, William N. "Parties and Nation-Building in America." *Political Parties and Political Development.* Eds. Joseph La Palombra and Myron Weiner. Princeton, N.J., 1966.†

464 CHAMBERS, William Nisbet. *Political Parties in a New Nation: The American Experience, 1776-1809.* New York, 1963.†

465 CHARLES, Joseph. *The Origins of the American Party System: Three Essays.* Williamsburg, Va., 1956.†

466 CUNNINGHAM, Noble, Jr. *The Jeffersonian Republicans: The Formation of Party Organization, 1789-1801.* Chapel Hill, N.C., 1957.†

467 GOODMAN, Paul. "The First American Party System." *The American Party System: Stages of Political Development.* Eds. William N. Chambers and Walter D. Burnham. New York, 1967.

468 HARTZ, Louis. *The Liberal Tradition in America.* New York, 1955.†

469 HOFSTADTER, Richard. *The American Political Tradition and the Men Who Made It.* New York, 1948.†

470 HOFSTADTER, Richard. *The Idea of a Party System: The Rise of Legitimate Opposition in the United States, 1780-1840.* Berkeley and Los Angeles, Cal., 1969.†

471 JOHNSON, E. A. J. "Federalism, Pluralism, and Public Policy." *J Econ Hist,* XXII (1962), 427-444.

472 KOCH, Adrienne. *Jefferson and Madison: The Great Collaboration.* New York, 1950.†

473 MALONE, Dumas. "Hamilton on Balance." *Proc Am Phil Soc,* CII (1958), 129-135.

474 MALONE, Dumas. *Thomas Jefferson as Political Leader.* Berkeley and Los Angeles, Cal., 1963.

475 MORRIS, Richard B. "Washington and Hamilton: A Great Collaboration." *Proc Am Phil Soc,* CII (1958), 107-116.

476 NICHOLS, Roy F. *The Invention of the American Political Parties.* New York, 1967.

477 ROBINSON, Edgar Eugene. *The Evolution of American Political Parties: A Sketch of Party Development.* New York, 1924.

478 ROSE, Lisle A. *Prologue to Democracy.* Lexington, Ky., 1968.

479 STEWART, Donald H. *The Opposition Press of the Federalist Period.* Albany, N.Y., 1969.

480 VAN BUREN, Martin. *Inquiry into the Origin and Course of Political Parties in the United States.* 1867. New York, 1967.

The Process of Elective Government

481 ARONSON, Sidney H. *Status and Kinship in the Higher Civil Service: Standards of Selection in the Administrations of John Adams, Thomas Jefferson, and Andrew Jackson.* Cambridge, Mass., 1964.

482 CHUTE, Marchette. *The First Liberty: A History of the Right to Vote in America, 1619-1850.* New York, 1969.

483 COMMAGER, Henry Steele. "Leadership in Eighteenth Century America & Today." *Daed,* XC (1961), 652-673.

484 CUNNINGHAM, Noble E., Jr. "Early Political Handbills in the United States." *Wm Mar Q,* XIV, 3d ser. (1957), 70-84.

485 CUNNINGHAM, Noble E., Jr. "John Beckley: An Early American Party Manager." *Wm Mar Q,* XIII, 3d ser. (1956), 40-52.

486 DALLINGER, Frederick William. *Nominations for Elective Office in the United States.* New York, 1897.

487 DANIELS, Bruce C. "Deference and Rotation in Selectmen's Offices in 18th-Century Connecticut." *Conn Hist Soc Bull,* XXXVII (1972), 92-96.

488 DeGRAZIA, Alfred. *Public and Republic: Political Representation in America.* New York, 1951.

489 EATON, Clement. "Southern Senators and the Right of Instruction, 1789-1860." *J S Hist,* XVIII (1952), 303-319.

490 GOODMAN, Paul. "Social Status of Party Leadership: The House of Representatives, 1797-1804." *Wm Mar Q,* XXV, 3d ser. (1968), 465-474.

491 HARRIS, P. M. G. "The Social Origins of American Leaders: The Demographic Foundations." *Perspectives Am Hist,* III (1969), 159-344.

492 LUETSCHER, George D. *Early Political Machinery in the United States.* Philadelphia, 1903.

493 McCORMICK, Richard P. *The History of Voting in New Jersey: A Study of the Development of Election Machinery 1664-1911.* New Brunswick, N.J., 1953.

494 McCORMICK, Richard P. "New Perspectives on Jacksonian Politics." *Am Hist Rev,* LXV (1960), 288-301.

495 McCORMICK, Richard P. "Suffrage Classes and Party Alignments: A Study in Voter Behavior." *Miss Val Hist Rev,* XLVI (1959), 397-410.

496 MUSHKAT, Jerome. *Tammany: The Evolution of a Political Machine, 1789-1865.* Syracuse, N.Y., 1971.

497 POLE, J. R. "Constitutional Reform and Election Statistics in Maryland, 1790-1812." *Md Hist Mag,* LV (1955), 275-292.

498 POLE, J. R. "Election Statistics in North Carolina, to 1861." *J S Hist,* XXIV (1958), 225-228.

499 POLE, J. R. "Election Statistics in Pennsylvania, 1790-1840." *Pa Mag Hist Biog,* LXXXII (1958), 217-219.

500 POLE, J. R. *Political Representation in England and the Origins of the American Republic.* New York, 1966.

501 POLE, J. R. "Representation and Authority in Virginia from the Revolution to Reform." *J S Hist,* XXIV (1958), 16-50.

502 POLE, J. R. "Suffrage and Representation in Maryland from 1776 to 1810: A Statistical Note and Some Reflections." *J S Hist,* XXIV (1958), 218-225.

503 POLE, J. R. "Suffrage Reform and the American Revolution in New Jersey." *Proc N J Hist Soc,* LXXIV (1956), 173-194.

504 POLE, J. R. "Suffrage and Representation in Massachusetts: A Statistical Note." *Wm Mar Q,* XIV, 3d ser. (1957), 560-592.

505 POLE, J. R. "The Suffrage in New Jersey, 1790-1807." *Proc N J Hist Soc,* LXXI (1953), 39-61.

506 ROSEBOOM, Eugene Holloway. *A History of Presidential Elections: From George Washington to Richard Nixon.* 3d ed. New York, 1970.†

507 RUDOLPH, Lloyd L. "The Eighteenth Century Mob in America and Europe." *Am Q,* XI (1959), 447-469.

508 SCHLESINGER, Arthur, Jr., Fred L. ISRAEL, and William P. HANSEN, eds. *History of American Presidential Elections.* 4 vols. New York, 1971.

509 SYDNOR, Charles S. *Gentlemen Freeholders: Political Practices in Washington's Virginia.* Chapel Hill, N.C., 1952.†

510 WILLIAMSON, Chilton. *American Suffrage from Property to Democracy, 1760-1860.* Princeton, N.J., 1960.

511 YOUNG, James Sterling. *The Washington Community 1800-1828.* New York and London, 1966.†

Regional and State Politics

512 AMMON, Harry. "The Formation of the Republican Party in Virginia, 1789-1796." *J S Hist,* XIX (1953), 283-310.

513 AMMON, Harry. "The Jeffersonian Republicans in Virginia: An Interpretation." *Va Mag Hist Biog,* LXXI (1963), 153-167.

514 BANNER, James M., Jr. *To the Hartford Convention: The Federalists and the Origin of Party Politics in Massachusetts, 1789-1815.* New York, 1969.

515 FEE, Walter R. *The Transition from Aristocracy to Democracy in New Jersey 1789-1829.* Somerville, N.J., 1933.

516 FERGUSON, Russell Jennings. *Early Western Pennsylvania Politics.* Pittsburgh, Pa., 1938.

517 FOX, Dixon Ryan. *The Decline of Aristocracy in the Politics of New York.* New York, 1919.†

518 GARDINER, C. Harvey, ed. *A Study in Dissent: The Warren-Gerry Correspondence, 1776-1792.* Carbondale, Ill., 1968.

519 GILPATRICK, Delbert Harold. *Jeffersonian Democracy in North Carolina, 1789-1816.* New York, 1931.

520 GOODMAN, Paul. *The Democratic-Republicans of Massachusetts: Politics in a Young Republic.* Cambridge, Mass., 1964.

521   GREEN, Fletcher Melvin. *Constitutional Development in the South Atlantic States, 1776-1860: A Study in the Evolution of Democracy.* Chapel Hill, N.C., 1930.†

522   HAMMOND, Jabez D. *The History of Political Parties in the State of New York.* 3 vols. Rev. ed. Syracuse, N.Y., 1852.

523   HOCKETT, Homer C. *Western Influences on Political Parties to 1825.* Columbus, Ohio, 1917.

524   MORSE, Anson Ely. *The Federalist Party in Massachusetts to the Year 1800.* Princeton, N.J., 1909.

525   MUNROE, John A. *Federalist Delaware, 1775-1815.* New Brunswick, N.J., 1954.

526   PRINCE, Carl E. *New Jersey's Jeffersonian Republicans: The Genesis of an Early Party Machine, 1789-1817.* Chapel Hill, N.C., 1967.†

527   RISJORD, Norman K. "The Virginia Federalists." *J S Hist,* XXXIII (1967), 486-517.

528   ROBINSON, William A. *Jeffersonian Democracy in New England.* New Haven, Conn., 1916.

529   ROSE, Lisle A. *Prologue to Democracy: The Federalists in the South, 1789-1800.* See 478.

530   SCHAPER, William A. "Sectionalism and Representation in South Carolina: A Sociological Study." *Ann Rep Am Hist Assn,* 1900. Washington, D.C., 1901, pp. 237-462.

531   TINKCOM, Harry M. *The Republicans and Federalists in Pennsylvania 1790-1801: A Study in National Stimulus and Local Response.* Harrisburg, Pa., 1950.

532   WAGSTAFF, Henry M. *Federalism in North Carolina.* Chapel Hill, N.C., 1910.

533   WELLING, James C. *Connecticut Federalism, or Aristocratic Politics in a Social Democracy.* New York, 1890.

534   WOLFE, John H. *Jeffersonian Democracy in South Carolina.* Chapel Hill, N.C., 1940.†

535   YOUNG, Alfred F. *The Democratic Republicans of New York: The Origins, 1763-1797.* Chapel Hill, N.C., 1967.

Attitudes and Ideologies

536   ADAIR, Douglass, and Marvin HARVEY. "Was Alexander Hamilton a Christian Statesman?" *Wm Mar Q,* XII, 3d ser. (1955), 308-329.

537   ALEXANDER, Edward P. "Jefferson and Kosciuszko: Friends of Liberty and of Man." *Pa Mag Hist Biog,* XCII (1968), 87-103.

538   ANDREWS, Stuart. "Thomas Jefferson and the French Revolution." *Hist Today,* XVIII (1968), 299-306.

539 APPLEBY, Joyce. "The Jefferson-Adams Rupture and the First French Translation of John Adams' Defence." *Am Hist Rev*, LXXIII (1968), 1084-1091.

540 BARLOW, Joel *Advice to the Privileged Orders in the Several States of Europe*. 1792. Ithaca, N.Y., 1956.†

541 BENTLEY, William. *The Diary of William Bentley, D.D., Pastor of the East Church, Salem, Massachusetts*. 4 vols. Salem, Mass., 1905-1914.

542 BROWN, Margaret L. "Mr. and Mrs. William Bingham of Philadelphia: Rulers of the Republican Court." *Pa Mag Hist Biog*, LXI (1937), 286-324.

543 CARTER, Edward C., II. "A 'Wild Irishman' under Every Federalist's Bed: Naturalization in Philadelphia, 1789-1806." *Pa Mag Hist Biog*, XCIV (1970), 331-346.

544 CLARK, Mary Elizabeth. *Peter Porcupine in America: The Career of William Cobbett, 1792-1800*. Philadelphia, 1939.

545 CROSS, Jack L. "John Marshall on the French Revolution and American Politics." *Wm Mar Q*, XII, 3d ser. (1955), 631-649.

546 DAVIS, Robert Ralph, J. "Diplomatic Plumage: American Court Dress in the Early National Period." *Am Q*, XX (1968), 164-179.

547 DAVIS, Robert Ralph, Jr. "Republican Simplicity: The Diplomatic Costume Question, 1789-1867." *C W Hist*, XV (1969), 19-29.

548 DURDEN, Robert F. "Joel Barlow and the French Revolution." *Wm Mar Q*, VIII, 3d ser. (1951), 327-354.

549 EVERETT, Edward G. "Some Aspects of Pro-French Sentiment in Pennsylvania, 1790-1800." *W Pa Hist Mag*, XLIII (1960), 23-41.

550 FÄY, Bernard. *The Revolutionary Spirit in France and America: A Study of the Intellectual Relations between France and the United States at the End of the Eighteenth Century*. New York, 1927.

551 FISCHER, David H. "The Myth of the Essex Junto." *Wm Mar Q*, XXI, 3d ser. (1964), 191-235.

552 GRISWOLD, Rufus Wilmot. *The Republican Court; or, American Society in the Days of Washington*. New York, 1855.

553 HANS, Nicholas. "Franklin, Jefferson, and the English Radicals at the End of the Eighteenth Century." *Proc Am Phil Soc*, XCVIII (1954), 406-426.

554 HAZEN, Charles Downer. *Contemporary Opinion of the French Revolution*. Baltimore, Md., 1897.

555 HOWE, John R., Jr. "Republican Thought and the Political Violence of the 1790's." *Am Q*, XIX (1947), 147-165.

556 HUTSON, James H. "John Adams' Title Campaign." *N Eng Q*, XLI (1968), 30-39.

557 HYSLOP, Beatrice F. "American Press Reports of the French Revolution, 1789-1794." *N Y Hist Soc Q*, LIII (1969), 34-63.

558 KNUDSON, Jerry W. "The Rage around Tom Paine. Newspaper Reaction to His Homecoming in 1802." *N Y Hist Soc Q*, LIII (1969), 34-63.

559 MASON, Alpheus Thomas. "The Federalist—A Split Personality." *Am Hist Rev*, LVII (1952), 625-643.

560 MORISON, Samuel Eliot. "Squire Ames and Doctor Ames." *N Eng Q*, I (1928), 5-31.

561 NASH, Gary B. "The American Clergy and the French Revolution." *Wm Mar Q*, XXII, 3d ser. (1965), 392-412.

562 PAINE, Thomas. *Rights of Man, Being an Answer to Mr. Burke's Attack on the French Revolution*. Baltimore, Md., 1791.

563 PALMER, R. R. "The Dubious Democrat: Thomas Jefferson in Bourbon France." *Pol Sci Q*, LXXII (1957), 388-404.

564 POLLIN, Burton R. "Godwin's Letter to Ogilvie, Friend of Jefferson, and the Federalist Propaganda." *J Hist Ideas*, XXVIII (1967), 432-444.

565 PROCHASKA, Franklyn K. "Thomas Paine's *The Age of Reason* Revisited." *J Hist Ideas*, XXXIII (1972), 561-576.

566 SMELSER, Marshall. "The Federalist Period as an Age of Passion." *Am Q*, X (1958), 391-419.

567 SMELSER, Marshall. "The Jacobin Phrenzy: Federalism and the Menace of Liberty, Equality, and Fraternity." *Rev Pol*, XIII (1951), 457-482.

568 SMELSER, Marshall. "The Jacobin Phrenzy: The Menace of Monarchy, Plutocracy, and Anglophobia, 1789-1798." *Rev Pol*, XXI (1959), 239-258.

569 WARREN, Charles. *Jacobin and Junto; or Early American Politics as Viewed in the Diary of Dr. Nathaniel Ames, 1758-1822*. Cambridge, Mass., 1931.

570 WEBSTER, T. S. "A New Yorker in the French Revolution: Stephen Thorn, Conspirator for a Canadian Revolution." *N Y Hist Soc Q*, LIII (1969), 251-272.

571 WHARTON Anne. *Social Life in the Early Republic*. Philadelphia, 1902.

572 WOODBURY, Margaret. *Public Opinion in Philadelphia: 1789-1801*. Northampton, Mass., 1920.

Popular Societies

573 ADELSON, Judah. "The Vermont Democratic-Republican Societies and the French Revolution." *Vt Hist*, XXXII (1968), 3-23.

574 JERNEGAN, Marcus D. "The Tammany Societies of Rhode Island." *Papers from the Historical Seminary of Brown University*, VIII (1897), 1-38.

575 KILROE, Edwin Patrick. *Saint Tammany and the Origin of the Society of Tammany or Columbian Order in the City of New York*. New York, 1913.

576 LINK, Eugene Perry. *Democratic-Republican Societies, 1790-1800*. New York, 1942.

577 MILLER, William. "The Democratic Societies and the Whiskey Insurrection." *Pa Mag Hist Biog*, LXII (1938), 324-349.

578 PAULSON, Peter. "The Tammany Society and the Jeffersonian Movement in New York City, 1795-1800." *N Y Hist*, XXXIV (1953), 72-84.

579 UTTER, William T. "Saint Tammany in Ohio: A Study in Frontier Politics." *Miss Val Hist Rev*, XV (1928), 321-340.

Émigrés

580 BALDRIDGE, Edwin R., Jr. "Talleyrand's Visit to Pennsylvania, 1795-1796." *Pa Hist*, XXXVI (1969), 145-160.

581 CHILDS, Francis S. *French Refugee Life in the United States, 1790-1800: An American Chapter of the French Revolution*. Baltimore, Md., 1940.

582 CLARKE, Thomas Wood. *Émigrés in the Wilderness*. New York, 1941.

583 EARL, John L. III. "Talleyrand in Philadelphia, 1794-1796." *Pa Mag Hist Biog*, XCI (1967), 282-298.

584 EMERSON, O. B. "The Bonapartist Exiles in Alabama." *Ala Rev*, XI (1958), 135-143.

585 HUTH, Hans, and Wilma J. PUGH, eds. "Talleyrand in America as a Financial Promotor, 1794-96." *Ann Rep Am Hist Assn*, 1941. Washington, D.C., 1942.

586 SWITZER, Richard, trans. *Chateaubriand's Travels in America*. Lexington, Ky., 1969.

Incidents of the Party Battle

587 BEASLEY, James R. "Emerging Republicanism and the Standing Order: The Appropriation Act Controversy in Connecticut, 1793-1795." *Wm Mar Q*, XXIX, 3d ser. (1972), 587-610.

588 BRADY, Patrick S. "The Slave Trade and Sectionalism in South Carolina, 1787-1808." *J S Hist*, XXXVIII (1972), 601-620.

589 BROWN, Dorothy M. "Maryland and the Federalist: Search for Unity." *Md Hist Mag*, LXIII (1968), 1-21.

590 CLARK, Malcolm C. "Federalism at High Tide: The Election of 1796 in Maryland." *Md Hist Mag*, LXI (1966), 210-230.

591 CLIFFORD, John Garry. "A Muddy Middle of the Road: The Politics of Edmund Randolph, 1790-1795." *Va Mag Hist Biog*, LXXX (1972), 286-311.

592 DeCONDE, Alexander. "Washington's Farewell Address, the French Alliance, and the Election of 1796." *Miss Val Hist Rev*, XLIII (1957), 641-658.

593 FÄY, Bernard. "Early Party Machinery in the United States: Pennsylvania in the Election of 1796." *Pa Mag Hist Biog*, LX (1936), 375-390.

594 FURLONG, Patrick J. "John Rutledge, Jr., and the Election of a Speaker of the House in 1799." *Wm Mar Q*, XXIV, 3d ser. (1967), 432-436.

595 HENDERSON, Dwight F., ed. "Georgia Federal Grand Jury Presentments, 1791-1796." *Ga Hist Q*, LV (1971), 282-292.

596 HOCKETT, Homer C. "Federalism and the West." *Essays in American History Dedicated to Frederick Jackson Turner*. Ed. Guy Stanton Ford. New York, 1951.

597 KLEIN, Frederic Shriver. "Jeffersonians in Local Politics along Pennsylvania-Maryland Border." *Pa Hist*, XXIV (1957), 15-28.

598 KOHN, Richard H. "General Wilkinson's Vendetta with General Wayne: Politics and Command in the American Army, 1791-1796." *Filson Club Hist Q*, XLV (1971), 361-372.

599 LYCAN, Gilbert L. "Alexander Hamilton and the North Carolina Federalists." *N C Hist Rev*, XXV(1948), 442-466.

600 MACLAY, William. *The Journal of William Maclay, United States Senator from Pennsylvania, 1789-1791*. Intro. Charles A. Beard. New York, 1927.

601 MILLER, William. "First Fruits of Republican Organization: Political Aspects of the Congressional Election of 1794." *Pa Mag Hist Biog*, LXIII (1939), 118-143.

602 PAULLIN, Charles Oscar. "The First Elections under the Constitution." *Iowa J Hist Pol*, II (1904), 3-33.

603 PERNICK, Martin S. "Politics, Parties, and Pestilence: Epidemic Yellow Fever in Philadelphia and the Rise of the First Party System." *Wm Mar Q*, XXIX, 3d ser. (1972), 559-586.

604 PHILLIPS, Ulrich B., ed. "South Carolina Federalist Correspondence, 1789-1797." *Am Hist Rev*, XIV (1909), 776-790.

605 PHILLIPS, Ulrich B. "The South Carolina Federalists." *Am Hist Rev*, XIV (1909), 529-543, 731-743.

606 RYAN, Mary P. "Party Formation in the United States Congress 1789 to 1796: A Quantitative Analysis." *Wm Mar Q*, XXVIII, 3d ser. (1971), 523-542.

607 WEHTJE, Myron F. "The Congressional Elections of 1799 in Virginia." *W Va Hist*, XXIX (1968), 251-273.

608 WHEELER, William Bruce. "The Baltimore Jeffersonians, 1788-1800: A Profile of Intra-Factional Conflict." *Md Hist Mag*, LXVI (1971), 153-168.

609 YOUNG, Alfred. "The Mechanics and the Jeffersonians: New York, 1789-1801." *Labor Hist*, V (1964), 247-276.

The Genet Affair

610 AMMON, Harry. "The Genet Mission and the Development of American Political Parties." *Miss Val Hist Rev*, LII (1966), 725-741.

611 BOWMAN, albert H. "Jefferson, Hamilton and American Foreign Policy." *Pol Sci Q*, LXXI (1956), 18-41.

612 MARSH, Philip. "James Monroe as 'Agricola' in the Genet Affair." *Va Mag Hist Biog*, LXII (1954), 472-476.

613 SPENCER, Donald S. "Appeals to the People: The Later Genet Affair." *N Y Hist Soc Q*, LIV (1970), 241-267.

614 THOMAS, Charles M. *American Neutrality in 1793*. New York, 1931.

The Whiskey Rebellion

615 BALDWIN, Leland D. *Whiskey Rebels: The Story of a Frontier Uprising.* Pittsburgh, Pa., 1939.†

616 BARBER, William D. " 'Among the Most *Techy Articles of Civil Policy*': Federal Taxation and the Adoption of the Whiskey Excise.'' *Wm Mar Q,* XXV, 3d ser. (1968), 58-84.

617 BRACKENRIDGE, Henry Marie. *History of the Western Insurrection, 1794.* 1859. New York, 1969.

618 COOKE, Jacob E. "The Whiskey Insurrection: A Re-Evaluation.'' *Pa Hist,* XXX (1963), 316-346.

619 JAMES, Alfred P. "A Political Interpretation of the Whiskey Insurrection.'' *W Pa Hist Mag,* XXXIII (1950), 90-101.

620 KOHN, Richard H. "The Washington Administration's Decision to Crush the Whiskey Rebellion.'' *J Amer Hist,* LIX (1972), 567-584.

The Jay Treaty

621 BEMIS, Samuel Flagg. *Jay's Treaty: A Study in Commerce and Diplomacy.* 1923. Rev. ed. New Haven, 1962.†

622 BHAGAT, G. "The Jay Treaty and the Indian Trade.'' *Essex Inst Hist Coll,* CVIII (1972), 153-172.

623 BOND, B. W. *The Monroe Mission to France, 1794-96.* Baltimore, Md., 1907.

624 BRANT, Irving. "Edmund Randolph, Not Guilty!'' *Wm Mar Q,* VII, 3d ser. (1950), 179-198.

625 COMBS, Jerald A. *The Jay Treaty: Political Battleground of the Founding Fathers.* Berkeley and Los Angeles, Cal., 1970.

626 "Edmund Randolph on the British Treaty.'' *Am Hist Rev,* XII (1907), 587-599.

627 FAUCHET, Joseph. "Mémoire sur les États Unis d'Amérique.'' Ed. Carl Ludwig Lokke. *Ann Rep Am Hist Assn,* 1936. Washington, D.C., 1938, pp. 83-123.

628 JAMES, James Alton. "French Diplomacy and American Politics, 1794-1795.'' *Ann Rep Am Hist Assn,* 1911. Washington, D.C., 1913, pp. 131-163.

629 MONROE, James. *A View of the Conduct of the Executive, in the Foreign Affairs of the United States, Connected with the Mission to the French Republic, during the Years, 1794, 5, and 6.* Philadelphia, 1797.

630 NEWCOMB, Josiah T. "New Light on Jay's Treaty.'' *Am J Int Law,* XXVIII (1934), 685-692.

631 OGG, Frederick Austin. "The Jay Treaty and the Slavery Interests of the United States.'' *Ann Rep Am Hist Assn,* 1901. Washington, D.C., 1902, pp. 273-298.

632 PERKINS, Bradford, ed. "Lord Hawkesbury and the Jay-Grenville Negotiations." *Miss Val Hist Rev,* XL (1953), 291-304.

633 RANDOLPH, Edmund. *A Vindication of Edmund Randolph.* 1795. New ed. with preface by P. U. Daniel, Jr. Richmond, Va., 1855.

634 SMELSER, Marshall. "The Passage of the Naval Act of 1794." *Mil Affairs,* XXII (1958), 1-12.

635 STERLING, David L. "A Federalist Opposes the Jay Treaty: The Letters of Samuel Bayard." *Wm Mary Q,* XVIII, 3d ser. (1961), 408-424.

636 WHITAKER, Arthur P. "Godoy's Knowledge of the Terms of the Jay Treaty." *Am Hist Rev,* XXXV (1930), 804-810.

XYZ and the Quasi-War with France

637 ALLEN, Gardiner Weld. *Our Naval War with France.* Boston, 1909.

638 AMES, Herman Vandenburgh, and John Bach McMASTER, eds. *XYZ Letters.* Philadelphia, 1899.

639 ANDERSON, William G. "John Adams, the Navy, and the Quasi-War with France." *Am Neptune,* XXX (1970), 117-132.

640 Carnegie Endowment for International Peace. *Documents Relating to the Controversy over Neutral Rights between the United States and France, 1797-1800.* Washington, D.C., 1917.

641 CLARFIELD, Gerard H. *Timothy Pickering and American Diplomacy, 1795-1800.* Columbia, Mo., 1969.

642 DeCONDE, Alexander. *The Quasi-War: The Politics and Diplomacy of the Undeclared War with France, 1797-1801.* New York, 1966.†

643 GERRY, Elbridge. *Letterbook, Paris, 1797-1798.* Ed. Russell W. Knight. Salem, Mass., 1966.

644 HILL, Peter P. *William Vans Murray, Federalist Diplomat: The Shaping of Peace with France 1797-1801.* Syracuse, N.Y., 1971.

645 JAMES, James Alton. "French Opinion as a Factor in Preventing War between France and the United States, 1795-1800." *Am Hist Rev,* XXX (1924), 44-56.

646 KRAMER, Eugene F. "John Adams, Elbridge Gerry, and the XYZ Affair." *Essex Inst Hist Coll,* XCIV (1958), 57-68.

647 KRAMER, Eugene F. "Some New Light on the XYZ Affair: Elbridge Gerry's Reasons for Opposing War with France." *N Eng Q,* XXIX (1956), 509-513.

648 KUEHL, John W. "Southern Reaction to the XYZ Affair: An Incident in the Emergence of American Nationalism." *Reg Ky Hist Sox,* LXX (1972), 21-49.

649 KUEHL, John W. "The XYZ Affair and American Nationalism: Republican Victories in the Middle Atlantic States." *Md Hist Mag,* LXVII (1972), 1-20.

650 KURTZ, Stephen G. "The French Mission of 1799-1800: Concluding Chapter in the Statecraft of John Adams." *Pol Sci Q,* LXXX (1965), 543-557.

651 LOGAN, Deborah Norris. *Memoir of Dr. George Logan of Stenton by His Widow.* Philadelphia, 1899.

652 Naval Records and Library Office. *Naval Documents Related to Quasi-War between the United States and France, 1797-1807.* 7 vols. Washington, D.C., 1935-1938.

653 ROBERTSON, William Spence. *The Life of Miranda.* 2 vols. Chapel Hill, N.C., 1929.

654 SAVAGEAU, David Le Pere. "The United States Navy and Its 'Half War' Prisoners, 1798-1801." *Am Neptune,* XXXI (1971), 159-176.

655 SCOTT, James Brown, ed. *The Controversy over Neutral Rights between the United States and France, 1797-1800.* New York, 1917.

656 TOLLES, Frederick B. "Unofficial Ambassador, George Logan's Mission to France, 1798." *Wm Mar Q,* VII, 3d ser. (1950), 3-25.

657 ZAHNISER, Marvin R. "The First Pinckney Mission to France." *S C Hist Mag,* LVI (1965), 205-217.

Alien and Sedition Acts

658 ANDERSON, Frank Maloy. "The Enforcement of the Alien and Sedition Acts." *Ann Rep Am Hist Assn,* 1912. Washington, D.C., 1914, pp. 115-126.

659 FORD, Worthington C., ed. "The Letters of William Duane." *Proc Mass Hist Soc,* XX, 2d ser. (1906), 257-394.

660 FORD, Worthington C., ed. *Thomas Jefferson and James Thomson Callender, 1798-1802.* Brooklyn, N.Y., 1897.

661 JELLISON, Charles A. "That Scoundrel Callender." *Va Mag Hist Biog,* LXVII (1959), 295-306.

662 KELLY, Alfred H. "Constitutional Liberty and the Law of Libel: A Historian's View." *Am Hist Rev,* LXXIV (1968), 429-452.

663 LEVY, Leonard W. *Legacy of Suppression: Freedom of Speech and Press in Early American History.* See 431.

664 LEVY, Leonard W. "Liberty and the First Amendment: 1790-1800." *Am Hist Rev,* LXVIII (1962), 22-37.

665 MILLER, John C. *Crisis in Freedom: The Alien and Sedition Acts.* Boston, 1951.†

666 MONTAGNO, George L. "Federalist Retaliation: The Sedition Trial of Matthew Lyon." *Vt Hist,* XXVI (1958), 3-16.

667 SMELSER, Marshall. "George Washington and the Alien and Sedition Acts." *Am Hist Rev,* LIX (1954), 322-335.

668 SMITH, James Morton. "Alexander Hamilton, the Alien Law, and Seditious Libel." *Rev Pol,* XVI (1954), 305-333.

669 SMITH, James Morton. "The Aurora and the Alien and Sedition Laws." Part I: "The Editorship of Benjamin Franklin Bache." Part II: "The Editorship of William Duane." *Pa Mag Hist Biog,* LXXVII (1953), 3-23, 123-155.

670 SMITH, James Morton. "The Federalist 'Saints' versus 'the Devil of Sedition': The Liberty Pole Cases of Dedham, Massachusetts, 1798-1799." *N Eng Q,* XXVIII (1955), 198-215.

671 SMITH, James Morton. *Freedom's Fetters: The Alien and Sedition Laws and American Civil Liberties.* Ithaca, N.Y., 1956.†

672 SMITH, James Morton. "John Adams Pardons William Durrell: A Note on Sedition Proceedings, 1798-1800." *N Y Hist Soc Q,* XL (1956), 176-182.

673 SMITH, James Morton. "President John Adams, Thomas Cooper, and Sedition: A Case Study in Suppression." *Miss Val Hist Rev,* XLII (1955), 438-465.

674 SMITH, James Morton. "The Sedition Law, Free Speech, and the American Political Process." *Wm Mar Q,* IX, 3d ser. (1952), 497-511.

675 WHARTON, Francis. *State Trials of the United States during the Administration of Washington and Adams.* Philadelphia, 1849.

Virginia and Kentucky Resolutions

676 ANDERSON, Frank Maloy. "Contemporary Opinion of the Virginia and Kentucky Resolutions." *Am Hist Rev,* V (1899), 45-63, 225-252.

677 KOCH, Adrienne, and Harry AMMON. "The Virginia and Kentucky Resolutions: An Episode in Jefferson's and Madison's Defense of Civil Liberties." *Wm Mar Q,* V, 3d ser. (1958), 145-176.

678 SMITH, James Morton. "The Grass Roots Origins of the Kentucky Resolutions." *Wm Mar Q,* XXVII, 3d ser. (1970), 221-245.

Election of 1800

679 BORDEN, Morton. "The Election of 1800: Charge and Countercharge." *Del Hist,* V (1952), 42-62.

680 CASSELL, Frank A. "General Samuel Smith and the Election of 1800." *Md Hist Mag,* LXIII (1968), 341-359.

681 HAYNES, Robert V. "The Revolution of 1800 in Mississippi." *J Miss Hist,* XIX (1957), 234-251.

682 JAMESON, J. Franklin, ed. "South Carolina in the Presidential Election of 1800." *Am Hist Rev,* IV (1898), 111-129.

683 KAPLANOFF, Mark D. "Religion and Righteousness: A Study of Federalist Rhetoric in the New Hampshire Election of 1800." *Hist N H,* XXIII (1968), 3-20.

684 LERCHE, Charles O., Jr. "Jefferson and the Election of 1800: A Case Study of the Political Smear." *Wm Mar Q,* V, 3d ser. (1948), 467-491.

685 MORSE, Anson D. "Causes and Consequences of the Party Revolution of 1800." *Ann Rep Am Hist Assn,* 1894. Washington, D.C., 1895, pp. 531-540.

686 O'BRIEN, Charles F. "The Religious Issue in the Presidential Campaign of 1800." *Essex Inst Hist Coll,* CVII (1971), 82-93.

687 PARTON, James. "The Presidential Election of 1800." *Atl Mo,* XVII (1873), 27-45.

Foreign Relations, 1789-1801

688 BEMIS, Samuel Flagg. *Pinckney's Treaty: America's Advantage from Europe's Distress, 1783-1800.* Rev. ed. New Haven, Conn., 1960.

689 BEMIS, Samuel Flagg. "Washington's Farewell Address: A Foreign Policy of Independence." *Am Hist Rev,* XXXIX (1934), 250-268.

690 BIZARDEL, Yvon, and Howard C. RICE, Jr. " 'Poor in Love Mr. Short.' " *Wm Mar Q,* XXI, 3d ser. (1964), 516-533.

691 BURT, A. L. *The United States, Great Britain and British North America, from the Revolution to the Establishment of Peace after the War of 1812.* See 66.

692 CANTOR, Milton. "A Connecticut Yankee in a Barbary Court: Joel Barlow's Algerian Letters to His Wife." *Wm Mar Q,* XIX, 3d ser. (1962), 86-109.

693 CANTOR, Milton. "Joel Barlow's Mission to Algiers." *Hist,* XXV (1963), 172-194.

694 CROSS, Jack L.*The London Mission: The First Critical Years.* East Lansing, Mich., 1968.

695 DeCONDE, Alexander. *Entangling Alliance: Politics and Diplomacy under George Washington.* Durham, N.C., 1958.

696 DeCONDE, Alexander, George L. MONTAGNO, and Joel LARUS. "Growing Pains of the New Republic." *Wm Mar Q,* XVII, 3d ser. (1960), 341-357.

697 ECHEVERRIA, Durand, ed. and trans. "General Collot's Plan for a Reconnaissance of the Ohio and Mississippi Valleys, 1796." *Wm Mar Q,* IX, 3d ser. (1952), 512-520.

698 FÄY, Bernard. *The Revolutionary Spirit in France and America: A Study of the Intellectual Relations between France and the United States at the End of the Eighteenth Century.* See 550.

699 GILBERT, Felix. *To the Farewell Address: Ideas of Early American Foreign Policy.* Princeton, N.J., 1961.† Paperback ed. title *The Beginnings of American Foreign Policy.* New York, 1965.

700 GRABER, Doris A. *Public Opinion, the President, and Foreign Policy: Four Case Studies from the Formative Years.* See 68.

701 HORSMAN, Reginald. "The British Indian Department and the Abortive Treaty of Lower Sandusky, 1793." *Ohio Hist Q,* LXX (1961), 189-213.

702 HORSMAN, Reginald. "The British Indian Department and the Resistance to General Anthony Wayne, 1793-1795." *Miss Val Hist Rev,* XLIX (1962), 269-290.

703 JACKSON, Melvin H. *Privateers in Charleston, 1793-1796: An Account of a French Palatinate in South Carolina.* Washington, D.C., 1969.

704 KAPLAN, Lawrence S. "The Consensus of 1789: Jefferson and Hamilton on American Foreign Policy." *S Atl Q,* LXXI (1972), 91-105.

705 LOOZE, Helene Johnson. *Alexander Hamilton and the British Orientation of American Foreign Policy, 1783-1803.* The Hague and Paris, 1969.

706 LYCAN, Gilbert L. *Alexander Hamilton and American Foreign Policy: A Design for Greatness.* Norman, Okla., 1970.

707 LYCAN, Gilbert L. "Alexander Hamilton's Florida Policy." *Fla Hist Q,* L (1971), 143-157.

708 LYON, E. Wilson. "The Directory and the United States." *Am Hist Rev,* XLIII (1938), 515-533.

709 LYON, E. Wilson. "The Franco-American Convention of 1800." *J Mod Hist,* XII (1940), 305-334.

710 MANNING, W. R. "The Nootka Sound Controversy." *Ann Rep Am Hist Assn,* 1904. Washington, D.C., 1905, pp. 279-478.

711 MARKOWITZ, Arthur A. "Washington's Farewell and the Historians: A Critical Review." *Pa Mag Hist Biog,* XCIV (1970), 173-191.

712 MURDOCH, Richard K. *The Georgia-Florida Frontier, 1793-1796: Spanish Reaction to French Intrigue and American Designs.* Berkeley, Cal., 1951.

713 NASATIR, Abraham P. *Spanish War Vessels on the Mississippi, 1792-1796.* New Haven, Conn., 1968.

714 PALTSITS, Vernon Hugo, ed. *Washington's Farewell Address.* New York, 1935.

715 PARTON, Dorothy M. *The Diplomatic Career of Joel Roberts Poinsett.* Washington, D.C., 1934.

716 PERKINS, Bradford. *The First Rapprochement: England and the United States, 1795-1805.* Philadelphia, 1955.

717 PETERSON, Merrill D. "Thomas Jefferson and Commercial Policy, 1783-1793." *Wm Mar Q,* XXII, 3d ser. (1965), 584-610.

718 RICE, Howard C. "James Swan: Agent of the French Republic, 1794-1796." *N Eng Q,* X (1937), 464-486.

719 RIPPY, J. Fred, and Angie DEBO. "The Historical Background of the American Policy of Isolation." *Smith Col Stud Hist,* IX (1924), 75-165.

720 RIPPY, J. Fred. *Joel Roberts Poinsett, Versatile American.* Durham, N.C., 1935.

721 SEARS, Louis Martin. *George Washington and the French Revolution.* Detroit, Mich., 1960.

722 THOMAS, Charles M. *American Neutrality in 1793.* See 614.

723 TRESCOTT, W. H. *The Diplomatic History of the Administrations of Washington and Adams, 1789-1801.* Boston, 1857.

724 TURNER, Frederick Jackson, ed. "Correspondence of the French Ministers to the United States, 1791-1797." *Ann Rep Am Hist Assn,* 1903. Washington, D.C., 1904.

725 TURNER, Frederick Jackson, ed. "Documents in the Blount Conspiracy, 1795-1797." *Am Hist Rev,* X (1905), 574-606.

726   TURNER, Frederick Jackson. "The Policy of France toward the Mississippi Valley in the Period of Washington and Adams." *Am Hist Rev*, X (1905), 249-279.

727   VARG, Paul A. *Foreign Policies of the Founding Fathers*. East Lansing, Mich., 1963.

728   WHITAKER, Arthur Preston. *The Mississippi Question, 1795-1803: A Study in Trade, Politics, and Diplomacy*. See 91.

729   WHITAKER, Arthur Preston. *The Spanish-American Frontier 1783-1795: The Westward Movement and the Spanish Retreat in the Mississippi Valley*. See 92.

730   WRIGHT, J. Leitch, Jr. "British Designs on the Old Southwest: Foreign Intrigue on the Florida Frontier, 1783-1803." *Fla Hist Q*, XLIV (1966), 265-284.

4. The Republican Era

General

731   ADAMS, Henry. *History of the United States during the Administration of Jefferson and Madison*. 9 vols. New York, 1889-1891. Abr. and Ed., Ernest Samuels. Chicago, 1967.†

732   BABCOCK, Kendrick Charles. *The Rise of American Nationality, 1811-1819*. New York, 1906.

733   BOWERS, Claude G. *Jefferson in Power: The Death Struggle of the Federalists*. Boston, 1936.†

734   CHANNING, Edward. *The Jeffersonian System, 1801-11*. New York, 1906.

735   DANGERFIELD, George. *The Era of Good Feelings*. New York, 1952.†

736   JOHNSON, Allen. *Jefferson and His Colleagues: A Chronicle of the Virginia Dynasty*. New Haven, Conn., 1921.

737   SMELSER, Marshall. *The Democratic Republic, 1801-1815*. New York, 1968.†

738   WALTERS, Raymond, Jr. *The Virginia Dynasty: The United States, 1801-1829*. Princeton, N.J., 1965.†

739   WHITE, Leonard D. *The Jeffersonians: A Study in Administrative History, 1801-1829*. New York, 1959.†

Politics

740   ADAMS, Henry, ed. *Documents Relating to New England Federalism, 1800-1815*. Boston, 1905.

741   AMMON, Harry. "James Monroe and the Election of 1808 in Virginia." *Wm Mar Q*, XX, 3d ser. (1963), 33-56.

742 BROWN, Charles Raymond. *The Northern Confederacy According to the Plans of the Essex Junto, 1796-1814*. Princeton, N.J., 1915.

743 BROWN, Everett Somerville, ed. *William Plumer's Memorandum of Proceedings in the United States Senate, 1803-1807*. 1923. New York, 1969.

744 COLE, Donald B. *Jacksonian Democracy in New Hampshire, 1800-1851*. See 98.

745 CUNNINGHAM, Noble E., Jr. *The Jeffersonian Republicans in Power, Party Operations, 1801-1809*. Chapel Hill, N.C., 1963.†

746 CUNNINGHAM, Noble E., Jr. "Who Were the Quids?" *Miss Val Hist Rev*, L (1963), 252-263.

747 ELSMERE, Jane. "The Notorious Yazoo Land Fraud Case." *Ga Hist Q*, LI (1967), 425-442.

748 FISCHER, David Hackett. *The Revolution of American Conservatism: The Federalist Party in the Era of Jeffersonian Democracy*. New York, 1965.†

749 HANYAN, Craig R. "De Witt Clinton and Partisanship: The Development of Clintonianism from 1811 to 1820." *N Y Hist Soc Q*, LVII (1972), 109-131.

750 HARRISON, Joseph H., Jr. "Oligarchs and Democrats: The Richmond Junto." *Va Mag Hist Biog*, LXXVIII (1970), 184-198.

751 HAYNES, George H., ed. "Letters of Samuel Taggart: Representative in Congress, 1803-1814." *Proc Am Ant Soc*, XXXIII, New Ser. (1923), 113-226.

752 HERNDON, G. Melvin. "The 1806 Survey of the North Carolina Coast, Cape Hatteras to Cape Fear." *N C Hist Rev*, XLIX (1972), 242-253.

753 HIGGINBOTHAM, Sanford W. *The Keystone in the Democratic Arch: Pennsylvania Politics, 1800-1816*. Harrisburg, Pa., 1952.

754 HUNT, Gaillard, ed. *The First Forty Years of Washington Society, Portrayed by the Family Letters of Mrs. Samuel Harrison Smith . . .* New York, 1906.

755 HUNT, Gaillard. "Office-Seeking during Jefferson's Administration." *Am Hist Rev*, III (1898), 270-291.

756 JORDAN, Daniel P., ed. "Congressional Electioneering in Early West Virginia: A Mini-War in Broadsides." *W Va Hist*, XXXIII (1971), 61-78.

757 KERBER, Linda K. *Federalists in Dissent: Imagery and Ideology in Jeffersonian America*. Ithaca, N.Y., 1970.

758 KNUDSON, Jerry W. "The Case of Albert Gallatin and Jeffersonian Patronage." *W Pa Hist Mag*, LII (1969), 241-250.

759 LEVY, Leonard. *Jefferson and Civil Liberties: The Darker Side*. Cambridge, Mass., 1963.

760 MACPHEE, Donald A. "The Yazoo Controversy: The Beginning of the 'Quid' Revolt." *Ga Hist Q*, XLIX (1965), 23-43.

761 MAGRATH, C. Peter. *Yazoo, Law and Politics in the New Republic: The Case of Fletcher v. Peck*. Providence, R.I., 1966.†

762 MALONE, Dumas. "Presidential Leadership and National Unity: The Jeffersonian Example." *J S Hist*, XXV (1969), 4-17.

763 MERRIAM, J. M. "Jefferson's Use of Executive Patronage." *Paps Am Hist Assn*, II (1887), no. 1, 47-52.

764 MORISON, Samuel Eliot. "First National Nominating Convention, 1808." *Am Hist Rev*, XVII (1912), 744-763.

765 POLE, J. R. "Jeffersonian Democracy and the Federalist Dilemma in New Jersey, 1798-1812." *Proc N J Hist Soc*, LXXIV (1956), 260-292.

766 PRENTISS, Harvey Putnam. *Timothy Pickering as the Leader of New England Federalism, 1800-1815*. Salem, Mass., 1934.

767 PRINCE, Carl E. "The Passing of the Aristocracy: Jefferson's Removal of the Federalists, 1801-1815." *Am Hist Rev*, LVII (1970), 563-575.

768 PRINCE, Carl E. "Patronage and a Party Machine: New Jersey Democratic-Republican Activists, 1801-16." *Wm Mar Q*, XXI, 3d ser. (1964), 571-578.

769 QUINCY, Josiah. *Memoir of the Life of John Quincy Adams*. Boston, 1860.

770 RISJORD, Norman K. *The Old Republicans: Southern Conservatism in the Age of Jefferson*. New York, 1965.

771 RULE, Henry B. "Henry Adams' Attack on Two Heroes of the Old South." *Am Q*, XIV (1962), 174-184.

772 SAPIO, Victor. "Maryland's Federalist Revival, 1808-1812." *Md Hist Mag*, LXIV (1969), 1-17.

773 SCANLON, James E. "A Sudden Conceit: Jefferson and the Louisiana Government Bill of 1804." *La Hist*, IX (1968), 139-162.

774 STAMPS, Norman L. "Party Government in Connecticut, 1800-1816." *Hist*, XVII (1955), 172-190.

Louisiana Purchase

775 ADAIR, Douglass. "Hamilton on the Louisiana Purchase: A Newly Identified Editorial from *The New York Evening Post*." *Wm Mar Q*, XII, 3d ser. (1955), 268-281.

776 ADAMS, Mary P. "Jefferson's Reaction to the Treaty of San Ildefonso." *J S Hist*, XXI (1955), 173-188.

777 ARENA, C. Richard. "Philadelphia-Mississippi Valley Trade and the Deposit Closure of 1802." *Pa Hist*, XXX (1963), 28-45.

778 BAILEY, Hugh C., and Bernard C. WEBER. "A British Reaction to the Treaty of San Ildefonso." *Wm Mar Q*, XVII, 3d ser. (1960), 242-246.

779 BROWN, Everett Somerville. *The Constitutional History of the Louisiana Purchase, 1803-1812*. Berkeley, Cal., 1920.

780 CHIDSEY, Donald Barr. *Louisiana Purchase*. New York, 1972.

781 CLAIBORNE, W. C. C. *Official Letter Books . . . 1801-1816*. Ed. Dunbar Rowland. 6 vols. Jackson, Miss., 1917.

782 "Dispatches from the United States Consulate in New Orleans, 1801-1803." *Am Hist Rev*, XXXII (1927), 801-824; XXXIII (1928), 331-359.

783 GOLD, Robert L. *Borderland Empires in Transition: The Triple-National Transfer of Florida*. Carbondale, Ill., 1969.

784 GUINNESS, Ralph B. "The Purpose of the Lewis and Clark Expedition." *Miss Val Hist Rev*, XX (1933), 90-100.

785 HARRISON, Lowell H. "John Breckinridge and the Acquisition of Louisiana." *La Stud*, VII (1968), 7-30.

786 KNUDSON, Jerry W. "Newspaper Reaction to the Louisiana Purchase: 'This New, Immense, Unbounded World.' " *Mo Hist Rev*, LXIII (1969), 182-213.

787 LYON, Elijah Wilson. *Louisiana in French Diplomacy, 1759-1804*. See 74.

788 LYON, Elijah Wilson. *The Man Who Sold Louisiana: The Career of François Barbé-Marbois*. Norman, Okla., 1942.

789 NICHOLS, Roy F. "The Louisiana Purchase: Challenge and Stimulus to American Democracy." *La Hist Q*, XXXVIII (1955), 1-25.

790 NUTTER, Charles. "Robert R. Livingston, the Forgotten Architect of the Louisiana Purchase." *Mo Hist Rev*, XLVIII (1954), 117-133.

791 PELZER, Louis. "Economic Factors in the Acquisition of Louisiana." *Proc Miss Val Hist Assn*, VI (1912-1913), 109-127.

792 SHOEMAKER, Floyd C. "The Louisiana Purchase, 1803, and the Transfer of Upper Louisiana to the United States, 1804." *Mo Hist Rev*, XLVIII (1953), 1-22.

793 SMITH, Ronald D. "Napoleon and Louisiana: Failure of the Proposed Expedition to Occupy and Defend Louisiana, 1801-1803." *La Hist*, XII (1971), 21-40.

794 SPRAGUE, Stuart Seely. "Jefferson, Kentucky and the Closing the Port of New Orleans, 1802-1803." *Reg Ky Hist Soc*, LXX (1972), 312-317.

795 WHITAKER, Arthur P. *The Mississippi Question, 1795-1803: A Study in Trade, Politics, and Diplomacy*. See 91.

796 WHITAKER, Arthur P. "New Light on the Treaty of San Lorenzo: An Essay in Historical Criticism." *Miss Val Hist Rev*, XV (1929), 435-454.

Republicans and the Marshall Court

797 BOYD, Julian P. "The Chasm that Separated Thomas Jefferson and John Marshall." *Essays on the American Constitution*. Ed. Gottfried Dietze. Englewood Cliffs, N.J., 1964.

798 CRAIGMYLE, Thomas Shaw. *John Marshall in Diplomacy and Law*. New York, 1933.

799 DODD, William E. "Chief Justice John Marshall and Virginia." *Am Hist Rev*, XII (1907), 776-787.

800 DUNNE, Gerald T. "Joseph Story: 1812 Overture." *Har Law Rev*, LXXVII (1963), 240-278.

801 ELLIS, Richard E. *The Jeffersonian Crisis: Courts and Politics in the Young Republic*. New York, 1971.

802 FARRAND, Max. "The Judiciary Act of 1801." *Am Hist Rev*, V (1900), 682-686.

803 FAULKNER, Robert Kenneth. *The Jurisprudence of John Marshall.* Princeton, N.J., 1968.

804 FRISCH, Morton J. "John Marshall's Philosophy of Constitutional Republicanism." *Rev Pol,* XX (1958), 34-45.

805 HOOKER, Richard J., ed. "John Marshall on the Judiciary, the Republicans, and Jefferson, March 4, 1801." *Am Hist Rev,* LIII (1948), 518-520.

806 HORTON, John T. *James Kent: A Study in Conservatism.* New York, 1939.

807 JACKSON, Percival E. *Dissent in the Supreme Court: A Chronology.* Norman, Okla., 1969.

808 JONES, William Melville, ed. *Chief Justice John Marshall: A Reappraisal.* Ithaca, N.Y., 1956.

809 KERBER, Linda K. "Oliver Wolcott: Midnight Judge." *Conn Hist Soc Bull,* XXXII (1967), 25-30.

810 KNUDSON, Jerry W. "The Jeffersonian Assault on the Federalist Judiciary, 1802-1805: Political Forces and Press Reaction." *Am J Legal Hist,* XIV (1970), 55-75.

811 KONEFSKY, Samuel Joseph. *John Marshall and Alexander Hamilton, Architects of the American Constitution.* New York, 1964.

812 LERNER, Max. "John Marshall and the Campaign of History." *Col Law Rev,* XXXIX (1939), 396-431.

813 LILLICH, Richard B. "The Chase Impeachment." *Am J Legal Hist,* IV (1960), 49-72.

814 MORGAN, Donald G. *Justice William Johnson, the First Dissenter: The Career and Constitutional Philosophy of a Jeffersonian Judge.* Columbia, S.C., 1954.

815 NEWMYER, R. Kent. "Joseph Story and the War of 1812: A Judicial Nationalist." *Hist,* XXVI (1964), 486-501.

816 RADABAUGH, John. "Spencer Roane and the Genesis of Virginia Judicial Review." *Am J Legal Hist,* VI (1962), 63-70.

817 ROPER, Donald. "Judicial Unanimity and the Marshall Court—A Road to Reappraisal." *Am J Legal Hist,* IX (1965), 118-134.

818 TURNER, Kathryn. "The Appointment of Chief Justice Marshall." *Wm Mar Q,* XVII, 3d ser. (1960), 143-163.

819 TURNER, Kathryn. "Federalist Policy and the Judiciary Act of 1801." *Wm Mar Q,* XXII, 3d ser. (1965), 3-32.

820 TURNER, Lynn W. "The Impeachment of John Pickering." *Am Hist Rev,* LIV (1949), 485-407.

The Burr Conspiracy

821 ABERNETHY, Thomas Perkins. *The Burr Conspiracy.* New York, 1954.

822 BEIRNE, Francis F. *Shout Treason: The Trial of Aaron Burr.* New York, 1959.

823 BURR, Samuel Engle, Jr. *Napoleon's Dossier on Aaron Burr: Proposals of Colonel Aaron Burr to the Emperor Napoleon from Les Archives Nationales, Paris, France, with Background and Retrospect.* San Antonio, Tex., 1969.

824 COX, Isaac Joslin. "General Wilkinson and His Later Intrigues with the Spaniards." *Am Hist Rev,* XIX (1914), 794-812.

825 FAULKNER, Robert K. "John Marshall and the Burr Trial." *J Am Hist,* LIII (1966), 246-258.

826 McCALEB, Walter. *The Aaron Burr Conspiracy: and, A New Light on Aaron Burr.* New York, 1966.

827 REED, V. B., and J. D. WILLIAMS, eds. *The Case of Aaron Burr.* New York, 1960.

Foreign Relations

General

828 BIERCK, Harold, Jr. "The First Instance of U.S. Foreign Aid:Venezuelan Relief in 1812." *Inter-Am Econ Affairs,* IX (1955), 47-59.

829 BOWMAN, Charles H., Jr. "Manuel Torres, a Spanish American Patriot in Philadelphia, 1796-1822." *Pa Hist,* XCIV (1970), 26-53.

830 BRADLEY, Jared W. "W. C. C. Claiborne and Spain: Foreign Affairs under Jefferson and Madison, 1801-1811." *La Hist,* XII (1971), 297-314; XIII (1972), 5-26.

831 BRANT, Irving. "Joel Barlow, Madison's Stubborn Minister." *Wm Mar Q,* XV, 3d ser. (1958), 438-451.

832 BRIGGS, Herbert Whittaker. *The Doctrine of Continuous Voyage.* Baltimore, Md., 1940.

833 CARR, Albert Z. *The Coming of War: An Account of the Remarkable Events Leading to the War of 1812.* Garden City, N.Y., 1960.

834 COX, Isaac Joslin. "Monroe and the Early Mexican Revolutionary Agents." *Ann Rep Am Hist Assn,* 1911. Washington, D.C., 1913, pp. 199-215.

835 COX, Isaac Joslin. *The West Florida Controversy, 1798-1813: A Study in American Diplomacy.* 1918. Gloucester, Mass., 1967.

836 DAVIS, Robert Ralph, Jr. "Republican Simplicity: The Diplomatic Costume Question, 1789-1867." See 547.

837 DYER, George B., and Charlotte L. DYER. "The Beginnings of a United States Strategic Intelligence System in Latin America, 1809-1826." *Mil Affairs,* XIV (1950), 65-83.

838 EGAN, Clifford L. "United States, France, and West Florida, 1803-1807." *Fla Hist Q,* XLVII (1969), 227-252.

839 EMMERSON, John Cloyd, Jr. *The Chesapeake Affair of 1807.* Portsmouth, Va., 1954.

840 GAINES, Edwin M. "The Chesapeake Affair: Virginians Mobilize to Defend National Honor." *Va Mag Hist Biog,* LXIV (1956), 131-142.

841 GRIFFIN, Charles Carroll. "Privateering from Baltimore during the Spanish American Wars of Independence." *Md Hist Mag,* XXXV (1940), 1-25.

842 GRIFFIN, Charles Carroll. *The United States and the Disruption of the Spanish Empire 1810-1822.* New York, 1937.

843 IRWIN, Roy Watkins. *The Diplomatic Relations of United States with the Barbary Pirates, 1776-1816.* See 72.

844 KAPLAN, Lawrence S. "Jefferson, the Napoleonic Wars, and the Balance of Power." *Wm Mar Q,* XIV, 3d ser. (1957), 196-217.

845 KAPLAN, Lawrence S. "Jefferson's Foreign Policy and Napoleon's Ideologues." *Wm Mar Q,* XIX, 3d ser. (1962), 344-359.

846 MARKS, Henry S., ed. "Boundary Disputes in the Republic of West Florida in 1810." *La Hist,* XII (1971), 355-365.

847 MORISON, Samuel Eliot, ed. "DuPont, Talleyrand, and French Spoliations." *Proc Mass Hist Stoc,* XLIX, 2d ser. (1915), 63-79.

848 PARKER, David W. "Secret Reports of John Howe, 1808." *Am Hist Rev,* XVII (1911), 70-102, 332-354.

849 PARTON, Dorothy M. *The Diplomatic Career of Joel Roberts Poinsett.* See 715.

850 PATRICK, Rembert Wallace. *Florida Fiasco: Rampart Rebels on the Georgia Florida Border, 1810-1815.* Athens, Ga., 1954.

851 PERKINS, Bradford. *Castlereagh and Adams: England and the United States, 1812-1823.* Berkeley, Cal., 1964.

852 PERKINS, Bradford. "George Canning, Great Britain, and the United States, 1807-1809." *Am Hist Rev,* LXIII (1957), 1-22.

853 PERKINS, Bradford. "George Joy, American Propagandist at London, 1805-1815." *N Eng Q,* XXXIV (1961), 191-210.

854 PERKINS, Bradford. *Prologue to War: England and the United States, 1805-1812.* 2d ed. Berkeley, Cal., 1968.†

855 PERKINS, Bradford. "Sir William Scott and the Essex." *Wm Mar Q,* XIII, 3d ser. (1956), 169-183.

856 RIPPY, J. Fred. *Joel Roberts Poinsett, Versatile American.* See 720.

857 RIPPY, J. Fred. *Rivalry of the United States and Great Britain over Latin America (1808-1830).* New York, 1964.

858 ROSMAN, Reginald. "British Indian Policy in the Northwest, 1807-1812." *Miss Val Hist Rev,* XLV (1958), 51-66.

859 SHULIM, Joseph I. "Thomas Jefferson Views Napoleon." *Va Mag Hist Biog,* LX (1952), 288-304.

860 SMITH, Jay D. "Commodore James Barron: Guilty as Charged [1807]?" *Proc U S Nav Inst,* XCIII (1967), 79-85.

861 STEEL, Anthony. "More Light on the Chesapeake." *Mar Mirror,* XXIX (1953), 243-265.

862 STEEL, Anthony. "Impressment in the Monroe-Pinckney Negotiation, 1806-1807." *Am Hist Rev,* LVII (1952), 352-369.

863 STEPHEN, James. *War in Disguise; or The Frauds of the Neutral Flags.* Repr. 3d ed. Ed. Francis Piggott. London, 1917.

864 TSIANG, I-mien. *The Question of Expatriation in America Prior to 1907.* Baltimore, Md., 1942.

865 WHITAKER, Arthur P. *The United States and the Independence of Latin America, 1800-1830.* Baltimore, Md., 1941.

866 ZIMMERMAN, James Fulton. *Impressment of American Seamen.* New York, 1925.

Commercial Reprisal and the Embargo

867 ALBION, Robert G. "Maritime Adventures of New York in the Napoleonic Era." *Essays in Modern English History in Honor of Wilbur Cortez Abbott.* Cambridge, Mass., 1941.

868 BRIGGS, Herbert Whittaker. *The Doctrine of Continuous Voyage.* See 832.

869 BROWN, Dorothy M. "Embargo Politics in Maryland." *Md Hist Mag,* LVIII (1963), 193-210.

870 BRYANT, William Cullen. *The Embargo; or, Sketches of the Times.* Ed. Thomas D. Mabbott. 1809. Gainesville, Fla., 1955.

871 CROSBY, Alfred W., Jr. *America, Russia, Hemp, and Napoleon: American Trade with Russia and the Baltic, 1783-1812.* Columbus, Ohio, 1965.

872 CROSBY, Alfred W. "American Trade with Mauritius in the Age of the French Revolution and Napoleon." *Am Neptune,* XXV (1965), 5-17.

873 CROUZET, François. "Wars, Blockade, and Economic Change in Europe, 1792-1815." *J Econ Hist,* XXIV (1964), 567-588.

874 DANIELS, G. W. "American Cotton Trade with Liverpool under the Embargo and Non-Intercourse Acts." *Am Hist Rev,* XXI (1916), 276-287.

875 FORBES, John D. "European Wars and Boston Trade, 1783-1815." *N Eng Q,* XI (1938), 709-730.

876 GALPIN, William F. "The American Grain Trade to the Spanish Peninsula, 1810-1814." *Am Hist Rèv,* XXVIII (1922), 24-44.

877 GALPIN, William F. "American Grain Trade under the Embargo of 1808." *J Econ Bus Hist,* II (1929), 71-100.

878 GALPIN, William F. *The Grain Supply of England during the Napoleonic Period.* New York, 1925.

879 GALPIN, William F. "The Grain Trade of New Orleans, 1804-1814." *Miss Val Hist Rev,* XIV (1928), 497-507.

880 HEATON, Herbert. "Non-Importation, 1806-1812." *J Econ Hist,* I (1941), 178-198.

881 HECKSCHER, Eli Filip. *The Continental System: An Economic Interpretation.* Ed. Harold Westergaard. London and New York, 1922.

882 JENNINGS, Walter Wilson. *The American Embargo, 1807-1809, with Particular Reference to Its Effect on Industry.* Iowa City, 1921.

883 LINGELBACH, William E. "England and Neutral Trade." *Mil Hist Econ*, II (1917), 153-178.

884 MELVIN, Frank Edgar. *Napoleon's Navigation System: A Study of Trade Control during the Continental Blockade*. New York, 1919.

885 PANCAKE, John S. "Baltimore and the Embargo, 1807-1809." *Md Hist Mag*, XLVII (1952), 173-187.

886 REINHOEL, John H., ed. "Some Remarks on the American Trade: Jacob Crowninshield to James Madison, 1806." *Wm Mar Q*, XVI, 3d ser. (1959), 83-118.

887 SEARS, Louis M. *Jefferson and the Embargo*. Durham, N.C., 1927.

888 "Smuggling in 1813-1814: A Personal Reminiscence." *Vt Hist*, XXXVIII (1970), 22-26.

889 WILTSE, Charles Maurice. *Thomas Jefferson on the Law of Nations*. Concord, N.H., 1935.

War of 1812

General

890 BABCOCK, Louis L. *War of 1812 on the Niagara Frontier*. Buffalo, N.Y., 1927.

891 BEIRNE, Francis F. *The War of 1812*. New York, 1949.

892 BROWN, Roger H. *The Republic in Peril: 1812*. New York, 1964.

893 COLES, Harry Lewis. *The War of 1812*. Chicago, 1965.†

894 GILPIN, Alec R. *The War of 1812 in the Old Northwest*. East Lansing, Mich., 1958.

895 GRIBBIN, William. "The War of 1812 and American Presbyterianism: Religion and Politics during the Second War with Britain." *J Presby Hist Soc*, XLVII (1969), 320-339.

896 HITSMAN, J. Mackay. "David Parrish and the War of 1812." *Mil Affairs*, XXVI (1963), 171-177.

897 HORSMAN, Reginald. *The War of 1812*. New York, 1969.

898 JACOBS, James Ripley, and Glenn TUCKER. *The War of 1812: A Compact History*. New York, 1969.

899 KAPLAN, Lawrence S. "France and the War of 1812." *J Amer Hist*, LVII (1970), 36-47.

900 LAWSON, Don. *The War of 1812: America's Second War for Independence*. London and New York, 1966.

901 LUCAS, Sir Charles Prestwood. *The Canadian War of 1812*. Oxford, England, 1906.

902 PAINE, Ralph Delahage. *The Fight for a Free Sea: A Chronicle of the War of 1812*. New Haven, Conn., 1920.

903　SAPIO, Victor A. *Pennsylvania and the War of 1812*. Lexington, Ky., 1970.

904　TUCKER, Glenn. *Poltroons and Patriots: A Popular Account of the War of 1812*. Indianapolis and New York, 1954.

905　WHITE, Patrick Cecil Telfer. *A Nation on Trial: America and the War of 1812*. New York, 1965.†

906　WILSON, Joseph Thomas. *The Black Phalanx*. 1890. New York, 1968.

907　ZASLOW, Morris, ed. *The Defended Border: Upper Canada and the War of 1812*. Toronto, 1964.

The Decision for War

908　ANDERSON, Dice R. "The Insurgents of 1811." *Ann Rep Am Hist Assn*, 1911. Washington, D.C., 1913, pp. 167-176.

909　BARLOW, William. "The Coming of the War of 1812 in Michigan Territory." *Mich Hist*, LIII (1969), 91-107.

910　BRANT, Irving. "Madison and the War of 1812." *Va Mag Hist Biog*, LXXIV (1966), 51-67.

911　COLEMAN, Christopher B. "The Ohio Valley in the Preliminaries of the War of 1812." *Miss Val Hist Rev*, VII (1920), 39-50.

912　GOODMAN, Warren H. "The Origins of the War of 1812: A Survey of Changing Interpretations." *Miss Val Hist Rev*, XXVIII (1941), 171-186.

913　GRIBBIN, William. "The Covenant Transformed: The Jeremiad Tradition and the War of 1812." *Church Hist*, XL (1971), 297-305.

914　HACKER, Louis M. "Western Land Hunger and the War of 1812." *Miss Val Hist Rev*, X (1924), 365-395.

915　HAMIL, Fred C. "Michigan in the War of 1812: Causes and Background of the War." *Mich Hist*, LXIV (1960), 257-291.

916　HATZENBUEHLER, Ronald L. "Party Unity and the Decision for War in the House of Representatives, 1812." *Wm Mar Q*, XXXIX, 3d ser. (1972), 367-390.

917　HORSMAN, Reginald. *The Causes of the War of 1812*. Philadelphia, 1962.†

918　HORSMAN, Reginald. "Western War Aims, 1811-1812." *Ind Mag Hist*, LIII (1957), 1-18.

919　JOHNSON, Leland R. "The Suspense Was Hell: The Senate Vote for War in 1812." *Ind Mag Hist*, LXV (1969), 247-267.

920　KAPLAN, Lawrence S. "France and Madison's Decision for War, 1812." *Miss Val Hist Rev*, L (1964), 652-671.

921　LATIMER, Margaret K. "South Carolina—A Protagonist of the War of 1812." *Am Hist Rev*, LXI (1956), 914-929.

922　LEWIS, Howard T. "A Re-Analysis of the Causes of the War of 1812." *Amer*, VI (1911), 506-516, 577-585.

923　PANCAKE, John S. " 'The Invisibles': A Chapter in the Opposition to President Madison." *J S Hist*, XXI (1955), 17-37.

924 PRATT, Julius W. *The Expansionists of 1812.* 1925. New York, 1949.

925 PRATT, Julius W. "Western Aims in the War of 1812." *Miss Val Hist Rev,* XII (1925), 36-50.

926 RISJORD, Norman K. "1812: Conservatives, War Hawks, and the Nation's Honor." *Wm Mar Q,* XVIII, 3d ser. (1961), 196-210.

927 SAPIO, Victor A. *Pennsylvania and the War of 1812.* See 903.

928 SMITH, Abbott. "Mr. Madison's War: An Unsuccessful Experiment in the Conduct of National Policy." *Pol Sci Q,* LVII (1942), 229-246.

929 SMITH, Theodore C. "War Guilt in 1812." *Proc Mass Hist Soc,* LXIV (1932), 319-345.

930 TAYLOR, George Rogers. "Agrarian Discontent in the Mississippi Valley Preceding the War of 1812." *J Pol Econ,* XXXIX (1931), 471-505.

931 TAYLOR, George Rogers. "Prices in the Mississippi Valley Preceding the War of 1812." *J Econ Bus Hist,* III (1930-1931), 148-163.

932 THWAITES, Reuben Gold. "The Ohio Valley Press before the War of 1812-15." *Proc Am Ant Soc,* XIX (1909), 309-368.

933 WILTSE, C. M. "The Authorship of the War Report of 1812." *Am Hist Rev,* XLIX (1944), 253-259.

Military Action

934 BROWN, Wilbur S. *The Amphibious Campaign for West Florida and Louisiana, 1814, 1815: A Critical Review of Strategy and Tactics at New Orleans.* University, Ala., 1969.

935 CARTER, Samuel, III. *Blaze of Glory: The Fight for New Orleans, 1814-1815.* New York, 1971.

936 CASSELL, Frank A. "Baltimore in 1813: A Study of Urban Defense in the War of 1812." *Mil Affairs,* XXXIII (1969), 349-361.

937 CASSELL, Frank A. "Response to Crisis: Baltimore in 1814." *Md Hist Mag,* LXVI (1971), 261-287.

938 CHIDSEY, Donald Barr. *The Battle of New Orleans: An Informal History of the War That Nobody Wanted: 1812.* New York, 1961.

939 DIETZ, Anthony G. "The Use of Cartel Vessels during the War of 1812." *Am Neptune,* XXVIII (1968), 165-194.

940 FORESTER, Cecil Scott. *The Age of Fighting Sail: The Story of the Naval War of 1812.* Garden City, N.Y., 1956.

941 GLOVER, Richard. "The French Fleet, 1807-1914; Britain's Problem; and Madison's Opportunity." *J Mod Hist,* XXXIX (1967), 233-252.

942 HITSMAN, J. Mackay. *The Incredible War of 1812: A Military History.* Toronto, 1965.

943 HOLLAND, James W. "Andrew Jackson and the Creek War: Victory at the Horseshoe." *Ala Rev,* XXI (1968), 243-275.

944 LATOUR, Arsène Lacarrière. *Historical Memoir of the War in West Florida and Louisiana, in 1814-15.* 1816. Gainesville, Fla., 1964.

945 LYMAN, Olin Linus. *Commodore Oliver Hazard Perry and the War on the Lakes.* New York, 1905.

946 MAHAN, Alfred T. *Sea Power in Its Relations to the War of 1812.* 2 vols. 2d ed. Boston, 1919.

947 MAHON, John K. "British Strategy and Southern Indians: War of 1812." *Fla Hist Q,* XLIV (1966), 285-302.

948 MILLS, James Cooke. *Oliver Hazard Perry and the Battle of Lake Erie.* Detroit, Mich., 1913.

949 MULLER, Charles Geoffrey. *The Darkest Day: 1814; The Washington-Baltimore Campaign.* Philadelphia, 1963.

950 MULLER, Charles Geoffrey. *The Proudest Day: Macdonough on Lake Champlain.* New York, 1960.

951 MURDOCH, Richard K. "Intelligence Reports of British Agents in the Long Island Sound Area, 1814-1815." *Am Neptune,* XXIX (1969), 187-197.

952 OWSLEY, Frank L., Jr. "British and Indian Activities in Spanish West Florida during the War of 1812." *Fla Hist Q,* XLVI (1967), 111-123.

953 OWSLEY, Frank L., Jr. "The Role of the South in the Grand Strategy in the War of 1812." *Tenn Hist Q,* XXXI (1972), 22-38.

954 PAULLIN, Charles Oscar, ed. *The Battle of Lake Erie: A Collection of Documents, Chiefly by Commodore Perry.* Cleveland, Ohio, 1918.

955 PRATT, J. W. "Fur Trade Strategy and the American Left Flank in the War of 1812." *Am Hist Rev,* XL (1935), 246-273.

956 ROWLAND, Eron Opha. *Andrew Jackson's Campaign against the British, or the Mississippi Territory in the War of 1812.* New York, 1926.

957 SMELSER, Marshall. "Tecumseh, Harrison, and the War of 1812." *Ind Mag Hist,* LXV (1969), 25-44.

958 SMITH, Theodore Clarke. *The Wars between England and America.* 1914. Port Washington, N.Y., 1969.

959 STACEY, C. P. "An American Plan for a Canadian Campaign." *Am Hist Rev,* XLVI (1941), 348-358.

960 WOEHRMANN, Paul. "National Response to the Sack of Washington." *Md Hist Mag,* LXVI (1971), 222-260.

Opposition to the War

961 ANDERSON, Frank Maloy. "A Forgotten Phase of the New England Opposition to the War of 1812." *Proc Miss Val Hist Assn,* VI (1912-1913), 176-188.

962 BANNER, James M., Jr. *To the Hartford Convention: The Federalists and the Origin of Party Politics in Massachusetts, 1789-1815.* See 514.

963 BRYNN, Edward. "Patterns of Dissent: Vermont's Opposition to the War of 1812." *Vt Hist,* XL (1972), 10-27.

964 BUTLER, Nicholas Murray. *The Effect of the War of 1812 upon the Consolidation of the Union.* Baltimore, Md., 1887.

965 CAREY, Mathew. *The Olive Branch; or Faults on Both Sides, Federal and Democratic.* Philadelphia, 1969. Repr. 10th ed.

966 CARTER, Edward C., II. "Mathew Carey and 'The Olive Branch,' 1814-1818." *Pa Mag Hist Biog,* LXXXIX (1965), 399-415.

967 CRUIKSHANK, Ernest Alexander. *The Political Adventures of John Henry: The Record of an International Imbroglio.* Toronto, 1936.

968 GRIBBIN, William. "American Episcopacy and the War of 1812." *Hist Mag P E Ch,* XXVIII (1969), 25-36.

969 LEMMON, Sarah McCulloh. "Dissent in North Carolina during the War of 1812." *N C Hist Rev,* XLIX (1972), 103-118.

970 MADONNA, G. Terry. "The Lancaster Federalists and the War of 1812." *J Lancaster Co Hist Soc,* LXXI (1967), 137-164.

971 MARTELL, J. S. "A Side Light on Federalist Strategy during the War of 1812." *Am Hist Rev,* XLII (1938), 553-566.

972 MORISON, Samuel Eliot. "Our Most Unpopular War [1812-1815]." *Proc Mass Hist Soc,* LXXX (1968), 38-54.

973 TALMADGE, John Erwin. "Georgia's Federalist Press and the War of 1812." *J S Hist,* XIX (1953), 488-500.

974 WEHTJE, Myron F. "Opposition in Virginia to the War of 1812." *Va Mag Hist Biog,* LXXVIII (1970), 65-86.

975 WILLIAMS, William A. "A Frontier Federalist and the War of 1812." *Pa Mag Hist Biog,* LXXVI (1952), 81-85.

The Peace Treaty

976 BEMIS, Samuel Flagg. *John Quincy Adams and the Foundations of American Foreign Policy.* See 61.

977 DANGERFIELD, George. *The Era of Good Feelings.* See 735.

978 ENGLEMAN, F. L. *The Peace of Christmas Eve.* New York, 1962.

979 JONES, Wilbur Devereux, ed. "A British View of the War of 1812 and the Peace Negotiations." *Miss Val Hist Rev,* XLV (1958), 481-487.

980 UPDYKE, Frank A. *The Diplomacy of the War of 1812.* Baltimore, Md., 1915.

5. Evolution of Government

President and Cabinet

981 BINKLEY, Wilfred E. *President and Congress.* New York, 19747.

982 BROWN, Burlie W. "The Cincinnatus Image in Presidential Politics." *Ag Hist,* XXXI (1957), 23-29.

983 CORWIN, Edward S. *The President–Office and Powers, 1787-1957: History and Analysis of Practice and Opinion.* 4th rev. ed. New York, 1957.

984 CUNLIFFE, Marcus. *American Presidents and the Presidency.* New York, 1972.

985 HART, James. *The American Presidency in Action: 1789.* New York, 1948.

986 HATCH, Louis Clinton. *A History of the Vice-Presidency of the United States.* Rev. and ed. Earl L. Shoup. New York, 1934.

987 HINSDALE, Mary Louise. *A History of the President's Cabinet.* Ann Arbor, Mich., 1911.

988 HUNT, Gaillard. *The Department of State of the United States: Its History and Functions.* New Haven, Conn., 1914.

989 JACKSON, Carlton. *Presidential Vetoes, 1792-1945.* Athens, Ga., 1967.

990 LEARNED, Henry Barrett. *The President's Cabinet: Studies in the Origin, Formation and Structure of an American Institution.* New Haven, Conn., 1912.

991 MILTON, George Fort. *Use of Presidential Power, 1789-1943.* Boston, 1944.

992 PATTERSON, Caleb Perry. *Presidential Government in United States: The Unwritten Constitution.* Chapel Hill, N.C., 1947.

993 POLLARD, James Edward. *The Presidents and the Press.* New York, 1947.

994 STANWOOD, Edward. *A History of the Presidency.* 2 vols. Rev. ed. Boston and New York, 1928.

995 STEINBERG, Alfred. *The First Ten: The Founding Presidents and Their Administrations.* Garden City, N.Y., 1967.

996 WARD, Harry M. *The Department of War, 1781-1795.* Pittsburgh, Pa., 1962.

Congress

997 ALEXANDER, De Alva Stanwood. *History and Procedure of the House of Representatives.* Boston, 1916.

998 FURLONG, Patrick J. "The Origins of the House Committee on Ways and Means." *Wm Mar Q,* XXV, 3d ser. (1968), 587-604.

999 HARLOW, Ralph Volney. *The History of Legislative Methods in the Period before 1825.* New Haven, Conn., 1917.

1000 HAYDEN, Joseph Ralston. *The Senate and Treaties, 1789-1817: The Development of Treaty-Making Functions of the United States Senate during Their Formative Period.* New York, 1920.

1001 HAYNES, George Henry. *The Senate of the United States, Its History and Practice.* 2 vols. 1938. New York, 1960.

1002 MORAN, Thomas Francis. *The Rise and Development of the Bicameral System in America.* Baltimore, Md., 1895.

Civil Service

1003 ARONSON, Sidney H. *Status and Kinship in the Higher Civil Service: Standards of Selection in the Administrations of John Adams, Thomas Jefferson, and Andrew Jackson.* See 481.

1004 CALDWELL, L. K. *The Administrative Theories of Hamilton and Jefferson.* Chicago, 1944.

1005 CULLINAN, Gerald. *The Post Office Department.* New York, 1968.

1006 FISH, Carl Russell. *The Civil Service and the Patronage.* New York, 1905.

1007 RICH, Wesley E. *The History of the United States Post Office to the Year 1829.* Cambridge, Mass., 1924.

1008 RIPER, Paul P. Van. *History of the United States Civil Service.* Evanston, Ill., 1958.

1009 SCOTT, Ann Herbert. *Census, U.S.A.: Fact Finding for the American People, 1790-1970.* New York, 1968.

1010 SHORT, Lloyd Milton. *The Development of National Administrative Organization in the United States.* Baltimore, Md., 1923.

1011 WHITE, Leonard D. *The Federalists: A Study in Administrative History.* See 457.

1012 WHITE, Leonard D. *The Jeffersonians: A Study in Administrative History.* See 739.

1013 WILLIAMS, Ralph C. *The United States Public Health Service, 1798-1950.* Washington, D.C., 1951.

Supreme Court

1014 BEARD, Charles A. *The Supreme Court and the Constitution.* 1912. Englewood Cliffs, N.J., 1952.†

1015 BOUDIN, Louis. *Government by Judiciary.* 2 vols. New York, 1932.

1016 CORWIN, Edward S. *John Marshall and the Constitution: A Chronicle of the Supreme Court.* New Haven, Conn., 1919.

1017 FRIEDMAN, Leon, and Fred L. ISRAEL. *The Justices of the United States Supreme Court, 1789-1969: Their Lives and Major Opinions.* 4 vols. New York, 1969.

1018 GOEBEL, Julius, Jr. *The Oliver Wendell Holmes Devise History of the Supreme Court of the United States.* Vol. I: *Antecedents and Beginnings to 1801.* New York, 1971.

1019 HAINES, Charles Grove. *The Role of the Supreme Court in American Government and Politics, 1798-1835.* Berkeley, Cal., 1944.

1020 MORGAN, Donald G. "The Origins of Supreme Court Dissent." *Wm Mar Q,* X, 3d ser. (1953), 353-377.

1021 MORGAN, Richard E. *The Supreme Court and Religion.* New York, 1972.

1022 MORRIS, Richard B. *John Jay, the Nation and the Court.* Boston, 1967.

1023 MYERS, Gustavus. *History of the Supreme Court of the United States.* Chicago, 1925.

1024 SCHMIDHAUSER, John Richard. *The Supreme Court as Final Arbiter in Federal-State Relations, 1789-1957.* Chapel Hill, N.C., 1958.

1025 STEAMER, Robert J. "The Legal and Political Genesis of the Supreme Court." *Pol Sci Q,* LXXVII (1962), 546-569.

1026 WARREN, Charles. *The Supreme Court in United States History.* 2 vols. Rev. ed. Boston, 1935.

Constitutional Interpretation

1027 BAUER, Elizabeth Kelley. *Commentaries on the Constitution, 1790-1860.* New York, 1952.

1028 CORWIN, Edward S. *The "Higher Law" Background of American Constitutional Law.* Ithaca, N.Y., 1959.† Reprinted from *Harvard Law Review,* 1928-1929.

1029 CROSSKEY, William W. *Politics and the Constitution.* 2 vols. Chicago, 1953.

1030 DODD, Walter Fairleigh. *The Revision and Amendment of State Constitutions.* Baltimore, Md., 1910.

1031 DOYLE, Mathis. "Chisholm v. Georgia: Background and Settlement." *J Am Hist,* LIV (1967), 19-29.

1032 ELAZAR, Daniel J. *American Federalism: A View from the States.* New York, 1966.

1033 ELAZAR, Daniel J. "Federal State Collaboration in the 19th Century United States." *Pol Sci Q,* LXXIX (1964), 248-281.

1034 McLAUGHLIN, Andrew Cunningham. *A Constitutional History of the United States.* New York, 1936.

1035 MUSMANNO, Michael Angelo. *Proposed Amendments to the Constitution: A Monograph on the Resolutions Introduced in Congress Proposing Amendments to the Constitution of the United States of America.* See 396.

1036 ROSSITER, Clinton. *Alexander Hamilton and the Constitution.* New York, 1964.

1037 SWISHER, Carl Brent. *American Constitutional Development.* New York, 1954.

1038 SWISHER, Carl Brent. *The Growth of Constitutional Power in the United States.* Chicago, 1946.†

1039 WRIGHT, Benjamin Fletcher. *The Growth of American Constitutional Law.* Boston, 1942.†

Law and the Legal Profession

1040 BROWN, Elizabeth G. *British Statutes in American Law, 1776-1836*. Ann Arbor, Mich., 1964.

1041 BUGBEE, Bruce Willis. *The Early American Law of Intellectual Property: The Historical Foundation of the United States Patent and Copyright Systems*. Ann Arbor, Mich., 1960.

1042 CHAPIN, Bradley. *The American Law of Treason: Revolutionary and Early National Origins*. Seattle, Wash., 1964.

1043 CHAPIN, Bradley. "Colonial and Revolutionary Origins of the American Law of Treason." *Wm Mar Q*, XVII, 3d ser. (1960), 3-21.

1044 CHROUST, Anton-Hermann. *The Rise of the Legal Profession in America*. 2 vols. Norman, Okla., 1965.

1045 CUMMINGS, Homer, and Carl McFARLAND. *Federal Justice: Chapters in the History of Justice and the Federal Executive*. New York, 1937.

1046 ELLIS, Richard E. *The Jeffersonian Crisis: Courts and Politics in the Young Republic*. See 801.

1047 ENGLISH, William F. *The Pioneer Lawyer and Jurist in Missouri*. Columbia, Mo., 1947.

1048 FLAHERTY, David H., ed. *Essays in the History of Early American Law*. Chapel Hill, N.C., 1969.

1049 GOEBEL, Julius, Jr. *The Law Practice of Alexander Hamilton: Documents and Commentary*. 2 vols. New York, 1964, 1969.

1050 HAAR, Charles, ed. *The Golden Age of American Law*. New York, 1965.

1051 HAMILTON, William Baskerville. *Anglo-American Law on the Frontier: Thomas Rodney and His Territorial Cases*. Durham, N.C., 1953.

1052 HORSNELL, M. E. "Spencer Roane and the Property of Rights: A Post-Revolutionary View." *W Va Hist*, XXX (1969), 586-597.

1053 HORWITZ, Morton J. "The Emergence of an Instrumental Conception of American Law, 1780-1820." *Perspectives Am Hist*, V (1971), 287-326.

1054 HURST, James Willard. *The Growth of American Law: The Law Makers*. Boston, 1950.

1055 LAWSON, John Davison, ed. *American State Trials: A Collection of the Important and Interesting Criminal Trials Which Have Taken Place in the United States*. 17 vols. St. Louis, Mo., 1914-1936.

1056 MEEHAN, Thomas R. "Courts, Cases and Counselors in Revolutionary and Post-Revolutionary Pennsylvania." *Pa Mag Hist Biog*, XCI (1967), 3-34.

1057 MILLER, Perry, and Gilbert EDDY, eds. *The Legal Mind in America: From Independence to the Civil War*. Garden City, N.Y., 1962.

1058 MORRIS, Richard Brandon. *Studies in the History of American Law, with Special Reference to the Seventeenth and Eighteenth Centuries*. New York, 1930.

1059 NASH, Gary B. "The Philadelphia Bench and Bar, 1800-1861." *Comp Stud Soc Hist*, VII (1965), 203-220.

1060 NETTELS, Curtis. "The Mississippi Valley and the Federal Judiciary, 1807-1837." *Miss Val Hist Rev,* XII (1925), 202-226.

1061 OTTENBERG, Louis. "Alexander Hamilton's First Court Case: Elizabeth Rutgers *v.* Joshua Waddington in the Mayor's Court of New York City, 1784." *N Y Hist Soc Q,* XLI (1957), 423-439.

1062 POUND, Roscoe. *The Formative Era of American Law.* Boston, 1938.†

1063 PRAGER, Frank D. "Trends and Developments in American Patent Law from Jefferson to Clifford (1790-1870)." *Am J Legal Hist,* VI (1962), 45-62.

1064 ROWLAND, Dunbar. *Courts, Judges, and Lawyers of Mississippi, 1798-1935.* Jackson, Miss., 1935.

1065 TREACY, Kenneth. "The Olmstead Case, 1778-1809." *W Pol Q,* X (1927), 675-691.

1066 WARREN, Charles. *A History of the American Bar.* Boston, 1911.

1067 WARREN, Charles. *History of the Harvard Law School and of Early American Legal Conditions in America.* 3 vols. New York. 1908.

Military Services

The Army

1068 AMBROSE, Stephen E. *Duty, Honor, Country: A History of West Point.* Baltimore, Md., 1966.

1069 BERNARDO, Joseph, and Eugene H. BACON. *American Military Policy: Its Development since 1775.* Harrisburg, Pa., 1955.

1070 BROWN, Alan S. "The Role of the Army in Western Settlement: Josiah Harmar's Command, 1785-1790." *Pa Mag Hist Biog,* XCIII (1969), 161-178.

1071 CALDWELL, Norman W. "The Enlisted Soldier at the Frontier Post, 1790-1814." *Mid-Am,* XXXVII (1955), 195-204.

1072 CALDWELL, Norman W. "The Frontier Army Officer, 1794-1814." *Mid-Am,* XXXVII (1955), 101-128.

1073 CUNLIFFE, Marcus. *Soldiers and Civilians: The Martial Spirit in America, 1775-1865.* Boston, 1968.†

1074 ESPOSITO, V. J. *West Point Atlas of American Wars.* New York, 1962.

1075 GOETZMANN, William H. *Army Exploration in the American West, 1803-1863.* New Haven, 1959.†

1076 HERR, Major General John K., and Edward S. WALLACE. *The Story of the U.S. Cavalry, 1775-1942.* Boston, 1953.

1077 HIGGINBOTHAM, Don. *The War of American Independence: Military Attitudes, Policies, and Practice, 1763-1789.* New York, 1971.

1078 HILL, Carter. *Roads, Rails, and Waterways: The Army Engineers and Early Transportation.* Norman, Okla., 1957.

1079 JACOBS, James Ripley. *The Beginning of the U.S. Army 1783-1812.* Princeton, N.J., 1947.

1080 KNOPF, Richard C., ed. *Anthony Wayne, A Name in Arms; Diplomat, Defender of Expansion Westward of a Nation: The Wayne-Knox-Pickering-McHenry Correspondence.* Pittsburgh, Pa., 1960.

1081 MAHON, John K. "Military Relations between Georgia and the United States, 1789-1794." *Ga Hist Q,* XLIII (1959), 138-155.

1082 PRUCHA, Francis Paul. *A Guide to the Military Posts of the United States, 1789-1895.* Madison, Wis., 1964.

1083 PRUCHA, Francis Paul. *The Sword of the Republic: The United States Army on the Frontier, 1783-1846.* New York, 1969.

1084 REDDICK, L. D. "The Negro Policy of the United States Army, 1775-1945." *J Neg Hist,* XXXIV (1949), 9-29.

1085 SMITH, Dwight L., ed. *From Greene Ville to Fallen Timbers: A Journal of the Wayne Campaign: July 28-September 14, 1794.* Indianapolis, 1952.

1086 THORNBROUGH, Gayle, ed. *Outpost on the Wabash, 1787-1791: Letters of Brigadier General Josiah Harmar and Major John Francis Hamtramak.* Indianapolis, 1957.

1087 WEIGLEY, Russel Frank. *History of the United States Army.* New York, 1967.

The Navy

1088 ALBION, Robert Greenlaugh, and Jesse Barnes POPE. *Sea Lanes in Wartime: The American Experience, 1775-1942.* New York, 1942.

1089 CHAPELLE, Howard I. *The History of the American Sailing Navy: The Ships and Their Development.* New York, 1949.

1090 FENTON, Alfred H. *Oliver Hazard Perry.* New York, 1944.

1091 FERGUSON, Eugene S. *Truxton of the Constellation: The Life of Commodore Thomas Truxton, U.S. Navy, 1775-1822.* Baltimore, Md., 1956.

1092 HAYES, Frederic H. "John Adams and American Sea Power." *Am Neptune,* XXV (1965), 35-45.

1093 HIRSCH, Charles B. "Gunboat Personnel on the Western Waters." *Mid-Am,* XXXIV (1952), 75-86.

1094 JONES, Robert F. "The Naval Thought and Policy of Benjamin Stoddert, First Secretary of the Navy, 1798-1801." *Am Neptune,* XXIV (1964), 61-64.

1095 LANGLEY, Harold D. "The Negro in the Navy and Merchant Service, 1798-1860." *J Neg Hist,* LII (1967), 273-286.

1096 LEWIS, Charles Lee. *The Romantic Decatur.* Philadelphia, 1937.

1097 Library of Congress. *The Naval Battles of the United States in the Different Wars with Foreign Nations, from the Commencement of the Revolution to the Present Time.* 7 vols. Boston, 1857.

1098 MACLAY, Edgar Stanton, *A History of American Privateers*. New York, 1924.

1099 MACLAY, Edgar Stanton. *A History of the United States Navy from 1775 to 1901*. 3 vols. New York, 1901.

1100 Naval Records and Library Office. *Naval Documents Related to the Barbary Powers, 1785-1807*. 6 vols. Washington, D.C., 1939-1944.

1101 PAULLIN, Charles Oscar. *Commodore John Rodgers, Captain, Commodore, and Senior Officer of the American Navy, 1773-1835*. Cleveland, Ohio, 1910.

1102 PAULLIN, Charles Oscar. *Diplomatic Negotiations of American Naval Officers, 1778-1883*. See 84.

1103 PAULLIN, Charles Oscar. *Paullin's History of Naval Administration, 1775-1911: A Collection of Articles from the U.S. Naval Institute*. Annapolis, Md., 1968.

1104 PRATT, Fletcher. *Preble's Boys*. New York, 1950.

1105 SMELSER, Marshall. *The Congress Founds the Navy, 1787-1798*. Notre Dame, Ind., 1959.

1106 SPROUT, Harold H., and Margaret SPROUT. *The Rise of American Naval Power, 1776-1918*. Princeton, N.J., 1939.†

6. American Leaders

Selected Biographies

1107 ADAMS, Henry. *John Randolph*. New York, 1899.

1108 ADAMS, Henry. *The Life of Albert Gallatin*. New York, 1943.

1109 AMMON, Harry. *James Monroe: The Quest for National Identity*. New York, 1971.

1110 ANDERSON, Dice Robins. *William Branch Giles: A Study in the Politics of Virginia and the Nation from 1790 to 1830*. Menasha, Wis., 1914.

1111 ANTHONY, Katharine Susan. *First Lady of the Revolution: The Life of Mercy Otis Warren*. Garden City, N.Y., 1958.

1112 ANTHONY, Katharine Susan. *Dolly Madison, Her Life and Times*. Garden City, N.Y., 1949.

1113 AUSTIN, James T. *The Life of Elbridge Gerry*. 2 vols. Boston, 1827-1829.

1114 BERNHARD, Winfred E. A. *Fisher Ames, Federalist and Statesman, 1758-1808*. Chapel Hill, N.C., 1965.

1115 BEVERIDGE, Albert J. *The Life of John Marshall*. 4 vols. Boston and New York, 1916-1919.

1116 BLACKWELL, Robert Lee. "Matthew Lyon, A Forgotten Patriot Recalled." *Filson Club Hist Q*, XLVI (1972), 219-240.

1117 BOARDMAN, Roger Sherman. *Roger Sherman, Signer and Statesman.* Philadelphia, 1938.

1118 BORDEN, Morton. *The Federalism of James A. Bayard.* New York, 1955.

1119 BRANT, Irving. *James Madison.* 6 vols. Indianapolis, 1941-1961.

1120 BRANT, Irving. *The Fourth President: A Life of James Madison.* Indianapolis and New York, 1970.

1121 CALLAHAN, North. *Henry Knox: General Washington's General.* New York, 1958.

1122 CASSELL, Frank A. *Merchant Congressman in the Young Republic: Samuel Smith of Maryland, 1752-1839.* Madison, Wis., 1971.

1123 CHINARD, Gilbert. *Honest John Adams.* 1933. Repr. with int. by Douglass Adair. Boston, 1964.

1124 CHITWOOD, Oliver Perry. *Richard Henry Lee: Statesman of the Revolution.* Morgantown, W.Va., 1968.

1125 CLARKSON, Paul S., and R. Samuel JETT. *Luther Martin of Maryland.* Baltimore, Md., 1970.

1126 CONWAY, Moncure Daniel. *The Life of Thomas Paine: With a History of His Literary, Political and Religious Career in America, France, and England.* 2 vols. New York, 1892.

1127 COX, Joseph W. *Champion of Southern Federalism: Robert Goodloe Harper of South Carolina.* Port Washington, N.Y., 1972.

1128 CUNLIFFE, Marcus. *George Washington: Man and Monument.* Boston, 1958.†

1129 DANGERFIELD, George. *Chancellor Robert R. Livingston of New York, 1746-1813.* New York, 1960.

1130 EAST, Robert A. *John Quincy Adams: The Critical Years, 1785-1794.* New York, 1962.

1131 ERNST, Robert. *Rufus King: American Federalist.* Chapel Hill, N.C., 1968.

1132 FLEXNER, James Thomas. *George Washington and the New Nation (1783-1793).* Boston, 1970.

1133 FREEMAN, Douglas Southall, John Alexander CARROLL, and Mary Wells ASHWORTH. *George Washington.* 7 vols. New York, 1948-1957. Abr. 1 vol. by Richard Howell. New York, 1968.

1134 GUILDAY, Peter Keenan. *The Life and Times of John Carroll, Archbishop of Baltimore, 1735-1815.* 2 vols. 1922. Westminster, Md., 1954.

1135 HANLEY, Thomas O'Brien. *Charles Carroll of Carrollton: The Making of a Revolutionary Gentleman.* Washington, D.C., 1970.

1136 HATCHER, William. *Edward Livingston: Jeffersonian Republican and Jacksonian Democrat.* Baton Rouge, La., 1940.

1137 HAWKE, David Freeman. *Benjamin Rush: Revolutionary Gadfly.* New York, 1971.

1138 HECHT, Marie B. *John Quincy Adams: A Personal History of an Independent Man.* New York, 1972.

1139 HIGGINSON, Thomas Wentworth. *Life and Times of Stephen Higginson.* Boston, 1907.

1140 KETCHAM, Ralph. *James Madison: A Biography.* New York, 1971.

1141 KING, Charles S. *The Life and Correspondence of Rufus King.* 6 vols. New York, 1894-1900.

1142 KIRK, Russell. *Randolph of Roanoke: A Study in Conservative Thought.* Chicago, 1951.

1143 LODGE, Henry Cabot. *Life and Letters of George Cabot.* Boston, 1878.

1144 LOSSING, Benson J. *The Life and Times of Philip Schuyler.* 2 vols. New York, 1872-1873.

1145 MALONE, Dumas. *Jefferson and His Time.* 4 vols. Boston, 1948-1970.

1146 MARSHALL, John. *An Autobiographical Sketch by John Marshall.* Ed. John Stokes Adams. Ann Arbor, Mich., 1937.

1147 MAYO, Bernard. *Henry Clay: Spokesman of the New West.* Boston, 1937.

1148 MILLER, John C. *Alexander Hamilton: Patriot in Paradox.* New York, 1959.

1149 MINTZ, Max M. *Gouverneur Morris and the American Revolution.* Norman, Okla., 1970.

1150 MITCHELL, Broadus. *Alexander Hamilton.* 2 vols. New York, 1957-1962.

1151 MORISON, Samuel E. *Life and Letters of Harrison Gray Otis, Federalist.* 2 vols. 1913. Rev. *Harrison Gray Otis, 1765-1848: The Urbane Federalist.* Boston, 1969.

1152 NOCK, Albert Jay. *Jefferson.* New York, 1926.

1153 PETERSON, Merrill D. *Thomas Jefferson and the New Nation: A Biography.* New York, 1970.

1154 PICKERING, Octavius, and C. W. UPHAM. *The Life of Timothy Pickering.* 4 vols. Boston, 1867-1873.

1155 PINKNEY, Helen R. *Christopher Gore: Federalist of Massachusetts, 1758-1827.* Barre, Mass., 1969.

1156 POWELL, John Harvey. *Richard Rush, Republican Diplomat, 1780-1859.* Philadelphia, 1942.

1157 ROGERS, George C., Jr. *Evolution of a Federalist: William Loughton Smith of Charleston.* Columbia, S.C., 1962.

1158 ROWLAND, K. M. *Life of Charles Carroll of Carrollton, 1737-1832, with His Correspondence and Public Papers.* 2 vols. New York, 1898.

1159 RUTLAND, Robert Allen. *George Mason: Reluctant Statesman.* Williamsburg, Va., 1961.

1160 SCHACHNER, Nathan. *Alexander Hamilton.* New York and London, 1946.†

1161 SCHULTZ, Harold S. *James Madison.* New York, 1970.

1162 SHIPTON, Clifford K. *Biographical Sketches of Those Who Attended Harvard College in the Classes 1756-1760 with Bibliographical and Other Notes. Sibley's Harvard Graduates.* Vol. XIV. Boston, 1968. Vol. XV. *1761-1763.* Boston, 1970. Vol. XVI. *1764-1767.* Boston, 1972.

1163 SHIPTON, Clifford K. *New England Life in the Eighteenth Century: Representative Biographies from Sibley's Harvard Graduates.* Cambridge, Mass., 1963.

1164 SMITH, Donald L. *John Jay: Founder of a State and Nation.* New York, 1968.

1165 SMITH, Page. *John Adams.* 2 vols. New York, 1963.

1166 SPARKS, Jared, ed. *The Life of Gouverneur Morris.* 3 vols. Boston, 1932.

1167 SPAULDING, E. Wilder. *His Excellency George Clinton: Critic of the Constitution.* New York, 1938.

1168 STEINER, Bruce E. *Samuel Seabury, 1729-1796: A Study in the High Church Tradition.* Athens, Ohio, 1972.

1169 STYRON, Arthur. *Last of the Cocked Hats: James Monroe of the Virginia Dynasty.* Norman, Okla., 1945.

1170 TOLLES, Frederick B. *George Logan of Philadelphia.* New York, 1953.

1171 TURNER, Lynn. *William Plumer of New Hampshire, 1759-1850.* Chapel Hill, N.C., 1962.

1172 WALTERS, Raymond, Jr. *Alexander James Dallas: Lawyer-Politician-Financier, 1759-1817.* Philadelphia, 1943.

1173 WALTERS, Raymond, Jr. *Albert Gallatin, Jeffersonian Financier and Diplomat.* New York, 1957.†

1174 WANDELL, Samuel Henry, and Meade MINNIGERODE. *Aaron Burr: A Biography.* New York, 1925.

1175 WELCH, Richard E. *Theodore Sedgwick, Federalist: A Political Portrait.* Middletown, Conn., 1965.

1176 WHITNEY, Janet. *Abigail Adams.* Boston, 1947.

1177 WILTSE, Charles M. *John C. Calhoun: Nationalist, 1782-1828.* Indianapolis, 1944.

1178 WOODRESS, James. *A Yankee's Odyssey: The Life of Joel Barlow.* Philadelphia, 1958.

1179 ZAHNISER, Marvin R. *Charles Cotesworth Pinckney: Founding Father.* Chapel Hill, N.C., 1967.

Selected Published Works

1180 ADAMS, John. *The Adams-Jefferson Letters: The Complete Correspondence between Thomas Jefferson and Abigail and John Adams.* Ed. Lester J. Cappon. 2 vols. Chapel Hill, N.C., 1959.

1181 ADAMS, John. *The Adams Papers.* Ed. L. H. Butterfield. Ser. 1: *Diary and Autobiography of John Adams.* 4 vols. Cambridge, Mass., 1961.† Supp. Cambridge, Mass., 1966. Ser. 2: *Adams Family Correspondence.* 2 vols. Cambridge, Mass., 1963.

1182 ADAMS, John. *The Works of John Adams, Second President of the United States.* Ed. Charles Francis Adams. 10 vols. Boston, 1850-1856.

1183 ADAMS, John Quincy. *The Writings of John Quincy Adams 1779-1823.* Ed. W. C. Ford. 7 vols. New York, 1913-1917.

1184 ADAMS, Samuel. *The Writings of Samuel Adams.* Ed. Harry Alonzo Cushing. 4 vols. New York, 1904-1908.

1185 AMES, Fisher. *Works of Fisher Ames: With a Selection from His Speeches and Correspondence.* Ed. Seth Ames. 2 vols. 1854. New York, 1969.

1186 BAYARD, James A. "The Papers of James A. Bayard, 1796-1815." Ed. Elizabeth Donnan. *Ann Rep Am Hist Assn,* 1913. Washington, D.C., 1915.

1187 CALHOUN, John C. *The Papers of John C. Calhoun.* Vol. I: *1801-1817.* Eds. Robert L. Meriwether and W. Edwin Hemphill. Columbia, S.C., 1959.

1188 CLAY, Henry. *The Papers of Henry Clay.* Eds. James F. Hopkins and Mary W. M. Hargreaves. Vols. I, II. Lexington, Ky., 1959, 1961.

1189 CLINTON, George. *Public Papers of George Clinton.* Eds. Hugh Hastings and J. A. Holden. 10 vols. New York, 1899-1914.

1190 FRANKLIN, Benjamin. *The Writings of Benjamin Franklin.* Ed. Albert Henry Smyth. 10 vols. 1905-1907. New York, 1970.

1191 GADSDEN, Christopher. *The Writings of Christopher Gadsden, 1746-1805.* Ed. Richard Walsh. Columbia, S.C., 1966.

1192 GALLATIN, Albert. *Selected Writings of Albert Gallatin.* Ed. E. James Ferguson. Indianapolis and New York, 1967.

1193 GALLATIN, Albert. *The Writings of Albert Gallatin.* Ed. Henry Adams. 3 vols. 1879. New York, 1960.

1194 GERRY, Elbridge. *Diary of Elbridge Gerry.* Ed. Claude G. Bowers. New York, 1927.

1195 HAMILTON, Alexander. *The Papers of Alexander Hamilton.* Eds. Harold C. Syrett and Jacob E. Cooke. 15 vols. to date. New York, 1961-

1196 HAMILTON, Alexander. *The Works of Alexander Hamilton.* Ed. Henry Cabot Lodge. 12 vols. New York, 1904.

1197 HIGGINSON, Stephen. "Letters of Stephen Higginson, 1783-1804." Ed. J. Franklin Jameson. *Ann Rep Am Hist Assn,* 1896. Washington, D.C., 1897, pp. 704-841.

1198 JAY, John. *The Correspondence and Public Papers of John Jay.* Ed. Henry P. Johnson. 4 vols. New York, 1890-1893.

1199 JEFFERSON, Thomas. *The Papers of Thomas Jefferson.* Ed. Julian P. Boyd. 17 vols. to date. Princeton, 1950-

1200 JEFFERSON, Thomas. *The Writings of Thomas Jefferson.* Eds. Andrew Adgate Lipscomb and Albert Ellery Bergh. 20 vols. Washington, D.C., 1903.

1201 MADISON, James. "James Madison's Autobiography." Ed. Douglass Adair. *Wm Mar Q*, II, 3d ser. (1945), 191-209.

1202 MADISON, James. *The Papers of James Madison*. Eds. William T. Hutchinson and William M. E. Raschal. 8 vols. to date. Chicago, 1962-

1203 MADISON, James. *The Writings of James Madison*. Ed. Gaillard Hunt. 9 vols. New York, 1900-1910.

1204 MARSHALL, John. *An Autobiographical Sketch by John Marshall*. Ed. J. S. Adams. See 1146.

1205 MASON, George. *The Papers of George Mason, 1725-1792*. Ed. Robert A. Rutland. 3 vols. Chapel Hill, N.C., 1970.

1206 MONROE, James. *The Autobiography of James Monroe*. Ed. Stuart Gerry Brown. Syracuse, N.Y., 1959.

1207 MONROE, James. *The Writings of James Monroe*. Ed. Stanislaus Hamilton. 7 vols. New York, 1898-1903.

1208 PAINE, Thomas. *The Complete Writings of Thomas Paine*. Ed. Philip S. Foner. 2 vols. New York, 1945.

1209 RUSH, Benjamin. *The Letters of Benjamin Rush*. Ed. L. H. Butterfield. 2 vols. Princeton, N.J., 1951.

1210 WARREN, James. "Warren-Adams Letters." *Coll Mass Hist Soc*, LXXII, LXXIII. 1917-1925. 2 vols. New York, 1972.

1211 WARREN, James. *A Study in Dissent: The Warren-Gerry Correspondence, 1776-1792*. Ed. Clinton Harvey Gardiner. See 518.

1212 WASHINGTON, George. *The Writings of George Washington from the Original Sources, 1745-1799*. Ed. John C. Fitzpatrick. 39 vols. Washington, D.C.,1931-1944.

1213 WILSON, James. *The Works of James Wilson*. Ed. Robert Green McCloskey. Cambridge, Mass., 1967.

7. The Writing of American History

1214 ARCHDEACON, Thomas. "Early American Social Structure: Changing Views and Emphasis." *N Eng Soc Stud Bull*, XXV (1968), 12-16.

1215 BENSON, Lee. *Turner and Beard: American Historical Writing Reconsidered*. See 308.

1216 BERKHOFER, Robert F. *A Behavioral Approach to Historical Analysis*. New York, 1969.

1217 BLINKOFF, Maurice. "The Influence of Charles Beard upon American Historiography." *Monographs in History*, XII. University of Buffalo Studies, no. 4 (1936), pp. 16-36.

1218 BROWN, Robert E. *Carl Becker on History and the American Revolution.* East Lansing, Mich., 1970.

1219 CALLCOTT, George H. *History in the United States, 1800-1860: Its Practice and Purpose.* Baltimore, Md., 1970.

1220 DIGGINS, John P. "Consciousness and Ideology in American History: The Burden of Daniel J. Boorstin." *Am Hist Rev,* LXXVI (1971), 99-118.

1221 DOLLAR, Charles M., and Richard J. JENSEN. *Historian's Guide to Statistics: Quantitative Analysis and Historical Research.* New York, 1971.

1222 FISCHER, David Hackett. *Historians' Fallacies: Toward a Logic of Historical Thought.* New York, 1970.

1223 GOTTSCHALK, Louis, ed. *Generalization in the Writings of the Committee on Historical Analysis of the Social Science Research Council.* Chicago, 1963.

1224 HOFSTADTER, Richard. *The Progressive Historians: Turner, Beard, Parrington.* New York, 1968.

1225 HOFSTADTER, Richard. "Parrington and the Jeffersonian Tradition." *J Hist Ideas,* II (1941), 391-400.

1226 KUKLICK, Bruce. "Myth and Symbol in American Studies." *Am Q,* XXIV (1972), 435-450.

1227 MERRENS, H. Roy. "Historical Geography and Early American History." *Wm Mar Q,* XXII, 3d ser. (1965), 529-548.

1228 SHALHOPE, Robert E. "Toward a Republican Synthesis: The Emergence of an Understanding of Republicanism in American Historiography." *Wm Mar Q,* XXIX, 3d ser. (1972), 49-80.

1229 SHAW, Peter. "Block Is Thicker than Irony: Henry Adams' History." *N Eng Q,* XL (1967), 163-187.

1230 STROUT, Cushing. *The Pragmatic Revolt in American History: Carl Becker and Charles Beard.* New Haven, Conn., 1958.

1231 SYRETT, Harold C. "Alexander Hamilton: History by Stereotype." *N Y Hist Soc Q,* XLIII (1959), 39-50.

1232 TASSEL, David D. Van. *Recording America's Past: An Interpretation of the Development of Historical Studies in America, 1607-1884.* Chicago, 1960.

1233 WISH, Harvey. *The American Historians: A Social-Intellectual History of the Writing of the American Past.* New York, 1960.

III. Social and Political Thought

1. Philosophy and Philosophical Ideas

1234 BECKER, Carl. *The Heavenly City of the Eighteenth Century Philosophers.* New Haven, Conn., 1932.†

1235 BLAU, Joseph L. *Men and Movements in American Philosophy.* New York, 1952.

1236 CRAGG, Gerald R. *Reason and Authority in the Eighteenth Century.* Cambridge, Mass., 1964.

1237 D'ELIA, Donald J. "Benjamin Rush, David Hartley, and the Revolutionary Uses of Psychology." *Proc Am Philos Soc,* CXIV (1970), 109-118.

1238 GABRIEL, Ralph H. "The Enlightenment Tradition." *The American Spirit, A Series of Addresses.* Ed. F. Ernest Johnson. New York, 1948.

1239 GAY, Peter. *The Enlightenment: An Interpretation.* 2 vols. New York, 1966, 1969.†

1240 KOCH, Adrienne. *The Philosophy of Thomas Jefferson.* New York, 1943.

1241 KOCH, Adrienne. "Pragmatic Wisdom and the American Enlightenment." *Wm Mar Q,* XVIII, 3d ser. (1961), 313-329.

1242 KUNITZ, Stephen J. "Benjamin Rush on Savagism and Progress." *Ethnohist,* XVII (1970), 31-42.

1243 PEARCE, Roy Harvey. *The Savages of America: A Study of the Indian and the Idea of Civilization.* Rev. ed. Baltimore, Md., 1965.

1244 SCHNEIDER, Herbert W. *A History of American Philosophy.* New York, 1946.†

1245 SHEEHAN, Bernard W. "Paradise and the Noble Savage in Jeffersonian Thought." *Wm Mar Q,* XXVI, 3d ser. (1969), 327-359.

1246 VAN ZANDT, Roland. *The Metaphysical Foundations of American History.* The Hague, 1959.

1247 WERKMEISTER, William Henry. *A History of Philosophical Ideas in America.* New York, 1949.

2. The American Mind

1248 ADAMS, Henry. *The United States in 1800.* (First 6 chap. Adams, *History of the United States.*) Ed. Dexter Perkins. Ithaca, N.Y., 1957.

1249 BARITZ, Loren. *City on a Hill: A History of Ideas and Myths in America.* New York, 1964.

1250 BARKER, Charles A. *American Convictions: Cycles of Public Thought, 1600-1850.* Philadelphia, 1970.

1251 BENSON, C. Randolph. *Thomas Jefferson as Social Scientist.* Rutherford, N.J., 1971.

1252 BERTHOFF, Rowland. *An Unsettled People: Social Order and Disorder in American History.* New York, 1971.

1253 BOORSTIN, Daniel J. *The Lost World of Thomas Jefferson.* New York, 1968.†

1254 BRANT, Irving. *James Madison and American Nationalism.* Princeton, N.J., 1968.

1255 BURNS, Edward McNall. *The American Idea of Mission: Concepts of National Purpose and Destiny.* New Brunswick, N.J., 1957.

1256 CALHOUN, Daniel H. *Professional Lives in America: Structure and Aspirations, 1750-1850.* Cambridge, Mass., 1965.

1257 CASH, Wilbur J. *The Mind of the South.* New York, 1941.†

1258 COMMAGER, Henry Steele, and Elmo GIORDANETTI. *Was America a Mistake? An Eighteenth-Century Controversy.* Columbia, S.C., 1967.

1259 CUNLIFFE, Marcus. *Soldiers and Civilians: The Martial Spirit in America, 1775-1865.* See 1073.

1260 CURTI, Merle. *The Growth of American Thought.* 1943. New York, 1964.

1261 CURTI, Merle. *The Roots of American Loyalty.* New York, 1946.†

1262 DAVIS, David Brion. *Homicide in American Fiction, 1798-1860: A Study in Social Values.* Ithaca, N.Y., 1957.

1263 DAVIS, Richard Beale. *Intellectual Life in Jefferson's Virginia, 1790-1830.* Chapel Hill, N.C., 1964.

1264 DELMAGE, E. E. "American Ideas of Progress, 1750-1860." *Proc Am Philos Soc,* XCI (1947), 309-18.

1265 EATON, Clement. *The Mind of the Old South.* Baton Rouge, La., 1964.†

1266 EBY, Cecil D. "America as 'Asylum': A Dual Image." *Am Q,* XIV (1962), 483-489.

1267 EISINGER, Chester E. "The Freehold Concept in Eighteenth-Century American Letters." *Wm Mar Q,* IV, 3d ser. (1947), 42-59.

1268 EKIRCH, Arthur A. *The Civilian and the Military.* New York, 1956.

1269 FRANKLIN, John Hope. *The Militant South, 1800-1861*. Cambridge, Mass., 1956.†

1270 GABRIEL, Ralph Henry. *The Course of American Democratic Thought*. 2d ed. New York, 1956.

1271 GOODMAN, Paul. "Ethics and Enterprise: The Values of a Boston Elite." *Am Q*, XVIII (1966), 437-451.

1272 GOVAN, Thomas P. "Agrarian and Agrarianism: A Study in the Use and Abuse of Words." *J S Hist*, XXX (1964), 35-47.

1273 HESSELTINE, William B. "Four American Traditions." *J S Hist*, XXVII (1961), 3-32.

1274 HOFSTADTER, Richard. *Anti-Intellectualism in American Life*. New York, 1963.†

1275 HUMPHREY, Edward F. *Nationalism and Religion in America, 1774-1789*. Boston, 1924.

1276 JONES, Howard Mumford. *Ideas in America*. Cambridge, Mass., 1944.

1277 JONES, Howard Mumford. "The Unity of New England Culture." *Proc Mass Hist Soc*, LXXIX (1967), 74-88.

1278 KIRK, Russell. "Randolph of Roanoke and the Mind of the South." *Hist Today*, II (1952), 632-640.

1279 KOHN, Hans. *American Nationalism: An Interpretive Essay*. New York, 1957.†

1280 LYND, Staughton. *Intellectual Origins of American Radicalism*. New York, 1968.†

1281 MARK, Irving, and Eugene L. SCHWAAB, eds. *The Faith of Our Fathers: An Anthology Expressing the Aspirations of the American Common Man, 1790-1860*. New York, 1952.

1282 MILLER, Perry. *The Life of the Mind from the Revolution to the Civil WAr*. London, 1965.†

1283 MILLER, Perry. *Nature's Nation*. Cambridge, Mass., 1967.

1284 MIYAKAWA, T. Scott. *Protestants and Pioneers: Individualism and Conformity on the American Frontier*. Chicago, 1964.

1285 MOORE, Arthur K. *The Frontier Mind: A Cultural Analysis of the Kentucky Frontiersman*. Lexington, Ky., 1957.†

1286 MYERS, Gustavus. *History of Bigotry in the United States*. New York, 1943.†

1287 NAGEL, Paul C. *One Nation Indivisible: The Union in American Thought, 1776-1861*. New York, 1964.

1288 NAGEL, Paul C. *This Sacred Trust: American Nationality, 1798-1898*. New York, 1971.

1289 PERSONS, Stow. *American Minds: A History of Ideas*. New York, 1958.

1290 PETERSON, Merrill D. *The Jeffersonian Image in the American Mind*. New York, 1960.

1291 POTTER, David. *People of Plenty: Economic Abundance and the American Character*. Chicago, 1958.

1292 SPENCER, Benjamin Townley. *The Quest for Nationality: An American Literary Campaign*. Syracuse, N.Y., 1957.

1293 SUTTON, Robert P. "Nostalgia, Pessimism, and Malaise: The Doomed Aristocrat in Late-Jeffersonian Virginia." *Va Mag Hist Biog*, LXXVI (1968), 41-55.

1294 TAYLOR, William R. *Cavalier and Yankee: The Old South and the American National Character*. New York, 1961.†

1295 TUVESON, Ernest Lee. *Redeemer Nation: The Idea of America's Millennial Role*. Chicago, 1968.

1296 WECTER, Dixon. *The Saga of American Society: A Record of Social Aspiration, 1608-1937*. New York, 1937.

1297 WILLIAMS, William Appleman. *The Contours of American History*. Cleveland, Ohio, 1961.†

1298 WISH, Harvey. *Society and Thought in Early America*. New York, 1950.

3. Political Thought

1299 ADAIR, Douglass. "The New Thomas Jefferson." *Wm Mar Q*, III, 3d ser. (1946), 123-133.

1300 BECKER, Carl. "What Is Still Living in the Political Philosophy of Thomas Jefferson." *Am Hist Rev*, XLVIII (1943), 691-706.

1301 BELOFF, Max. *Jefferson and American Democracy*. New York, 1949.

1302 BRADLEY, Harold W. "The Political Thinking of George Washington." *J S Hist*, XI (1945), 469-486.

1303 CARPENTER, Jesse Thomas. *The South as a Conscious Minority, 1789-1861: A Study in Political Thought*. New York, 1930.

1304 COLBOURN, H. Trevor. "Thomas Jefferson's Use of the Past." *Wm Mar Q*, XV, 3d ser. (1958), 56-70.

1305 DAUER, Manning J., and Hans HAMMOND. "John Taylor: Democrat or Aristocrat." *J Pol*, VI (1944), 381-403.

1306 DETWEILER, Philip F. "The Changing Reputation of the Declaration of Independence: The First 50 Years." *Wm Mar Q*, XIX, 3d ser. (1962), 557-574.

1307 DRELL, Bernard. "John Taylor of Caroline and the Preservation of an Old Social Order." *Va Mag Hist Biog*, XLVI (1938), 285-298.

1308 FINK, Zera S. *The Classical Republicans*. Evanston, Ill., 1945.

1309 GAINES, Pierce Welch, comp. *Political Works of Concealed Authorship Relating to the United States, 1789-1810, with Attributions*. 3d ed. Hamden, Conn., 1972.

1310 GRISWOLD, A. Whitney. "The Agrarian Democracy of Thomas Jefferson." *Am Poli Sci Rev,* XL (1946), 657-681.

1311 GRISWOLD, A. Whitney. "Jefferson's Republic: The Rediscovery of Democratic Philosophy." *Fortune,* XLI (1950), 111.

1312 HACKER, Louis M. *Alexander Hamilton in the American Tradition.* New York, 1957.

1313 HANDLER, Edward. *America and Europe in the Political Thought of John Adams.* Cambridge, Mass., 1964.

1314 HARASZTI, Zoltán. *John Adams and the Prophets of Progress.* Cambridge, Mass., 1952.

1315 HOWE, John R., Jr. *The Changing Political Thought of John Adams.* Princeton, N.J., 1966.

1316 JACOBSON, Norman. "The Anti-Rationalist Heritage in America: Political Realism and the Age of Reason." *Rev Pol,* XV (1953), 446-469.

1317 KAPLAN, Lawrence S. *Jefferson and France: An Essay on Politics and Political Ideas.* New Haven, Conn., 1967.

1318 KENYON, Cecilia. "Alexander Hamilton: Rousseau of the Right." *Pol Sci Q,* LXXIII (1958), 161-178.

1319 KETCHAM, Ralph L. "James Madison and the Nature of Man." *J Hist Ideas,* XIX (1958), 62-76.

1320 KOCH, Adrienne. "Hamilton and Power." *Yale Rev,* LXVII (1958), 537-551.

1321 KOCH, Adrienne. *Power, Morals, and the Founding Fathers: Essays in the Interpretation of the American Enlightenment.* Ithaca, N.Y., 1961.†

1322 KURTZ, Stephen G. "The Political Science of John Adams, A Guide to His Statecraft." *Wm Mar Q,* XXV, 3d ser. (1968), 605-613.

1323 LIPSET, Seymour Martin, and Earl RAAB. *The Politics of Unreason: Right-Wing Extremism in America, 1790-1970.* New York, Evanston, Ill., and London, 1970.

1324 LIPSKY, George A. *John Quincy Adams: His Theory and Ideas.* New York, 1950.

1325 LIVINGSTON, John D. "Alexander Hamilton and the American Tradition." *Mid W J Pol Sci,* I (1957), 209-224.

1326 McCLOSKY, Robert G. "American Political Thought and the Study of Politics." *Am Poli Sci Rev,* LI (1957), 115-129.

1327 MALONE, Dumas. "Mr. Jefferson and the Traditions of Virginia." *Va Mag Hist Biog,* LXXV (1967), 131-142.

1328 MALONE, Dumas. "The Relevance of Mr. Jefferson." *Va Q Rev,* XXXVII (1961), 332-349.

1329 MERRIAM, Charles Edward. *A History of American Political Theories.* 1903. New York, 1968.

1330 MUDGE, Eugene Ten Broeck. *The Social Philosophy of John Taylor of Caroline: A Study in Jeffersonian Democracy.* New York, 1939.

1331 OSTRANDER, Gilman. *The Rights of Man in America, 1606-1861.* Columbia, Mo., 1960.

1332   PADOVER, Saul K. "Madison as a Political Thinker." *Soc Res*, XX (1953), 32-54.

1333   PAINE, Thomas. *Rights of Man, Being an Answer to Mr. Burke's Attack on the French Revolution.* See 562.

1334   RIEMER, Neal. "The Republicanism of James Madison." *Pol Sci Q*, LXIX (1954), 45-64.

1335   ROBATHAN, Dorothy M. "John Adams and the Classics." *N Eng Q*, XIX (1946), 91-98.

1336   ROSSITER, Clinton. "The Legacy of John Adams." *Yale Rev*, XLVI (1957), 528-550.

1337   ROSSITER, Clinton. "The Political Theory of Benjamin Franklin." *Pa Mag Hist Biog*, LXXVI (1952), 259-293.

1338   SMILEY, David L. "Revolutionary Origins of the South's Constitutional Defenses." *N C Hist Rev*, LXIV (1967), 256-269.

1339   SPURLIN, Paul Merrill. *Montesquieu in America, 1760-1801.* Baton Rouge, La., 1940.

1340   SPURLIN, Paul Merrill. *Rousseau in America, 1760-1809.* Baton Rouge, La., 1969.

1341   STEWART, Donald H., and George P. Clark. "Misanthrope or Humanitarian? John Adams in Retirement." *N Eng Q*, XXVIII (1955), 216-236.

1342   STOURZH, Gerald. *Alexander Hamilton and the Idea of Republican Government.* Stanford, Cal., 1970.

1343   WERNER, John M. "David Hume and America." *J Hist Ideas*, XXXIII (1972), 439-456.

1344   WHEALEN, John J. "James Harrington and American Liberalism, 1789-1800." *Hist Bull*, XXXII (1954), 143-152.

1345   WILTSE, Charles Maurice. *The Jeffersonian Tradition in American Democracy.* Chapel Hill, N.C., 1935.

1346   WILTSE, Charles Maurice. *Thomas Jefferson: A Study in the Philosophy of the State.* Ithaca, N.Y., 1932.

4. American and Foreign Cultures

1347   APPLEBY, Joyce. "America as a Model for the Radical French Reformers of 1789." *Wm Mar Q*, XXVIII, 3d ser. (1971), 267-287.

1348   BROWN, Esther E. *The French Revolution and the American Man of Letters.* Columbia, Mo., 1951.

1349   BROWN, Marvin Luther. *American Independence through Prussian Eyes.* Durham, N.C., 1958.

1350   CHINARD, Gilbert, ed. *George Washington as the French Knew Him.* Princeton, N.J., 1940.

1351 DOLL, Eugene Edgar. *American History as Interpreted by German Historians from 1770 to 1815*. Philadelphia, 1949.

1352 DOUGLASS, Elisha P. "German Intellectuals and the American Revolution." *Wm Mar Q*, XVII, 3d ser. (1960), 200-218.

1353 ECHEVERRIA, Durand. *Mirage in the West: A History of the French Image of American Society to 1815*. Princeton, N.J., 1957.

1354 FIELD, James A., Jr. *America and the Mediterranean World, 1776-1882*. Princeton, N.J., 1969.

1355 FRIEDRICH, Carl J. *The Impact of American Constitutionalism Abroad*. Boston, 1967.

1356 HOFFMAN, Philip G. "Australia's Debt to the American Revolution." *Hist*, XVII (1955), 143-156.

1357 JONES, Howard Mumford. *America and French Culture, 1750-1848*. Chapel Hill, N.C., 1927.

1358 LOVELAND, Anne C. *Emblem of Liberty: The Image of Lafayette in the American Mind*. Baton Rouge, La., 1971.

1359 McDERMOTT, John Francis, ed. *Frenchmen and French Ways in the Mississippi Valley*. Urbana, Ill., 1969.

1360 MIDDLETON, Richard. "British Historians and the American Revolution." *J Am Stud*, V (1971), 43-58.

1361 MILLER, Stuart Creighton. *The Unwelcome Immigrant: The American Image of the Chinese, 1785-1882*. Berkeley, Cal., 1969.

1362 MORRIS, Richard B. *The Emerging Nation and the American Revolution*. New York, 1970.

1363 PAULSTON, Roland G. "French Influence in American Institutions of Higher Learning, 1784-1825." *Hist Educ Q*, VIII (1968), 229-245.

1364 POCHMANN, Henry August. *German Culture in America: Philosophical and Literary Influence, 1600-1900*. Madison, Wis., 1957.

1365 RAYBACK, J. G. "French Comment on the Pennsylvania Constitution of 1776." *Pa Mag Hist Biog*, LXXVI (1952), 311-325.

1366 ROSENTHAL, Lewis. *America and France: The Influence of the United States on France in the XVIIIth Century*. New York, 1882.

1367 SHULIM, Joseph I. *The Old Dominion and Napoleon Bonaparte: A Study in American Opinion*. New York, 1952.

IV. Geographical Expansion

1. General

1368 BILLINGTON, Ray Allen. *The American Frontiersman.* Oxford, England, 1954.

1369 BILLINGTON, Ray Allen. *Westward Expansion: A History of the American Frontier.* New York, 1967.

1370 CARUSO, John Anthony. *The Appalachian Frontier: America's First Surge Westward.* Indianapolis, 1959.

1371 CLARK, Thomas D. *Frontier America: The Story of the Westward Movement.* 2d ed. New York, 1969.

1372 COLEGROVE, Kenneth W. "Attitude of Congress toward the Pioneers of the West from 1789 to 1820." *Iowa J Hist Pol,* VIII (1910), 3-129.

1373 EBLEN, Jack Ericson. *The First and Second United States Empires: Governors and Territorial Government, 1784-1912.* Pittsburgh, Pa., 1968.

1374 GATES, Charles M. "The West in American Diplomacy." *Miss Val Hist Rev,* XXVI (1940), 499-510.

1375 GATES, Paul. "Tenants of the Log Cabin." *Miss Val Hist Rev,* XLIX (1962), 3-31.

1376 HORSMAN, Reginald. *The Frontier in the Formative Years 1783-1815.* New York, 1970.†

1377 JAKIE, John A. "The American Bison and the Human Occupance of the Ohio Valley." *Proc Am Phil Soc,* CII (1968), 299-305.

1378 LYNCH, William O. "The Mississippi Valley and Its History." *Miss Val Hist Rev,* XXVI (1939), 3-20.

1379 MIYAKAWA, T. Scott. *Protestants and Pioneers: Individualism and Conformity on the American Frontier.* See 1284.

1380 MOORE, Arthur K. *The Frontier Mind: A Cultural Analysis of the Kentucky Frontiersman.* See 1285.

1381 NETTELS, Curtis. "The Mississippi Valley and the Constitution." *Miss Val Hist Rev,* XI (1924), 332-357.

1382 NETTELS, Curtis. "The Mississippi Valley and the Federal Judiciary, 1807-1837." See 1060.

1383 PHILBRICK, Francis S. *The Rise of the West, 1754-1830.* New York, 1965.†

1384 SMITH, Henry Nash. *Virgin Land: The American West as Symbol and Myth.* Cambridge, Mass., 1950.

1385 TERRELL, John Upton. *The Six Turnings: Major Changes in the American West, 1806-1834.* Glendale, Cal., 1968.

1386 VAN EVERY, Dale. *Ark of Empire: The American Frontier, 1784-1803.* New York, 1963.†

1387 VAN EVERY, Dale. *The Final Challenge: The American Frontier, 1804-1845.* New York, 1964.

1388 WERTENBAKER, Thomas J. "The Molding of the Middle West." *Am Hist Rev,* LIII (1948), 223-234.

2. Sociology of the Frontier

1389 ABERNETHY, Thomas P. "Democracy and the Southern Frontier." *J S Hist,* IV (1938), 3-13.

1390 ALLEN, Harry C. *Bush and Backwoods: A Comparison of the Frontier in Australia and the United States.* East Lansing, Mich., 1959.

1391 BARTLETT, Richard A. "Freedom and the Frontier: A Pertinent Re-Examination." *Mid-Am,* XL (1958), 131-138.

1392 BILLINGTON, Ray Allen. *America's Frontier Heritage.* New York, 1966.†

1393 BILLINGTON, Ray Allen. "Frederick Jackson Turner: The Image and the Man." *W Hist Q,* III (1972), 137-152.

1394 BILLINGTON, Ray Allen. *The Genesis of the Frontier Thesis: A Study in Historical Creativity.* San Marino, Cal., 1971.

1395 CRAVEN, Avery O. "The 'Turner' Theories and the South." *J S Hist,* V (1939), 291-314.

1396 CURTI, Merle. *The Making of an American Community: A Case Study of Democracy in a Frontier Community.* Stanford, Cal., 1959.†

1397 ELKINS, Stanley, and Eric McKITRICK. "A Meaning for Turner's Frontier." Part I: "Democracy in the Old Northwest." Part II: "The Southwest Frontier and New England." *Pol Sci Q,* LXIX (1954), 321-353, 565-602.

1398 ESAREY, Logan. "The Pioneer Aristocracy." *Ind Mag Hist,* XIII (1917), 270-287.

1399 EVANS, Paul D. "The Frontier in American Development: A Review." *N Y Hist,* LII (1971), 51-61.

1400 HOFSTADTER, Richard. "Turner and the Frontier Myth." *Am Sch,* XVIII (1949), 433-443.

1401 JACOBS, Wilbur R., John W. CAUGHEY, and Joe B. FRANTZ. *Turner, Bolton, and Webb: Three Historians of the American Frontier.* Seattle, Wash., 1965.

1402 LEWIS, Archibald R., and Thomas F. McGANN. *The New World Looks at Its History: Proceedings of the Second International Congress of Historians of the United States and Mexico.* Austin, Tex., 1963.

1403 NORDROFF, Ellen von. "The American Frontier as a Safety Valve—The Life, Death, Reincarnation, and Justification of a Theory." *Ag Hist,* XXXVI (1962), 123-142.

1404 SHANNON, Fred A. "A Post Mortem on the Labor-Safety-Valve Theory." *Ag Hist,* XVII (1945), 31-37.

1405 TURNER, Frederick Jackson. *The Frontier in American History.* New York, 1941.†

1406 TURNER, Frederick Jackson. *The Significance of Sections in American History.* New York, 1932.

1407 WELTER, Rush. "The Frontier West as Image of American Society, 1776-1860." *Pac N W Q,* LII (1961), 1-7.

1408 WINKS, Robin W. *The Myth of the American Frontier: Its Relevance to America, Canada and Australia.* Leicester, England, 1971.

1409 WOLF, George D. *The Fair Play Settlers of the West Branch Valley, 1769-1784: A Study of Frontier Ethnography.* Harrisburg, Pa., 1969.

1410 WRIGHT, Benjamin F. "American Democracy and the Frontier." *Yale Rev,* XX (1930), 349-365.

1411 WRIGHT, Benjamin F. "Political Institutions and the Frontier." *Sources of Culture in the Middle West.* Ed. Dixon Ryan Fox. New York, 1934.

3. Western Exploration

1412 BAILEY, Francis. *Journal of a Tour in Unsettled Parts of North America in 1796 and 1797.* Ed. Jack D. L. Holmes. Carbondale, Ill., 1969.

1413 BAKELESS, John Edwin, ed. *The Journals of Lewis and Clark: A New Selection with an Introduction.* New York, 1964.

1414 BAKELESS, John Edwin. *Lewis and Clark, Partners in Discovery.* New York, 1947.

1415 BREBNER, John Bartlet. *The Explorers of North America, 1492-1806.* London, 1933.†

1416 GOETZMANN, William H. *Army Exploration in the American West, 1803-1863.* See 1075.

1417 HAWGOOD, John A. *America's Western Frontiers: The Story of the Explorers and Settlers Who Opened the Trans-Mississippi West.* New York, 1967.

1418 HOLLON, W. Eugene. *The Lost Pathfinder, Zebulon Montgomery Pike.* Norman, Okla., 1949.

1419 JACKSON, Donald, ed. *Letters of the Lewis and Clark Expedition: With Related Documents, 1783-1854.* Urbana, Ill., 1962.

1420 LEWIS, G. Malcolm. "Early American Exploration and Cis-Rocky Mountain Desert, 1803-1823." *Great Plains J,* V (1965), 1-11.

1421 McDERMOTT, John Francis, ed. *Travelers on the Western Frontier.* Urbana, Ill., 1970.

1422 McMASTER, John Bach, ed. *The Trail Makers.* 17 vols. New York, 1903-1905.

1423 PIKE, Zebulon Montgomery. *Journals, with Letters and Related Documents.* Ed. Donald Jackson. 2 vols. Norman, Okla., 1966.

1424 STUART, Robert. *The Discovery of the Oregon Trail: Robert Stuart's Narrative of His Overland Trip Eastward from Astoria in 1812-13.* Ed. Philip Ashton Rollins. New York and London, 1935.

1425 THWAITES, Reuben G., ed. *Early Western Travels, 1748-1846.* 32 vols. Cleveland, Ohio, 1904-1907.

1426 WHITEBROOK, Robert Ballard. *Coastal Exploration of Washington.* Palo Alto, Cal., 1959.

1427 WILLIAMS, Samuel C., ed. *Early Travels in the Tennessee Country, 1540-1800.* Johnson City, Tenn., 1928.

4. The Northwestern and New England Frontier

1428 ACKERKNECHT, Erwin H. *Malaria in the Upper Mississippi Valley, 1760-1900.* Baltimore, Md., 1945.

1429 ALVORD, Clarence Walworth. *The Illinois Country, 1673-1818.* 1920. Chicago, 1965.

1430 BARNHART, John D. "Sources of Southern Migration into the Old Northwest." *Miss Val Hist Rev,* XXII (1935), 49-62.

1431 BARNHART, John D. "Southern Contributions to the Social Order of the Old Northwest." *N C Hist Rev,* XVII (1940), 237-248.

1432 BARNHART, John D., and Dorothy L. RIKER. *Indiana to 1816: The Colonial Period.* Indianapolis, 1971.

1433 BUCK, Solon J., and Elizabeth H. HAWTHORN. *The Planting of Civilization in Western Pennsylvania.* Pittsburgh, Pa., 1939.

1434 CARUSO, John Anthony. *The Great Lakes Frontier: An Epic of the Old Northwest.* Indianapolis, 1961.

1435 DOWNES, Randolph C. *Frontier Ohio, 1788-1803.* Columbus, Ohio, 1935.

1436 DUNN, Jacob Piatt. *Indiana and Indianas: A History of Aboriginal and Territorial Indiana and the Century of Statehood.* 5 vols. Chicago, 1919.

1437 FARRELL, David. "Settlement along the Detroit Frontier, 1760-1796." *Mich Hist,* LII (1968), 89-108.

1438 FROST, James A. *Life on the Upper Susquehanna, 1783-1860*. New York, 1951.

1439 GILPIN, Alec R. *The Territory of Michigan, 1805-1837*. East Lansing, Mich., 1970.

1440 HIGGINS, Ruth L. *Expansion in New York, with Especial Reference to the Eighteenth Century*. Columbus, Ohio, 1931.

1441 MILLER, James McDonald. *The Genesis of Western Culture: The Upper Ohio Valley 1800-1825*. Repr. New York, 1969.

1442 SCHAFER, Joseph. "High Society in Pioneer Wisconsin." *Wis Mag Hist*, XX (1937), 447-461.

1443 SHIPTON, Clifford K. "The New England Frontier." *N Eng Q*, X (1937), 25-36.

1444 SMITH, Norman W. "A Mature Frontier: The New Hampshire Economy, 1790-1850." *Hist N H*, XXIV (1969), 3-16.

1445 UTTER, William T. *The Frontier State, 1803-1825* [Ohio]. Columbus, Ohio, 1942.

1446 UTTER, William T. "Saint Tammany in Ohio: A Study in Frontier Politics." *Miss Val Hist Rev*, XV (1928), 321-340.

1447 WINTHER, Oscar O. *The Great Northwest: A History*. 2d ed. New York, 1950.

1448 WRIGHT, J. E., and Doris S. CORBETT. *Pioneer Life in Western Pennsylvania*. Pittsburgh, Pa., 1940.

5. The Southwestern and Florida Frontier

1449 ABERNETHY, Thomas Perkins. *From Plantation to Frontier in Tennessee: A Study in Frontier Democracy*. Chapel Hill, N.C., 1932.

1450 ABERNETHY, Thomas P. "Social Relations and Political Control in the Old Southwest." *Miss Val Hist Rev*, XVI (1930), 529-537.

1451 ABERNETHY, Thomas P. *Three Virginia Frontiers*. Baton Rouge, La., 1940.

1452 BAGOT, D. Huger. "The South Carolina Up Country at the End of the Eighteenth Century." *Am Hist Rev*, XXVIII (1923), 682-698.

1453 BARNHART, John D. *Valley of Democracy: The Frontier versus the Ohio Valley, 1775-1818*. Bloomington, Ind., 1953.

1454 BREVARD, Caroline Mays, and James Alexander ROBERTSON. *A History of Florida, from the Treaty of 1763 to Our Own Times*. 2 vols. Deland, Fla., 1924-25.

1455 CARRIGAN, Jo Ann. "Impact of Epidemic Yellow Fever on Life in Louisiana." *La Hist*, IV (1963), 5-34.

1456 CLARK, Thomas D. *A History of Kentucky*. New York, 1937.

1457 DAVENPORT, F. Garvin. *Ante-Bellum Kentucky: A Social History, 1800-1860.* Oxford, Ohio, 1943.

1458 DAVIS, Charles S. *The Cotton Kingdom of Alabama.* Montgomery, Ala., 1939.

1459 DICK, Everett. *The Dixie Frontier from the First Transmontaine Beginnings to the Civil War.* New York, 1948.†

1460 ELLSWORTH, Lucius F., ed. *The Americanization of the Gulf Coast, 1803-1850.* Pensacola, Fla., 1972.

1461 FOREMAN, Grant. *Indians and Pioneers: The Story of the American Southwest before 1830.* New Haven, Conn., 1930.

1462 FORTIER, Alcée. *A History of Lousiana.* 4 vols. New York, 1904.

1463 HAGY, James R. "The First Attempt to Settle Kentucky: Boone in Virginia." *Filson Club Hist Q,* XLIV (1970), 227-234.

1464 HAMER, Philip M., ed. *Tennessee: A History, 1673-1932.* 4 vols. New York, 1933.

1465 HAMILTON, William B. "The Southwestern Frontier, 1795-1817: An Essay in Social History." *J S Hist,* X (1944), 389-403.

1466 HATFIELD, Joseph T. "Governor William Charles Cole Claiborne, Indians, and Outlaws in Frontier Mississippi, 1801-1802." *J Miss Hist,* XXVII (1965), 323-350.

1467 LOWERY, Charles D. "The Great Migration to the Mississippi Territory, 1798-1819." *J Miss Hist,* XXX (1968), 173-192.

1468 LYNCH, William O. "The Westward Flow of Southern Colonists before 1861." *J S Hist,* IX (1943), 303-327.

1469 OWSLEY, Frank. "The Pattern of Migration and Settlement on the Southern Frontier." *J S Hist,* XI (1945), 147-176.

1470 POSEY, Walter B., ed. "Kentucky, 1790-1815: As Seen by Bishop Francis Asbury." *Filson Club Hist Q,* XXXI (1957), 333-348.

1471 RICE, Otis K. *The Alleghany Frontier: West Virginia Beginnings, 1730-1830.* Lexington, Ky., 1970.

1472 ROBERTSON, James Alexander. *Louisiana under the Rule of Spain, France and the United States, 1785-1807.* 2 vols. Cleveland, Ohio, 1911.

1473 ROWLAND, Dunbar. *Courts, Judges, and Lawyers of Mississippi, 1798-1935.* See 1064.

1474 ROWLAND, Dunbar. *History of Mississippi, the Heart of the South.* 2 vols. Chicago, 1925.

1475 SIEBERT, Wilbur H. "Kentucky's Struggle with Its Loyalist Proprietors." See 276.

1476 SIEBERT, Wilbur H. "The Loyalists in West Florida and the Natchez District." See 278.

1477 WATLINGTON, Patricia. "Discontent in Frontier Kentucky." *Reg Ky Hist Soc,* LXV (1967), 77-93.

6. *Economic and Urban Development of the Frontier*

1478   ATHERTON, Lewis E. *The Pioneer Merchant in Mid-America.* Columbia, Mo., 1939.

1479   BALD, F. Clever. *Detroit's First American Decade, 1796 to 1805.* Ann Arbor, Mich., 1948.

1480   BALDWIN, Leland D. "Shipbuilding on the Western Waters, 1793-1817." *Miss Val Hist Rev,* XX (1933), 29-44.

1481   BENTON, Elbert J. *Cultural Story of an American City.* Cleveland, Ohio, 1943-1946.

1482   BERRY, Thomas Senior. *Western Prices before 1861: A Study of the Cincinnati Market.* Cambridge, Mass., 1943.

1483   BINING, Arthur C. "The Rise of Iron Manufacturing in Western Pennsylvania." *W Pa Hist Mag,* XVI (1933), 235-256.

1484   BUCK, Solon J. "Frontier Economy in Southwestern Pennsylvania." *Ag Hist,* X (1936), 14-24.

1485   CHITTENDEN, Hiram Martin. *The American Fur Trade of the Far West.* 3 vols. Stanford, Cal., 1954.

1486   CLARK, John G. *The Grain Trade in the Old Northwest.* Urbana, Ill., 1966.

1487   DOUDS, Howard C. "Merchants and Merchandising in Pittsburgh, 1759-1800." *W Pa Hist Mag,* XX (1937), 123-132.

1488   EISTERHOLD, John A. "Lumber and Trade in the Lower Mississippi Valley and New Orleans, 1800-1860." *La Hist,* XIII (1972), 71-91.

1489   FULLER, George N. *Economic and Social Beginnings of Michigan: A Study of the Settlement of the Lower Peninsula during the Territorial Period, 1805-1837.* East Lansing, Mich., 1916.

1490   GALPIN, William F. "The Grain Trade of New Orleans, 1804-1814." See 879.

1491   HAEGER, John D. "The American Fur Company and the Chicago of 1812-1835." *J Ill State Hist Soc,* LXI (1968), 117-139.

1492   HENLEIN, Paul C. *Cattle Kingdom in the Ohio Valley, 1783-1860.* Lexington, Ky., 1959.

1493   HOPKINS, James F. *History of the Hemp Industry in Kentucky.* Lexington, Ky., 1951.

1494   HUNTER, Louis C. "Factors in the Early Pittsburgh Iron Industry." *Facts and Factors in Economic History.* Comp. Former Students of Edwin Francis Gay. Cambridge, Mass., 1932.

1495   JAMES, D. Clayton. *Antebellum Natchez.* Baton Rouge, La., 1968.

1496   KIRKPATRICK, R. L. "Professional, Religious, and Social Aspects of St. Louis Life, 1804-1816." *Mo Hist Rev,* XLIV (1950), 373-386.

1497 KOHLMEIER, Albert Ludwig. *The Old Northwest as the Keystone of the Arch of American Federal Union: A Study in Commerce and Politics.* Bloomington, Ind., 1938.

1498 MACKINTOSH, W. A. "Some Aspects of a Pioneer Economy." *Can J Econ Pol Sci,* II (1936), 457-463.

1499 MAYO, Bernard. "Lexington: Frontier Metropolis." *Historiography and Urbanization: Essays in Honor of W. Stull Holt.* Ed. Eric F. Goldman. Baltimore, 1941.

1500 PIERCE, Besse L. *A History of Chicago.* 3 vols. New York, 1937-1957.

1501 QUAIFE, Milo Milton. *Chicago and the Old Northwest, 1763-1835: A Study of the Evolution of the Northwest Frontier, Together with a History of Fort Dearborn.* Chicago, 1913.

1502 REISER, Catherine E. *Pittsburgh's Commercial Development, 1800-1850.* Harrisburg, Pa., 1951.

1503 REPS, John W. *Town Planning in Frontier America.* Princeton, N.J., 1969.

1504 STEVENS Wayne E. *The Northwest Fur-Trade, 1763-1800.* Urbana, Ill., 1928.

1505 STEVENS, Wayne E. "The Organization of the British Fur Trade, 1760-1800." *Miss Val Hist Rev,* III (1916), 172-202.

1506 VER HOEFF, Mary. *The Kentucky Mountains, Transportation and Commerce, 1750-1911: A Study in the Economic History of a Coal Field.* Louisville, Ky., 1911.

1507 WADE, Richard C. *The Urban Frontier: The Rise of Western Cities, 90-1830.* Cambridge, Mass., 1959.†

1508 WADE, Richard C. "Urban Life in Western America, 1790-1830." *Am Hist Rev,* LXIV (1958), 14-30.

1509 WEISENBURGER, Frances P. "The Urbanization of the Middle West: Town and Village in the Pioneer Period." *Ind Mag Hist,* XLI (1945), 19-30.

7. Frontier Leaders: Biographies

1510 AMBLER, Charles Henry. *George Washington and the West.* Chapel Hill, N.C., 1936.

1511 BAKELESS, John. *Background to Glory: The Life of George Rogers Clark.* Philadelphia, 1957.

1512 BASSETT, John Spencer. *The Life of Andrew Jackson.* 2 vols. 1925. Hamden, Conn., 1967.

1513 BRUCE, Henry Addington. *Daniel Boone and the Wilderness Road.* New York, 1910.

1514 CHAMBERS, William Nisbet. *Old Bullion Benton: Senator from the New West: Thomas Hart Benton, 1782-1858.* Boston, 1956.

1515 CLEAVES, Freeman. *Old Tippecanoe: William Henry Harrison and His Times.* New York, 1939.

1516 DRIVER, Carl Samuel. *John Sevier, Pioneer of the Old Southwest.* Chapel Hill, N.C., 1932.

1517 HARRISON, Lowell H. *John Breckinridge: Jeffersonian Republican.* Louisville, Ky., 1969.

1518 HOLMES, Jack D. L. *Gayoso: The Life of a Spanish Governor in the Mississippi Valley, 1789-1799.* Baton Rouge, La., 1965.

1519 JACOBS, James Ripley. *Tarnished Warrier, Major-General James Wilkinson.* New York, 1938.

1520 JAMES, James Alton. *The Life of George Rogers Clark.* Chicago, 1928.

1521 JAMES, Marquis. *Andrew Jackson: The Border Captain.* New York, 1933.†

1522 JELLISON, Charles A. *Ethan Allen: Frontier Rebel.* Syracuse, N.Y., 1969.

1523 JORDAN, Weymouth T. *George Washington Campbell of Tennessee: Western Statesman.* Tallahassee, Fla., 1955.

1524 MASON, Kathryn Harrod. *James Harrod of Kentucky.* Baton Rouge, La., 1951.

1525 PRICE, Robert. *Johnny Appleseed: A Man of Myth.* [John Chapman, 1775-1845]. Bloomington, Ind., 1954.

1526 SEARS, Alfred Byron. *Thomas Worthington: Father of Ohio Statehood.* Columbus, Ohio, 1958.

1527 TALBERT, Charles Gano. *Benjamin Logan: Kentucky Frontiersman.* Lexington, Ky., 1962.

1528 THOMAS, Samuel W. "William Croghan, Sr. [1752-1822]: A Pioneer Kentucky Gentleman." *Filson Club Hist Q,* XLIII (1969), 30-61.

1529 VAN EVERY, Dale. *Men of the Western Waters.* Boston, 1956.

1530 WILBUR, James Benjamin. *Ira Allen, Founder of Vermont, 1751-1814.* Boston, 1928.

1531 WOODFORD, Frank B., and Albert HYMA. *Frontier Ambassador: Gabriel Richard.* Detroit, Mich., 1958.

8. Indians

Indian-White Relations

1532 ABBOTT, Martin. "Indian Policy and Management in the Mississippi Territory, 1798-1817." *J Miss Hist,* XVI (1952), 153-169.

1533 BEAVER, R. Pierce. *Church, State, and the American Indians: Two and a Half Centuries of Partnership in Missions Between Churches and Government.* St. Louis, Mo., 1966.

1534   CAUGHEY, John Walton. *McGillivray of the Creeks*. Norman, Okla., 1938.

1535   COLEMAN, Kenneth. "Federal Indian Relations in the South, 1781-1789." *Chron Okla*, XXXV (1957), 435-458.

1536   COLEY, C. J. "Creek Treaties, 1790-1832." *Ala Rev*, XI (1958), 163-176.

1537   CORKRAN, David H. *The Carolina Indian Frontier*. Columbia, S.C., 1970.

1538   COTTERILL, R. S. "Federal Indian Management in the South, 1789-1825." *Miss Val Hist Rev*, XX (1933), 333-352.

1539   FENTON, William N. *American Indian and White Relations to 1830: Needs & Opportunities for Study*. Chapel Hill, N.C., 1957.

1540   HALLOWELL, Alfred I. "Impact of the American Indian on American Culture." *Am Anthro*, LIX (1957), 201-217.

1541   HORSMAN, Reginald. "American Indian Policy in the Old Northwest, 1783-1812." See 254.

1542   HORSMAN, Reginald. *Expansion and American Indian Policy, 1783-1812*. East Lansing, Mich., 1967.

1543   KAPPLER, Charles J., ed. *Indian Affairs, Laws and Treaties*. 5 vols. Washington, D.C., 1903-1941.

1544   MORRIS, Wayne. "Traders and Factories on the Arkansas Frontier, 1805-1822." *Ark Hist Q*, XXVIII (1969), 28-48.

1545   NICHOLS, Roger L. "The Army and the Indians 1800-1830—A Reappraisal: The Missouri Valley Example." *Pac Hist Rev*, XLI (1972), 151-168.

1546   PATTERSON, Palmer. "The Colonial Parallel: A View of Indian History." *Ethnohist*, XVIII (1971), 1-17.

1547   PEAKE, Ora Brooks. *A History of the United States Indian Factory, 1795-1822*. Denver, Colo., 1954.

1548   PHILLIPS, Edward H. "Timothy Pickering at His Best: Indian Commissioner, 1790-1794." *Essex Inst Hist Coll*, CII (1966), 163-202.

1549   POUND, Merritt Bloodworth. *Benjamin Hawkins–Indian Agent*. Athens, Ga., 1951.

1550   PRUCHA, Francis Paul. *American Indian Policy in the Formative Years: The Indian Trade and Intercourse Acts, 1780-1834*. Cambridge, Mass., 1962.†

1551   PURSER, Joyce. "The Administration of Indian Affairs in Louisiana, 1803-1820." *La Hist*, V (1964), 401-419.

1552   SHEEHAN, Bernard W. "Indian-White Relations in Early America: A Review Essay." *Wm Mar Q*, XXVI, 3d ser. (1969), 267-286.

1553   TUCKER, Glenn. *Tecumseh: Vision of Glory*. Indianapolis, 1956.

1554   WASHBURN, Wilcomb E. "A Moral History of Indian-White Relations: Needs and Opportunities for Study." *Ethnohist*, IV (1957), 47-61.

1555   WASHBURN, Wilcomb E. *Red Man's Land–White Man's Law: A Study of the Past and Present Status of the American Indian*. New York, 1971.

1556   WRIGHT, J. Leitch, Jr. *William Augustus Bowles, Director General of the Creek Nation*. Athens, Ga., 1967.

Indian Society

1557 BERKHOFER, Robert F., Jr. "Protestants, Pagans and Sequences among the North American Indians, 1760-1860." *Ethnohist,* X (1963), 201-232.

1558 BERKHOFER, Robert F., Jr. *Salvation and the Savage: An Analysis of Protestant Missions and American Indian Response, 1787-1862.* Lexington, Ky., 1965.

1559 BROWN, John P. *Old Frontiers: The Story of the Cherokee Indians from Earliest Times to the Date of Their Removal to the West, 1838.* Kingsport, Tenn., 1938.

1560 COTTERILL, R. S. *The Southern Indians: The Story of the Civilized Tribes before Removal.* Norman, Okla., 1954.

1561 DeFOREST, John W. *History of the Indians of Connecticut: From the Earliest Known Period to 1850.* 1851. Hamden, Conn., 1964.

1562 EWERS, John C. *Indian Life on the Upper Missouri.* Norman, Okla., 1968.

1563 FOREMAN, Grant. *The Five Civilized Tribes.* Naramax, Okla., 1934.†

1564 HUNTER, John D. *Manners and Customs of Several Indian Tribes Located West of the Mississippi.* 1823. Minneapolis, Minn., 1957.

1565 McMANUS, John C. "An Economic Analysis of Indian Behavior in the North American Fur Trade." *J Econ Hist,* XXXII (1972), 36-53. Disc. Stephen Salsbury and Earl Finbar Murphy. *Ibid.,* pp. 92-97.

1566 MILFORT, Louis. *Memoirs: Or, A Quick Glance at My Various Travels and My Sojourn in the Creek Nation.* Ed., trans. Ben C. McCary. Savannah, 1972.

1567 REID, John Philip. *A Law of Blood: The Primitive Law of the Cherokee Nation.* New York, 1970.

1568 SECOY, Frank Raymond. *Changing Military Patterns on the Great Plains.* Seattle, Wash., 1953.

1569 SPICER, Edward H. *Cycles of Conquest: The Impact of Spain, Mexico, and the United States on the Indians of the Southwest, 1533-1960.* Tucson, Ariz., 1962.

1570 STEARN, E. Wagner, and E. ALLEN. *The Effect of Smallpox on the Destiny of the American Indian.* Boston, 1945.

1571 SWANTON, John Reed. "Early History of the Creek Indians and Their Neighbors. " *Bur Am Ethno Bull,* LXXIII (1922).

1572 SWANTON, John Reed. *The Indians of the Southeastern United States.* Washington, D.C., 1946.

1573 WARING, Antonio J., ed. *Laws of the Creek Nation.* Athens, Ga., 1960. (Written down in 1825.)

1574 WOODWARD, Grace Steele. *The Cherokees.* Norman, Okla., 1963.

9. The Far West

1575 BANCROFT, Hugh Herbert. *History of the Pacific States of North America.* 34 vols. San Francisco, 1882-1890.

1576 BARRY, Louise. *The Beginning of the West: Annals of the Kansas Gateway to the American West, 1540-1854.* Topeka, Kans., 1972.

1577 CAREY, Charles Henry. *A General History of Oregon Prior to 1861.* 2 vols. Portland, Ore., 1935-1936.

1578 CARUTHERS, J. Wade. "The Seaborne Frontier to California 1796-1850." *Am Neptune,* XXIX (1969), 81-101.

1579 CAUGHEY, John Walton. *History of the Pacific Coast of North America.* New York, 1938.

1580 CLELAND, R. G. "Asiatic Trade and the American Occupation of the Pacific Coast." *Ann Rep Am Hist Assn,* 1914. Washington, D.C., 1914, pp. 281-289.

1581 COUGHLIN, Magdalen. "Boston Smugglers on the Coast [1797-1821]: An Insight into the American Acquisition of California." *Calif Hist Soc Q,* XLVI (1967), 99-120.

1582 CREER, Leland Hargrave. "Spanish-American Slave Trade in the Great Basin, 1800-1853." *N M Hist Rev,* XXIV (1950), 171-183.

1583 DICK, Everett. *Vanguards of the Frontier: A Social History of the Northern Plains and Rocky Mountains from the Earliest White Contacts to the Coming of the Homemaker.* New York, 1941.†

1584 FOLEY, William E. *A History of Missouri.* Vol. I: *1673-1820.* Columbia, Mo., 1971.

1585 FRANCHÈRE, Gabriel. *Journal of a Voyage on the North West Coast of North America during the Years 1811, 1812, 1813, and 1814.* Ed. W. Kaye Lamb. Toronto, 1969.

1586 FULLER, George Washington. *A History of the Pacific Northwest.* 2d ed. New York, 1938.

1587 HOWAY, Frederic W., ed. "Voyages of 'Columbia' to Northwest Coast 1787-90 and 1790-93." *Coll Mass Hist Soc,* LXXIX (1941), 1-495.

1588 NASATIR, A. P., ed. *Before Lewis and Clark: Documents Illustrating the History of the Missouri, 1785-1804.* 2 vols. St. Louis, Mo., 1952.

1589 OGDEN, Adele. *The California Sea Otter Trade, 1784-1848.* Berkeley, Cal., 1941.

1590 ROSS, Alexander. *The Fur Hunters of the Far West: A Narrative of Adventures in the Oregon and Rocky Mountains.* Ed. Milo M. Quaife. Chicago, 1924.

1591 SCOTT, H. W. *A History of the Oregon Country.* 6 vols. Cambridge, Mass., 1924.

1592 SIBLEY, Marilyn M. *Travelers in Texas, 1761-1860.* Austin, Tex., 1967.

1593 SKINNER, Constance Lindsay. *Adventures of Oregon: A Chronicle of the Fur Trade.* New Haven, Conn., 1921.

1594 WEBER, David J. *The Taos Trappers: The Fur Trade in the Far Southwest, 1540-1846.* Norman, Okla., 1971.

10. The Pacific Ocean and the Orient

1595 AHMAT, Sharon. "The Rhode Island Java Trade, 1799-1836." *R I Hist,* XXIV (1965), 1-10.

1596 AUGUR, Helen. *Passage to Glory: John Ledyard's America.* Garden City, N.Y., 1946.

1597 BHAGAT, G. *Americans in India 1784-1860.* New York, 1970.

1598 BRADLEY, Harold Whitman. *The American Frontier in Hawaii, 1789-1843.* Palo Alto, Cal., 1942.

1599 DANTON, George H. *The Cultural Contacts of the United States and China: The Earliest Sino-American Culture Contacts, 1784-1844.* New York, 1931.

1600 DENNETT, Tyler. *Americans in Eastern Asia.* New York, 1941.

1601 DODGE, Ernest Stanley. *New England and the South Seas.* Cambridge, Mass., 1965.

1602 DOWNS, Jacques M. "American Merchants and the China Opium Trade, 1800-1840." *Bus Hist Rev,* XLII (1968), 418-442.

1603 DULLES, Foster Rhea. *The Old China Trade.* Boston, 1930.

1604 DULLES, Foster Rhea. *Yankees and Samurai: America's Role in the Emergence of Modern Japan, 1791-1900.* New York, 1965.

1605 KALB, Marvin, and Elie ABEL. *The Roots of Involvement: The U.S. in Asia, 1784-1971.* New York, 1971.

1606 KIMBALL, Gertrude S. *The East-India Trade of Providence from 1787-1807.* Providence, R.I., 1896.

1607 KIRKER, James. *Adventures to China: Americans in the Southern Ocean, 1792-1812.* New York, 1970.

1608 LATOURETTE, Kenneth Scott. "The History of Early Relations between the United States and China, 1784-1844." *Trans Conn Acad Art Sci,* XXII (1917), 10-209.

1609 LATOURETTE, Kenneth Scott. "Voyages of American Ships to China, 1784-1844." *Trans Conn Acad Art Sci,* XXVIII (1927), 237-271.

1610 MORISON, Samuel Eliot. "Boston Traders in the Hawaiian Islands, 1789-1823." *Proc Mass Hist Soc,* LIV, 2d ser. (1920), 9-47.

1611 MUDGE, Jean McClure. *Chinese Export Porcelain for the American Trade, 1785-1835.* Newark, Del., 1962.

1612 PARKINSON, Cyril Northgate. *Trade in the Eastern Seas 1793-1813.* Cambridge, England, 1937.

1613 PHILLIPS, James Duncan. *Pepper and Pirates: Adventures in the Sumatra Pepper Trade of Salem.* Boston, 1949.

1614 PHILLIPS, James Duncan. *Salem and the Indies: East India Voyages of Salem Vessels Before 1800.* Salem, Mass., 1943.

1615 RYDELL, Raymond A. *Cape Horn to the Pacific: The Rise and Decline of an Ocean Highway.* Berkeley, Cal., 1952.

1616 STRAUSS, W. Patrick. *Americans in Polynesia, 1783-1842.* East Lansing, Mich., 1963.

1617 TATE, E. Mowbray. "American Merchant and Naval Contacts with China, 1784-1850." *Am Neptune,* XXXI (1971), 177-191.

1618 VER STEEG, Clarence L. "Financing and Outfitting the First United States Ship to China." *Pac Hist Rev,* XXII (1953), 1-12.

V. Material and Economic Growth

1. Demography

Population

1619 American Council of Learned Societies. "Report of Committee on Linguistic and National Stocks in the Population of the United States." *Ann Rep Am Hist Assn,* 1931. Washington, D.C., 1932.

1620 CASSEDY, James H. *Demography in Early America: Beginnings of the Statistical Mind, 1600-1800.* Cambridge, Mass., 1969.

1621 CHICKERING, Jesse. *A Statistical View of the Population of Massachusetts from 1765 to 1840.* Boston, 1846.

1622 EVERSLEY, D. E. C. "Population, Economy and Society." *Population in History.* Eds. David V. Glass and D. E. C. Eversley. London, 1965.

1623 FRIIS, Herman R. "A Series of Population Maps of the Colonies and the United States, 1625-1790." *Geog Rev,* XXX (1940), 463-479.

1624 GREENE, Evarts B., and Virginia D. HARRINGTON, *American Population before the Federal Census of 1790.* New York, 1932.

1625 JAFFE, A. J. "Differential Fertility in the White Population in Early America." *J Heredity,* XXXI (1940), 407-411.

1626 KLIMM, Lester E. *The Relation between Certain Population Changes and the Physical Environment in Hampden, Hampshire, and Franklin Counties, Massachusetts, 1790-1929.* Philadelphia, 1933.

1627 LEE, Everett, and Michael LALLI. "Population." Comments by George Rogers Taylor. *The Growth of the Seaport Cities 1790-1825.* Ed. David T. Gilchrist. Charlottesville, Va., 1967.

1628 MAYER, Kurt B. *Economic Development and Population Growth in Rhode Island.* Providence, R.I., 1953.

1629 POTTER, J. "The Growth of Population in America, 1760-1860." *Population in History.* Eds. David V. Glass and D. E. C. Eversley. See 1622.

1630 THOMPSON, Warren S., and Pascal K. WHELPTON. *Population Trends in the United States.* New York, 1933.

1631 United States Bureau of the Census. *A Century of Population Growth, from the First Census of the United States to the Twelfth, 1790-1900.* Washington, D.C., 1909.

1632 VINOVSKIS, Maris A. "Mortality Rates and Trends in Massachusetts before 1860." *J Econ Hist,* XXXII (1972), 184-213. Disc. J. J. Spengler and Richard Sutch. *Ibid.,* pp. 214-218.

1633 WILSON, Harold F. "Population Trends in Northwestern New England, 1790-1930." *Geog Rev,* XXIV (1934), 272-277.

1634 YASUBA, Yasukichi. *Birth Rates of the White Population in the United States, 1800-1860.* Baltimore, Md., 1962.

Immigration

1635 BERTHOFF, Rowland T. *British Immigrants in Industrial America, 1790-1950.* Cambridge, Mass., 1953.

1636 CARTER, Edward C., II. "A 'Wild Irishman' under Every Federalist's Bed: Naturalization in Philadelphia, 1789-1806." See 543.

1637 COMMONS, John Rogers. *Races and Immigrants in America.* 1907. New York, 1967.

1638 FRANKLIN, Frank G. "The Legislative History of Naturalization in the United States, 1776-1795." *Ann Rep Am Hist Assn,* 1901. Washington, 1902, pp. 299-318.

1639 GORDON, Milton M. "Assimilation in America: Theory and Reality." *Daed,* XC (1961), 263-285.

1640 HANDLIN, Oscar. *Boston's Immigrants, 1790-1880: A Study in Acculturation.* Rev. ed. Cambridge, Mass., 1959.†

1641 HANSEN, Marcus L. *The Atlantic Migration, 1607-1860: A History of the Continuing Settlement of the United States.* Cambridge, Mass., 1940.†

1642 HEATON, Herbert. "The Industrial Immigrant in the United States, 1783-1812." *Proc Am Phil Soc,* XCV (1951), 519-527.

1643 LUCAS, Henry S. *Netherlanders in America: Dutch Immigration to the United States and Canada, 1789-1950.* Ann Arbor, Mich., 1955.

1644 MARRARO, Howard R. "Italo-Americans in Eighteenth Century New York." *N Y Hist,* XXI (1940), 316-323.

1645 MARRARO, Howard R. "Italo-Americans in Pennsylvania in the Eighteenth Century." *Pa Hist,* VII (1940), 159-166.

1646 MILLER, Stuart Creighton. *The Unwelcome Immigrant: The American Image of the Chinese, 1785-1882.* See 1361.

1647 NIEHAUS, Earl F. *The Irish in New Orleans, 1800-1860.* Baton Rouge, La., 1965.

1648 ROWLEY, William E. "The Irish Aristocracy of Albany, 1798-1878." *N Y Hist,* LII (1971), 275-304.

1649 SCOTT, Franklin Daniel. *The Peopling of America: Perspectives on Immigration.* Washington, D.C., 1972. Pub. 1963, 1966 as *Emigration and Immigration.*

1650 TAYLOR, Philip. *The Distant Magnet: European Emigration to the U.S.A.* New York, 1971.

1651 WITTKE, Carl. *We Who Built America: The Saga of the Immigrant.* New York, 1939.†

Internal Migration

1652 BARNHART, John D. "Sources of Southern Migration into the Old Northwest." See 1430.

1653 BUTTERFIELD, Roy L. "On the American Migrations." *N Y Hist,* XXXVIII (1957), 368-386.

1654 ELLIS, David M. "The Yankee Invasion of New York, 1783-1850." *N Y Hist,* XXXII (1951), 1-17.

1655 FOX, Dixon Ryan. *Yankees and Yorkers.* New York, 1940.

1656 GOODRICH, Carter, and Sol DAVISON. "The Wage Earners in the Western Movement." *Pol Sci Q,* L (1935), 161-185; LI (1936), 61-116.

1657 HOLBROOK, Stewart H. *The Yankee Exodus: An Account of Migration from New England.* New York, 1950.†

1658 LOWERY, Charles D. "The Great Migration to the Mississippi Territory, 1798-1819." See 1467.

1659 LYNCH, William O. "The Westward Flow of Southern Colonists before 1861." See 1468.

1660 OWSLEY, Frank. "The Pattern of Migration and Settlement on the Southern Frontier." See 1469.†

1661 ROSENBERRY, Lois (Kimball) Mathews. *The Expansion of New England: Spread of New England Settlement and Institutions to the Mississippi River, 1620-1865.* Boston, 1909.

1662 ROSENBERRY, Lois (Kimball) Mathews. *Migrations from Connecticut Prior to 1800.* Tercentenary Commission of the State of Connecticut, XXVIII. New Haven, Conn., 1934.

1663 STILWELL, Lewis D. *Migration from Vermont, 1776-1860.* Montpelier, Vt., 1948.

1664 THORNTHWAITE, C. Warren, and Helen I. SLENTZ. *Internal Migration in the United States*. Philadelphia, 1934.

1665 WOOTEN, Hugh Hill. "Westward Migration from Iredell County, 1800-1850." *N C Hist Rev*, XXX (1953), 61-71.

1666 YARBROUGH, William H. *Economic Aspects of Slavery in Relation to Southern and Southwestern Migration*. Nashville, Tenn., 1932.

2. Economic Development

General

Interpretive and General Studies

1667 ANDREANO, Ralph L., ed. *New Views on American Economic Development: A Selective Anthology of Recent Work*. Cambridge, Mass., 1965.

1668 BJORK, Gordon C. "The Weaning of the American Economy: Independence, Market Changes, and Economic Development." *J Econ Hist*, XXIV (1964), 541-560.

1669 BRUCHEY, Stuart. "The Business Economy of Marketing Change, 1790-1840: A Study of Sources of Efficiency." *Ag Hist*, XLVI (1972), 211-226.

1670 BRUCHEY, Stuart. *The Roots of American Economic Growth, 1607-1861: An Essay in Social Causation*. New York, 1965.†

1671 CALLENDER, Guy S., ed. *Selections from the Economic History of the United States, 1765-1860*. Boston, 1909.

1672 CARUTHERS, J. Wade. "Influence of Maritime Trade in Early American Development: 1750-1830." *Am Neptune*, XXIX (1969), 199-210.

1673 Conference on Research in Income and Wealth. *Output, Employment, and Productivity in the United States after 1800*. New York, 1966.

1674 Conference on Research in Income and Wealth. *Trends in the American Economy in the Nineteenth Century*. Princeton, N.J., 1960.

1675 EAST, Robert A. "The Business Entrepreneur in a Changing Colonial Economy, 1763-1795." *Tasks Econ Hist*, suppl. *J Econ Hist*, VI (1946), 16-27.

1676 HAMMOND, Bray. *Banks and Politics in America, from the Revolution to the Civil War*. Princeton, N.J., 1957.†

1677 HAWK, Emory Q. *Economic History of the South*. New York, 1934.

1678 KNAPP, Joseph G. *The Rise of American Cooperative Enterprise, 1620-1920*. Danville, Ill., 1969.

1679 LEBERGOTT, Stanley. *Manpower in Economic Growth: The American Record since 1800*. New York, 1964.

1680 McMASTER, John B. "The Struggle for Commercial Independence, 1783-1812." *Cambridge Modern History*, VII. Cambridge, England, 1903.

1681 NETTELS, Curtis P. *The Emergence of a National Economy, 1775-1815.* New York, 1962.†

1682 NORTH, Douglass C. *The Economic Growth of the United States, 1790-1860.* Englewood Cliffs, N.J., 1961.†

1683 NORTH, Douglass C. *Growth and Welfare in the American Past.* Englewood Cliffs, N.J., 1966.†

1684 OLIVER, John W. *History of American Technology (1607-1955).* New York, 1956.

1685 PITKIN, Timothy. *A Statistical View of the Commerce of the United States.* New York, 1967. Facsimile of 1816 ed.

1686 REZNECK, Samuel. "The Rise and Early Development of Industrial Consciousness in the United States, 1760-1830." *J Econ Bus Hist,* IV (1932), 784-811.

1687 ROCHESTER, Anna. *American Capitalism 1607-1800.* New York, 1949.

1688 SEYBERT, Adam. *Statistical Annals of the United States, 1789-1818.* 1818. York, 1967.

1689 SMITH, Walter Buckingham, and Arthur Harrison COLE. *Fluctuations in American Business, 1790-1860.* Cambridge, Mass., 1935.

1690 THISTLETHWAITE, Frank. *The Anglo-American Connection in the Early Nineteenth Century.* See 89.

1691 WILKINS, Mira. *The Emergence of Multinational Enterprise: American Business Abroad from the Colonial Era to 1914.* Cambridge, Mass., 1970.

1692 WILLIAMS, William Appleman. "The Age of Mercantilism: An Interpretation of the American Political Economy, 1763-1828." *Wm Mar Q,* XV, 3d ser. (1958), 419-437.

Economic Thought

1693 AIKEN, John R. "Benjamin Franklin, Karl Marx, and the Labor Theory of Value." *Pa Mag Hist Biog,* XC (1966), 378-384.

1694 BOURNE, Edward G. "Alexander Hamilton and Adam Smith." *Q J Econ,* VIII (1894), 328-344.

1695 COXE, Tench. *A View of the United States of America in a Series of Papers Written at Various Times, in the Years Between 1787 and 1794.* New York, 1965.

1696 DORFMAN, Joseph. *The Economic Mind in American Civilization, 1606-1933.* 5 vols. New York, 1946-1959.

1697 GRAMPP, William D. "A Reexamination of Jeffersonian Economics." *S Econ J,* XII (1946), 263-282.

1698 MILLER, Harry E. *Banking Theories in the United States before 1860.* Cambridge, Mass., 1927.

1699 MINTS, Lloyd Wynn. *A History of Banking Theory in Great Britain and the United States.* Chicago, 1945.

1700 SELEKMAN, Benjamin M., and Sylvia K. SELEKMAN. "Mathew Carey." *Har Bus Rev,* XIX (1941), 326-341.

1701 SPENGLER, Joseph. "The Political Economy of Jefferson, Madison, and Adams." *American Studies in Honor of William Kenneth Boyd.* Ed. David K. Jackson. Durham, N.C., 1940.

1702 STONE, Richard Gabriel. *Hezekiah Niles as an Economist.* Baltimore, Md., 1933.

1703 WETZEL, William Achenbach. *Benjamin Franklin as an Economist.* Baltimore, Md., 1895.

1704 WILHITE, Virgle Glenn. *Founders of American Economic Thought and Policy.* New York, 1958.

The Role of Government

1705 CALLENDER, Guy S. "The Early Transportation and Banking Enterprises of the States in Relation to the Growth of Corporations." *Q J Econ,* XVII (1902), 111-162.

1706 DOWD, Mary Jane. "The State in the Maryland Economy, 1776-1807." *Md Hist Mag,* LVII (1962), 90-132, 229-258.

1707 ELAZAR, Daniel J. "Banking and Federalism in the Early American Republic." *Huntington Lib Q,* XXVIII (1965), 301-320.

1708 FOLMSBEE, Stanley John. *Sectionalism and Internal Improvements in Tennessee, 1796-1845.* Knoxville, Tenn., 1939.

1709 GOODRICH, Carter. *The Government and the Economy, 1783-1861.* New York, 1967.†

1710 GOODRICH, Carter. *Government Promotion of American Canals and Railroads 1800-1890.* New York, 1960.

1711 HANDLIN, Oscar, and Mary Flug HANDLIN. *Commonwealth: A Study of the Role of Government in the American Economy: Massachusetts, 1775-1861.* Rev. ed. Cambridge, Mass., 1969.

1712 HANDLIN, Oscar. "Laissez-Faire Thought in Massachusetts, 1790-1880." *Tasks Econ Hist,* supp. *J Econ Hist,* III (1943), 55-65.

1713 HARTZ, Louis. *Economic Policy and Democratic Thought: Pennsylvania, 1776-1860.* Cambridge, Mass., 1948.

1714 HARTZ, Louis. "Laissez-Faire Thought in Pennsylvania, 1776-1860." *Tasks Econ Hist,* supp. *J Econ Hist,* III (1943), 66-77.

1715 HEATH, Milton S. *Constructive Liberalism: The Role of the State in Economic Development in Georgia to 1860.* Cambridge, Mass., 1954.

1716 HEATH, Milton S. "Laissez-Faire in Georgia, 1732-1860." *Tasks Econ Hist,* supp. *J Econ Hist,* III (1943), 78-100.

1717 HUTCHINS, John G. B. *The American Maritime Industries and Public Policy, 1789-1914: An Economic History.* Cambridge, Mass., 1941.

1718 MILLER, Nathan. *The Enterprise of a Free People: Aspects of Economic Development in New York during the Canal Period, 1792-1838.* Ithaca, N.Y., 1962.

1719 MORRIS, Richard B. *Government and Labor in Early America.* New York, 1946.†

1720 SEAVOY, Ronald E. "Laws to Encourage Manufacturing: New York Policy and the 1811 General Incorporation Statute." *Bus Hist Rev,* XLVI (1972), 85-95.

1721 YOUNG, Jeremiah Simeon. *A Political and Constitutional Study of the Cumberland Road.* Chicago, 1902.

1722 ZEIS, Paul M. *American Shipping Policy.* Princeton, N.J., 1938.

Urban Development

1723 BARHET, James L. "Growth of New York and Suburbs since 1790." *Sci Monthly,* XI (1920), 404-418.

1724 BALDWIN, Leland D. *Pittsburgh: The Story of a City.* Pittsburgh, Pa., 1937.

1725 BLAKE, Nelson M. *Water for the Cities: A History of the Urban Water-Supply Problem in the United States.* Syracuse, N.Y., 1956.

1726 BRYAN, Wilhelmus Boyart. *A History of the National Capital, from Its Foundation through the Period of the Adoption of the Organic Act.* 2 vols. New York, 1914-1916.

1727 CLARK, John G. *New Orleans 1718-1812: An Economic History.* Baton Rouge, La., 1970.

1728 EBERLEIN, Harold D., and Cortlandt HUBBARD. *Portrait of a Colonial City: Philadelphia, 1670-1838.* Philadelphia, 1939.

1729 GILCHRIST, David T., ed. *The Growth of the Seaport Cities, 1790-1825.* See 1627.

1730 GINSBERG, Stephen F. "The Police and Fire Protection in New York City: 1800-1850." *N Y Hist,* LII (1971), 133-150.

1731 GREEN, Constance McLaughlin. *Washington, Village and Capital, 1800-1878.* Princeton, N.J., 1963.

1732 HANDLIN, Oscar, and John BURCHARD, eds. *The Historian and the City.* Cambridge, Mass., 1963.

1733 LEMON, James T. "Urbanization and the Development of Eighteenth-Century Southeastern Pennsylvania and Adjacent Delaware." *Wm Mar Q,* XXIV, 3d ser. (1967), 501-542.

1734 MOORE, Gay M. *Seaport in Virginia: George Washington's Alexandria.* Richmond, Va., 1949.

1735 OBERHOLTZER, Ellis P. *Philadelphia, A History of the City and Its People.* 4 vols. Philadelphia, 1912.

1736 OSTERWEIS, Rollin G. *Three Centuries of New Haven, 1638-1938.* New Haven, Conn., 1953.

1737 PHILLIPS, James Duncan. *Salem and the Indies: The Story of the Great Commercial Era of the City.* Boston, 1947.

1738 POMERANTZ, Sidney. *New York: An American City, 1783-1803: A Study of Urban Life.* New York, 1938.

1739 PRED, Allan R. *The Spatial Dynamics of United States Urban-Industrial Growth, 1800-1914: Interpretive and Theoretical Essays.* Cambridge, Mass., 1966.

1740 REPS, John W. *The Making of Urban America: A History of City Planning in the United States.* Princeton, N.J., 1965.

1741 REPS, John W. *Town Planning in Frontier America.* See 1503.

1742 SCHARF, John Thomas. *The Chronicles of Baltimore: Being a Complete History of "Baltimore Town" and Baltimore City from the Earliest Period to the Present Time.* Baltimore, Md., 1874.

1743 SCHARF, J. Thomas, and Thompson WESTCOTT. *History of Philadelphia.* 3 vols. Philadelphia, 1884.

1744 SEMMES, Raphael. *Baltimore as Seen by Visitors, 1783-1860.* Baltimore, Md., 1953.

1745 STOKES, I. N. Phelps. *The Iconography of Manhattan Island, 1498-1909.* 6 vols. New York, 1915-1928.

1746 TAYLOR, George Rogers. "American Urban Growth Preceding the Railway Age." *J Econ Hist,* XXVII (1967), 309-339.

1747 WARNER, Sam Bass, Jr. "If All the World Were Philadelphia: A Scaffolding for Urban History, 1774-1930." *Am Hist Rev,* LXXIV (1968), 26-43.

1748 WARNER, Sam Bass, Jr. *The Private City: Philadelphia in Three Periods of Its Growth.* Philadelphia, 1968.

1749 WEBER, Adna F. *The Growth of Cities in the Nineteenth Century: A Study in Statistics.* New York, 1899.

1750 WHITEHILL, Walter Muir. *Boston: A Topographical History.* Cambridge, Mass., 1959.

1751 WILKENFELD, Bruce M. "The New York City Common Council, 1689-1800." *N Y Hist,* LII (1971), 249-273.

1752 WILSON, James G., ed. *The Memorial History of the City of New York, from Its First Settlement to the Year 1892.* 4 vols. New York, 1892-1893.

1753 WINSOR, Justin, ed. *The Memorial History of Boston, 1630-1880.* 4 vols. Boston, 1880-1881.

Wages and Prices

1754 ADAMS, Donald R., Jr. "Some Evidence on English and American Wage Rates, 1790-1830." *J Econ Hist,* XXX (1970), 499-520.

1755 ADAMS, Donald R., Jr. "Wage Rates in the Early National Period: Philadelphia, 1785-1830." *J Econ Hist,* XXVIII (1968), 404-417.

1756 ADAMS, T. M. *Prices Paid by Farmers for Goods and Services and Received by Them for Farm Products, 1790-1871: Wages of Farm Labor, 1780-1937.* Burlington, Vt., 1939.

1757 BERRY, Thomas Senior. *Western Prices before 1861: A Study of the Cincinnati Market.* See 1482.

1758   BEZANSON, Anneobaad. GRAY, and M. HUSSEY. *Wholesale Prices in Philadelphia, 1784-1861.* 2 vols. Philadelphia, 1936-1937.

1759   COLE, Arthur Harrison. *Wholesale Commodity Prices in the United States, 1700-1861* (with statistical supplement). 1938. Cambridge, Mass., 1969.

1760   PETERSON, Arthur G. *Historical Study of Prices Received by Producers of Farm Products in Virginia, 1801-1927.* Washington, D.C., 1929.

1761   TAYLOR, George Rogers. "Wholesale Commodity Prices at Charleston, South Carolina, 1796-1861." *J Econ Bus Hist,* IV (1932), 848-876.

1762   United States Bureau of Labor Statistics. *History of Wages in the United States from Colonial Times to 1928.* Bull. 499. Washington, D.C., 1929.

1763   VINOVSKIS, Maris A. "The 1789 Life Table of Edward Wigglesworth." *J Econ Hist,* XXXI (1971), 570-590.

1764   WARREN, G. F., F. A. PEARSON, and H. M. STOKER. *Wholesale Prices for 213 Years, 1720-1932.* Ithaca, N.Y., 1932.

Bankruptcy and Imprisonment for Debt

1765   COLEMAN, Peter J. "The Insolvent Debtor in Rhode Island, 1745-1828." *Wm Mar Q,* XXII, 3d ser. (1965), 413-434.

1766   CONANT, H. J. "Imprisonment for Debt in Vermont: A History." *Vt Q,* XIX, n.s. (1951), 67-81.

1767   FEER, Robert A. "Imprisonment for Debt in Massachusetts before 1800." *Miss Val Hist Rev,* XLVIII (1961), 252-269.

1768   RANDALL, Edwin T. "Imprisonment for Debt in America: Fact and Fiction." *Miss Val Hist Rev,* XXXIX (1952), 89-102.

1769   REMINGTON, Harold. *A Treatise on the Bankruptcy Law of the United States.* 3 vols. Charlottesville, Va., 1908-1910.

1770   WARREN, Charles. *Bankruptcy in United States History.* Cambridge, Mass., 1935.

Labor and Indentured Servitude

1771   BERNSTEIN, Leonard. "The Working People of Philadelphia from Colonial Times to the General Strike of 1835." *Pa Mag Hist Biog,* LXXIV (1950), 322-339.

1772   COMMONS, John R., et al. *History of Labour in the United States.* 4 vols. New York, 1918-1935.

1773   DULLES, Foster R. *Labor in America: A History.* New York, 1949.

1774   FONER, Philip Sheldon. *History of the Labor Movement in the United States.* 4 vols. New York, 1947-1965.

1775   FORBES, Allan W. "Apprenticeship in Massachusetts: Its Early Importance and Later Neglect." *Worc Hist Soc Pub,* II, New Ser. (1936), 5-25.

1776   GEISER, Karl Frederick. *Redemptions and Indentured Servant, in the Colony and Commonwealth of Pennsylvania.* New Haven, Conn., 1901.

1777 GRIFFIN, Richard W. "Poor White Laborers in Southern Cotton Factories, 1789-1865." *S C Hist Mag,* LXI (1960), 26-40.

1778 HERRICK, Cheesman A. *White Servitude in Pennsylvania: Indentured and Redemption Labor in Colony and Commonwealth.* Philadelphia, 1926.

1779 LYND, Staughton, and Alfred YOUNG. "After Carl Becker: The Mechanics and New York City Politics, 1774-1801." See 130.

1780 McCORMAC, Eugene I. *White Servitude in Maryland, 1634-1820.* Baltimore, Md., 1904.

1781 MILLER, William. "The Effects of the American Revolution on Indentured Servitude." *Pa Hist,* VII (1940), 131-141.

1782 MONTGOMERY, David. "The Working Classes of the Pre-Industrial American City, 1780-1830." *Labor Hist,* IX (1968), 3-22.

1783 MORRIS, Richard B. "White Bondage in Ante-Bellum South Carolina." *S C Hist Geneal Mag,* LXIX (1948), 191-207.

1784 MOTLEY, James M. *Apprenticeship in American Trade Unions.* Baltimore, Md., 1907.

1785 PELLING, Henry. *American Labor.* Chicago, 1960.†

1786 PERLMAN, Selig. *A History of Trade Unionism in the United States.* New York, 1922.

1787 PILLSBURY, William M. "Earning a Living 1788-1818: Jeb Danforth, Cabinetmaker." *R I Hist,* XXXI (1972), 81-93.

1788 RAYBACK, Joseph G. *A History of American Labor.* New York, 1959.†

1789 SULLIVAN, William A. *The Industrial Worker in Pennsylvania, 1800-1840.* Harrisburg, Pa., 1955.

1790 WALSH, Richard. *Charleston's Sons of Liberty: A Study of the Artisans, 1763-1789.* See 202.

Social Structure

1791 BERTHOFF, Rowland. "The American Social Order: A Conservative Hypothesis." *Am Hist Rev,* LXV (1960), 495-514.

1792 KULIKOFF, Allan. "The Progress of Inequality in Revolutionary Boston." *Wm Mar Q,* XXVIII, 3d ser. (1971), 375-412.

1793 LAND, Aubrey C. "Economic Base and Social Structure: The Northern Chesapeake in the Eighteenth Century." *J Econ Hist,* XXV (1965), 639-654.

1794 LEMON, James T. *The Best Poor Man's Country: A Geographical Study of Early Southeastern Pennsylvania.* Baltimore, Md., 1972.

1795 LEMON, James T., and Gary B. NASH. "The Distribution of Wealth in Eighteenth-Century America: A Century of Changes in Chester County, Pennsylvania, 1693-1802." *J Soc Hist,* II (1968), 1-24.

1796 MAIN, Jackson T. "The Distribution of Property in Post-Revolutionary Virginia." *Miss Val Hist Rev,* LXI (1954), 241-258.

1797 MAIN, Jackson T. "The One Hundred." See 189.

1798 MAIN, Jackson T. *The Social Structure of Revolutionary America.* Princeton, N.J., 1965.

1799   MAIN, Jackson T. "Trends in Wealth Concentration before 1860." *J Econ Hist*, XXXI (1971), 445-447.

1800   NASH, Gary B. *Class and Society in Early America*. Englewood Cliffs, N.J., 1970.†

1801   OAKS, Robert F. "Big Wheels in Philadelphia: DuSimitiere's List of Carriage Owners." *Pa Mag Hist Biog*, XCV (1971), 351-362.

1802   SOLTOW, Lee. "Economic Inequality in the United States in the Period from 1790 to 1860." *J Econ Hist*, XXXI (1971), 822-839.

1803   SUTTON, Robert P. "Sectionalism and Social Structure: A Case Study of Jeffersonian Democracy." *Va Mag Hist Biog*, LXXX (1972), 70-84.

Agriculture

General

1804   BIDWELL, Percy W., and John I. FALCONER. *History of Agriculture in the Northern United States, 1620-1860*. New York, 1941.

1805   CHAMBERS, Jonathan D., and G. E. MINGAY. *The Agricultural Revolution, 1750-1880*. London, 1966.

1806   CONNOR, L. G. "A Brief History of the Sheep Industry in the United States." *Ann Rep Am Hist Assn*, 1918. Washington, D.C., 1921, pp. 89-197.

1807   CRAVEN, Avery O. *Soil Exhaustion as a Factor in the Agricultural History of Virginia and Maryland, 1606-1860*. Urbana, Ill., 1925.

1808   DOWDEY, Clifford. *The Great Plantation: A Profile of Berkeley Hundred and Plantation Virginia from Jamestown to Appomattox*. New York, 1957.

1809   ELLIS, David Maldwyn. *Landlords and Farmers in the Hudson-Mohawk Region, 1790-1850*. Ithaca, N.Y., 1946.

1810   GATES, Paul W. "Problems of Agricultural History 1796-1840." *Ag Hist*, XLVI (1972), 33-58.

1811   GRAY, Lewis Cecil. *History of Agriculture in the Southern United States to 1860*. 2 vols. Washington, D.C., 1933.

1812   HIGBEE, Edward C. "The Three Earths of New England." *Geog Rev*, XLII (1952), 425-438.

1813   HORSFALL, Frank, Jr. "Horticulture in Eighteenth-Century America." *Ag Hist*, XLIII (1969), 159-167.

1814   HULBERT, A. B. *Soil: Its Influence on the History of the United States, with Special Reference to Migration and the Scientific Study of Local History*. New Haven, Conn., 1930.

1815   JENSEN, Merrill. "The American Revolution and American Agriculture." *Ag Hist*, XLIII (1969), 107-124.

1816   LAND, Aubrey C. "Economic Behavior in a Planting Society: The 18th Century Chesapeake." *J S Hist*, XXXIII (1967), 469-485.

1817 LAND, Aubrey C. "The Tobacco Staple and the Planter's Problems: Technology, Labor, and Crops." *Ag Hist*, XLIII (1969), 69-82.

1818 LEMON, James T. "The Agricultural Practices of National Groups in Eighteenth Century Southeastern Pennsylvania." *Geog Rev*, LVI (1966), 467-496.

1819 LEMON, James T. "Household Consumption in Eighteenth-Century America and Its Relationship to Production and Trade: The Situation among Farmers in Southeastern Pennsylvania." *Ag Hist*, XLI (1967), 67-70.

1820 MOORE, John Hebron. "Mississippi's Search for a Staple Crop." *J Miss Hist*, XXIX (1967), 371-385.

1821 MOORE, John Hebron. "A Review of Lewis C. Gray's *History of Agriculture in the United States to 1860.*" *Ag Hist*, XLVI (1972), 19-27. Comments by Neill A. McNall. *Ibid.*, pp. 29-32.

1822 PAPENFUSE, Edward C., Jr. "Planter Behavior and Economic Opportunity in a Staple Economy." *Ag Hist*, XLVI (1972), 297-311.

1823 PARKS, Roger N. "Comments on Change in Agriculture, 1790-1840." *Ag Hist*, XLVI (1972), 173-180.

1824 RASMUSSEN, Wayne D. "History of Agriculture in the Northern United States, 1620-1860 Revisited." *Ag Hist*, XLVI (1972), 9-17. Comments by Neill A. McNall. *Ibid.*, pp. 29-32.

1825 ROBERT, Joseph C. *The Story of Tobacco in America.* New York, 1949.†

1826 ROBERT, Joseph C. *The Tobacco Kingdom: Plantation, Market and Factory in Virginia and North Carolina, 1800-1860.* Durham, N.C., 1938.

1827 SCARBOROUGH, William K. *The Overseer: Plantation Management in the Old South.* Baton Rouge, La., 1966.

1828 SCHAFER, Joseph. *The Social History of American Agriculture.* New York, 1936.

1829 SITTERSON, Joseph Carlyle. *Sugar Country: The Cane Sugar Industry in the South, 1753-1950.* Lexington, Ky., 1953.

1830 WATKINS, James Lawrence. *King Cotton: A Historical and Statistical Review, 1790-1908.* New York, 1908.

1831 WOODMAN, Harold D. *King Cotton and His Retainers: Financing and Marketing the Cotton Crop of the South, 1800-1925.* Lexington, Ky., 1968.

Agricultural Reform

1832 BIDWELL, Percy W. "The Agricultural Revolution in New England." *Am Hist Rev*, XXVI (1921), 683-702.

1833 BRANDENBURG, David J. "A French Aristocrat Looks at American Farming." *Ag Hist*, XXXII (1958), 155-165.

1834 BRUCE, Kathleen. "Virginian Agricultural Decline to 1860: A Fallacy." *Ag Hist*, VI (1932), 3-13.

1835 CRAVEN, A. O. "John Taylor and Southern Agriculture." *J S Hist*, IV (1938), 137-147.

1336 DESTLER, Chester McArthur. "The Gentleman Farmer and the New Agriculture: Jeremiah Wadsworth." *Ag Hist*, XLVI (1972), 135-153.

1837 KELSEY, Darwin P., ed. *Farming in the New Nation: Interpreting American Agriculture, 1790-1840.* Washington, D.C., 1972. Reprint.

1838 KNIGHT, Franklin, ed. *Letters on Agriculture from His Excellency George Washington, President of the United States, to Arthur Young.* Washington, D.C., 1847.

1839 LOEHR, Rodney C. "Arthur Young and American Agriculture." *Ag Hist*, XLIII (1969), 43-56.

1840 LOEHR, Rodney. "The Influence of English Agriculture on American Agriculture, 1775-1825." *Ag Hist*, XI (1937), 3-16.

1841 MARTI, Donald B. "Early Agricultural Societies in New York: The Foundations of Improvement." *N Y Hist*, XLVIII (1967), 313-331.

1842 PURSELL, Carroll W., Jr. "E. I. du Pont and the Merino Mania in Delaware, 1805-1815." *Ag Hist*, XXXVI (1962), 91-100.

1843 SCOVILLE, Warren C. "Did Colonial Farmers 'Waste' Our Land?" *S Econ J*, XX (1953), 178-181.

1844 TOLLES, Frederick B. "George Logan and the Agricultural Revolution." *Proc Am Phil Soc*, XCV (1951), 589-598.

1845 TRUE, Rodney H. "The Early Development of Agricultural Societies in the United States." *Ann Rep Am Hist Assn*, 1920. Washington, D.C., 1925, pp. 293-306.

1846 WATSON, W. C., ed. *Men and Times of the Revolution: Or, Memoirs of Elkanah Watson.* New York, 1856.

1847 WOODWARD, Carl R. "A Discussion of Arthur Young and American Agriculture." *Ag Hist*, XLIII (1969), 57-67.

Land Policy and Speculation

1848 BAILEY, Kenneth P. *The Ohio Company of Virginia and the Westward Movement 1748-1792: A Chapter in the History of the Colonial Frontier.* Glendale, Cal., 1939.

1849 BILLINGTON, Ray A. "The Origin of the Land Speculator as a Frontier Type." *Ag Hist*, XIX (1945), 204-212.

1850 BOYD, J. P. "Connecticut's Experiment in Expansion: The Susquehanna Company, 1753-1803." *J Econ Bus Hist*, IV (1931), 38-69.

1851 CHAZANOFF, William. *Joseph Ellicott and the Holland Land Company: The Opening of Western New York.* Syracuse, N.Y., 1970.

1852 COTTERILL, R. S. "The National Land System in the South: 1803-1812." *Miss Val Hist Rev*, XVI (1930), 495-506.

1853 COTTERILL, R. S. "The South Carolina Land Cession." *Miss Val Hist Rev*, XII (1925), 376-384.

1854 CUTLER, W. P., and J. P. CUTLER. *Life Journals and Correspondence of Rev. Manasseh Cutler.* 2 vols. Cincinnati, Ohio, 1888.

1855 ELSMERE, Jane. "The Notorious Yazoo Land Fraud Case." See 747.

1856 EVANS, Paul Demund. *The Holland Land Company*. Buffalo, N.Y., 1924.

1857 GATES, Paul W., and Robert W. SWENSON. *History of Public Land Law Development*. Washington, D.C., 1968.

1858 GATES, Paul W. "The Role of the Land Speculator in Western Development." *Pa Mag Hist Biog*, LXVI (1942), 314-333.

1859 HENDERSON, Elizabeth K. "The Northwestern Lands of Pennsylvania, 1790-1812." *Pa Mag Hist Biog*, LX (1936), 131-160.

1860 HIBBARD, Benjamin H. *A History of the Public Land Policies*. New York, 1939.†

1861 LeDUC, Thomas. "History and Appraisal of United States Land Policy to 1862." *Land Use Policy and Problems in the United States*. Ed. Howard W. Ottson. Lincoln, Neb., 1963.

1862 LEWIS, George E. *The Indiana Company, 1763-1798: A Study in Eighteenth Century Frontier Land Speculation and Business Venture*. Glendale, Cal., 1941.

1863 LIVERMORE, Shaw. *Early American Land Companies: Their Influence on Corporate Development*. New York, 1939.

1864 LUTZ, Paul V. "Land Grants for Service in the Revolution." See 258.

1865 ROBBINS, Roy M. *Our Landed Heritage: The Public Domain, 1776-1936*. Princeton, N.J., 1936.†

1866 ROBERTS, Frances C. "Politics and Public Land Disposal in Alabama's Formative Period." *Ala Rev*, XXII (1969), 163-174.

1867 ROHRBOUGH, Malcolm J. *The Land Office Business: The Settlement and Administration of American Public Lands, 1799-1837*. New York, 1968.

1868 TREAT, Payson J. *The National Land System, 1785-1820*. New York, 1910.

1869 TURNER, Orasmus. *History of the Pioneer Settlement of Phelps and Gorham's Purchase and Morris' Reserve*. Rochester, N.Y., 1852.

1870 WHITAKER, Arthur P. "The Muscle Shoals Speculation, 1783-1789." *Miss Val Hist Rev*, XIII (1926), 365-386.

1871 WHITAKER, Arthur P., ed. "The South Carolina Yazoo Company." *Miss Val Hist Rev*, XVI (1929), 383-394.

1872 WILKINSON, Norman B. "Robert Morris and the Treaty of Big Tree." *Miss Val Hist Rev*, XL (1953), 257-278.

Transportation and Internal Improvements

1873 AMBLER, Charles H. *A History of Transportation in the Ohio Valley*. Glendale, Cal., 1932.

1874 BALDWIN, Leland D. *The Keelboat Age on Western Waters*. Pittsburgh, Pa., 1941.

1875 COLLES, Christopher. *A Survey of the Roads of the United States of America 1789*. Ed. Walter W. Ristow. Cambridge, Mass., 1961. (The earliest American road guide.)

1876 CRITTENDEN, Charles C. "Inland Navigation in North Carolina, 1763-1789." *N C Hist Rev*, VIII (1931) 145-154.

1877 CRITTENDEN, Charles C. "Means of Communication in North Carolina, 1763-1789." *N C Hist Rev*, VIII (1931), 373-383.

1878 CRITTENDEN, Charles C. "Overland Travel and Transportation in North Carolina, 1763-1789." *N C Hist Rev*, VIII (1931), 239-257.

1879 DUNBAR, Seymour. *A History of Travel in America*. 4 vols. Indianapolis, 1915.

1880 DURRENBERGER, Joseph Austin. *Turnpikes: A Study of the Toll Road Movement in the Middle Atlantic States and Maryland*. Valdosta, Ga., 1931.

1881 EARLE, Alice Morse. *Stage-Coach and Tavern Days*. New York, 1900.

1882 GRAY, Ralph D. *The National Waterway: A History of the Chesapeake and Delaware Canal, 1769-1965*. Urbana, Ill., 1967.

1883 GRAY, Ralph D. "Philadelphia and the Chesapeake and Delaware Canal, 1769-1823." *Pa Mag Hist Biog*, LXXXIV (1960), 401-423.

1884 HARLOW, Alvin F. *Old Towpaths: The Story of the American Canal Era*. New York, 1926.

1885 HARTSOUGH, Mildred L. *From Canoe to Steel Barge on the Upper Mississippi*. Minneapolis, Minn., 1934.

1886 HOLMES, Oliver W. "The Turnpike Era." *History of the State of New York*. Ed. Alexander C. Flick. New York, 1934. V, 257-924.

1887 HULBERT, Archer B. *The Paths of Inland Commerce: A Chronicle of Trail, Road, and Waterway*. New Haven, 1920.

1888 JORDAN, Philip D. *The National Road*. 1948. Magnolia, Mass., 1967.

1889 LANE, Wheaton J. *From Indian Trail to Iron Horse: Travel and Transportation in New Jersey, 1620-1860*. Princeton, N.J., 1939.

1890 LANE, Wheaton J. "The Turnpike Movement in New Jersey." *Proc N J Hist Soc*, LIII (1936), 19-52.

1891 MACGILL, Caroline E., et al. *History of Transportation in the United States before 1860*. New York, 1948.

1892 MARLOWE, George F. *Coaching Roads of Old New England*. New York, 1945.

1893 MILLER, Nathan. *The Enterprise of a Free People: Aspects of Economic Development in New York during the Canal Period, 1792-1838*. See 1718.

1894 MYERS, Richmond E. "The Early Turnpikes of the Susquehanna Valley." *Pa Hist*, XXI (1954), 248-259.

1895 PHILLIPS, Ulrich Bonnell. *A History of Transportation in the Eastern Cotton Belt to 1860*. New York, 1908.

1896 PUSEY, William Allen. *The Wilderness Road to Kentucky, Its Location and Features*. New York, 1921.

1897 ROBERTS, Christopher. *The Middlesex Canal, 1793-1860*. Cambridge, Mass., 1938.

1898 SHAW, Ronald E. *Erie Water West: A History of the Erie Canal, 1792-1854*. Lexington, Ky., 1966.

1899 SHUMWAY, George. *Conestoga Wagon, 1750-1850: Freight Carrier for 100 Years of America's Westward Expansion*. 2d ed. York, Pa., 1966.

1900 VER HOEFF, Mary. *The Kentucky Mountains, Transportation and Commerce, 1750-1911: A Study in the Economic History of a Coal Field*. See 1506.

1901 WAITLEY, Douglas. *Roads of Destiny: The Trails that Shaped a Nation*. Washington, D.C., 1970.

1902 WARD, George Washington. *The Early Development of the Chesapeake and Ohio Canal Project*. Baltimore, Md., 1899.

1903 WOOD, Frederic J. *The Turnpikes of New England*. Boston, 1919.

1904 WOODFOLK, George R. "Rival Urban Communication Schemes for the Possession of the Northwest Trade, 1783-1800." *Mid-Am*, XXXVIII (1956), 214-232.

Public Finance

1905 ADAMS, Henry Carter. *Taxation in the United States, 1789-1816*. Baltimore, Md., 1884.

1906 BALINSKY, Alexander. *Alexander Gallatin: Fiscal Theories and Policies*. New Brunswick, N.J., 1958.

1907 BAYLEY, Rafael A. *History of the National Loans of the United States, from July 4, 1776 to June 30, 1880*. Washington, D.C., 1881.

1908 BENSON, George C. S., et al. *The American Property Tax: Its History, Administration, and Economic Impact*. Claremont, Cal., 1965.

1909 BOLLES, Albert S. *The Financial History of the United States from 1774 to . . . 1885*. 3 vols. New York, 1879-1886.

1910 DEWEY, Davis Rich. *Financial History of the United States*. 12th ed. New York, 1934.

1911 ELLIOTT, Jonathan. *The Funding System of the United States and Great Britain, with Some Tabular Facts of Other Nations Touching the Same Subject*. Washington, D.C., 1845.

1912 FERGUSON, E. James. *The Power of the Purse: A History of American Public Finance, 1776-1790*. Chapel Hill, N.C., 1961.

1913 KIMMEL, Lewis H. *Federal Budget and Fiscal Policy, 1789-1958*. Washington, D.C., 1959.

1914 RATCHFORD, B. U. *American State Debts*. Durham, N.C., 1941.

1915 RATNER, Sidney. *American Taxation: Its History as a Social Force in Democracy*. New York, 1942.†

1916 TAUS, Esther Rogoff. *Central Banking Functions of the United States Treasury, 1789-1941*. New York, 1943.

1917 TIMBERLAKE, Richard H., Jr. "The Specie Standard and Central Banking in the United States before 1860." *J Econ Hist*, XXI (1961), 318-341.

1918 TRESCOTT, Paul B. "Federal-State Financial Relations, 1790-1860." *J Econ Hist*, XV (1955), 227-245.

Tariff

1919 ELLIOTT, Orrin Leslie. *The Tariff Controversy in the United States, 1789-1833.* Palo Alto, Cal., 1892.

1920 HILL, William. "The First Stages of the Tariff Policy of the United States." *Pub Am Econ Assn,* VIII (1893), 452-614.

1921 KAISER, Carl W., Jr. *History of the Academic Protectionist-Free Trade Controversy in America before 1860.* Philadelphia, 1939.

1922 PREYER, Norris W. "Southern Support of the Tariff of 1816: A Reappraisal." *J S Hist,* XXV (1959), 306-322.

1923 SETSER, Vernon G. *The Commercial Reciprocity Policy of the United States, 1774-1829.* See 87.

1924 STANWOOD, Edward. *American Tariff Controversies in the Nineteenth Century.* 2 vols. Boston and New York, 1903.

1925 TAUSSIG, Frank William. *The Tariff History of the United States.* 8th ed. New York and London, 1931.

Financial Institutions

1926 BRADBURY, M. L. "Legal Privilege and the Bank of North America." *Pa Mag Hist Biog,* XCVI (1972), 139-166.

1927 BROWN, Kenneth L. "Stephen Girard's Bank." *Pa Mag Hist Biog,* LXVI (1942), 29-55.

1928 CAROTHERS, Neil. *Fractional Money: A History of the Small Coins and Fractional Paper Currency of the United States.* New York, 1930.

1929 CARTER, E. C., II. "The Birth of a Political Economist: Mathew Carey and the Recharter Fight of 1810-1811." *Pa Hist,* XXXIII (1966), 274-288.

1930 CLARKE, M. St. Clair, and D. A. HALL. *Legislative and Documentary History of the Bank of the United States, Including the Original Bank of North America.* Washington, D.C., 1832.

1931 FENSTERMAKER, J. Van. *The Development of American Commercial Banking, 1782-1837.* Kent, Ohio, 1965.

1932 FENSTERMAKER, J. Van. "The Statistics of American Commercial Banking, 1782-1818." *J Econ Hist,* XXV (1965), 400-413.

1933 GILLINGHAM, Harold E. *Marine Insurance in Philadelphia, 1721-1800.* Philadelphia, 1933.

1934 GREEF, Albert O. *The Commercial Paper House in the United States.* Cambridge, Mass., 1937.

1935 HAMMOND, Bray. *Banks and Politics in America, from the Revolution to the Civil War.* See 1676.

1936 HELDERMAN, Leonard C. *National and State Banks: A Study of Their Origins.* Boston, 1931.

1937 HEPBURN, Alonzo Barton. *A History of Currency in the United States, with a Brief Description of the Currency Systems of All Commercial Nations*. 1915. New York, 1967.

1938 HIDY, Ralph W. "Anglo-American Merchant Bankers." *J Econ Hist,* I (1941), 53-66.

1939 HOLDSWORTH, John Thom, and Davis R. DEWEY. *The First and Second Banks of the United States*. Washington, D.C., 1911.

1940 JAMES, F. Cyril. "The Bank of North America and the Financial History of Philadelphia." *Pa Mag Hist Biog*, LXIV (1940), 56-87.

1941 LAUGHLIN, James Lawrence. *The History of Bimetallism in the United States*. 4th ed. New York, 1900.

1942 LEWIS, Lawrence, Jr. *A History of the Bank of North America*. Philadelphia, 1882.

1943 MARTIN, J. G. *Seventy-Three Years History of the Boston Stock Market (1798-1871)*. Boston, 1871.

1944 MASSEY, J. Earl. *America's Money: The Story of Our Coins and Currency*. New York, 1968.

1945 MORGAN, H. Wayne. "The Origins and Establishment of the First Bank of the United States." *Bus Hist Rev*, XXX (1956), 472-492.

1946 MUSCALUS, John A. *The Use of Banking Enterprise in the Financing of Public Education, 1796-1866*. Philadelphia, 1945.

1947 REDLICH, Fritz. *The Molding of American Banking: Men and Ideas*. 2 vols. New York, 1951.

1948 REUBENS, Beatrice G. "Burr, Hamilton, and the Manhattan Company." *Pol Sci Q*, LXXII (1957), 578-607; LXXIII (1958), 100-125.

1949 SCHWARTZ, Anna J. "The Beginning of Competitive Banking in Philadelphia, 1782-1809." *J Pol Econ*, LV (1947), 417-431.

1950 SOBEL, Robert. *The Big Board: A History of the New York Stock Market*. New York, 1965.†

1951 SPARKS, Earl S. *History and Theory of Agricultural Credit in the United States*. New York, 1932.

1952 TRESCOTT, Paul B. *Financing American Enterprise: The Story of Commercial Banking*. New York, 1963.

1953 WALTERS, Raymond, Jr. "The Origins of the Second Bank of the United States." *J Pol Econ*, LIII (1945), 115-131.

1954 WILSON, Janet. "The Bank of North America and Pennsylvania Politics, 1781-1787." See 205.

Commerce: Foreign and Domestic

1955 BUCK, Norman S. *The Development of the Organization of Anglo-American Trade, 1800-1850*. New Haven, Conn., 1925.

1956 BURON, Edmond. "Statistics on Franco-American Trade, 1778-1806." *J Econ Bus Hist*, IV (1932), 571-580.

1957 CHECKLAND, S. G. "American versus West Indian Traders in Liverpool, 1793-1815." *J Econ Hist*, XVIII (1958), 141-160.

1958 CLAUDER, Anna C. *American Commerce as Affected by the Wars of the French Revolution and Napoleon, 1793-1812*. Philadelphia, 1932.

1959 COATSWORTH, John H. "American Trade with European Colonies in the Caribbean and South America, 1790-1812." *Wm Mar Q*, XXIV, 3d ser. (1967), 243-266.

1960 GALEY, John H. "Salem's Trade with Brazil, 1801-1870." *Essex Inst Hist Coll*, CVII (1971), 198-219.

1961 GARES, Albert J. "Stephen Girard's West Indian Trade, 1789-1812." *Pa Mag Hist Biog*, LXXII (1948), 311-342.

1962 GARRETT, Jane N. "Philadelphia and Baltimore, 1790-1840: A Study of Intra-Regional Unity." *Md Hist Mag*, LV (1960), 1-13.

1963 GOEBEL, Dorothy Burne. "British Trade to the Spanish Colonies, 1796-1823." *Am Hist Rev*, XLIII (1938), 288-320.

1964 JOHNSON, Emory R., T. W. VAN METRE, G. G. HUEBNER, and D. S. HANCHETT. *History of Domestic and Foreign Commerce of the United States*. 2 vols. Washington, D.C., 1915.

1965 JONES, Fred M. "Middlemen in the Domestic Trade in the United States, 1800-1860." *Stud Soc Sci* (Ill.), Urbana, 1937, pp. 1-68.

1966 LEACH, Mac Edward. "Notes on American Shipping Based on Records of the Court of the Vice-Admiralty of Jamaica, 1776-1812." *Am Neptune*, XX (1960), 44-48.

1967 LIPPINCOTT, Isaac. *Internal Trade of the United States, 1700-1860*. Chicago, 1916.

1968 LIVINGWOOD, James Weston. *The Philadelphia-Baltimore Trade Rivalry, 1780-1860*. Harrisburg, Pa., 1947.

1969 LOSSE, Winifred J. "The Foreign Trade of Virginia, 1789-1809." *Wm Mar Q*, I, 3d ser. (1944), 161-178.

1970 MARTIN, Margaret E. "Merchants and Trade of the Connecticut River Valley, 1750-1820." *Smith Col Stud Hist*, 1939.

1971 MORISON, Samuel Eliot. *Maritime History of Massachusetts, 1783-1860*. Boston, 1921.†

1972 NICHOLS, Roy F. "Trade Relations and the Establishment of the United States Consulates in Latin America, 1779-1809." *His-Am Hist Rev*, XIII (1933), 291-313.

1973 PITKIN, Timothy. *A Statistical View of the Commerce of the United States*. See 1685.

1974 RAPP, Marvin A. "New York's Trade on the Great Lakes, 1800-1840." *N Y Hist*, XXXIX (1958), 22-33.

1975 VAN METRE, T. W. *An Outline of the Development of the Internal Commerce of the United States, 1789-1900*. Baltimore, Md., 1913.

Shipping and Maritime Industries

1976 CHAPELLE, Howard Irving. *History of American Sailing Ships*. New York, 1935.

1977 HOHMAN, Elmo Paul. *The American Whaleman: A Study of Life and Labor in the Whaling Industry*. New York, 1928.

1978 INNIS, Harold A. *The Cod Fisheries: The History of an International Economy*. New Haven, Conn., 1940.

1979 McFARLAND, Raymond. *A History of the New England Fisheries*. Philadelphia, 1911.

1980 MARVIN, Winthrop Lippitt. *The American Merchant Marine: Its History and Romance from 1620-1902*. New York, 1902.

1981 MORRISON, John H. *History of New York Ship Yards*. New York, 1909.

1982 PAINE, Ralph D. *The Old Merchant Marine: A Chronicle of American Ships and Sailors*. New Haven, Conn., 1921.

1983 TOWER, Walter S. *A History of the American Whale Fishery*. Philadelphia, 1907.

Business Corporations

1984 CALLENDER, Guy S. "The Early Transportation and Banking Enterprises of the States in Relation to the Growth of Corporations." See 1705.

1985 DAVIS, Joseph Stancliffe. *Essays in the Earlier History of American Corporations*. 2 vols. Cambridge, Mass., 1917.

1986 DEWEY, John. "The Historic Background of Corporate Legal Personality." *Yale Law J*, XXV (1926), 655-673.

1987 DODD, Edwin M. *American Business Corporations until 1890: With Special Reference to Massachusetts*. Cambridge, Mass., 1954.

1988 EVANS, George H., Jr. *Business Incorporations in the United States, 1800-1943*. New York, 1948.

1989 HAAR, Charles. "Legislative Regulation of New York Industrial Corporations, 1800-1850." *N Y Hist*, XXII (1941), 191-207.

1990 HANDLIN, Oscar, and Mary HANDLIN. "Origins of the American Business Corporation." *J Econ Hist*, V (1945), 1-23.

1991 HURST, James Willard. *The Legitimacy of the Business Corporation in the Law of the United States, 1780-1970*. Charlottesville, Va., 1970.

1992 KESSLER, W. C. "Incorporation in New England: A Statistical Study, 1800-1875." *J Econ Hist*, VIII (1948), 43-62.

1993 LIVERMORE, Shaw. "Unlimited Liability in Early American Corporations." *J Pol Econ*, XLIII (1935), 674-687.

Manufactures and Mining

1994 BATTISON, Edwin A. "Eli Whitney and the Milling Machine." *Smithsonian J Hist*, I (1966), 9-34.

1995 BINING, Arthur Cecil. *Pennsylvania Iron Manufacture in the Eighteenth Century*. Harrisburg, Pa., 1938.

1996 BISHOP, John Leander. *A History of American Manufactures from 1608 to 1860*. 2 vols. 1861-1864. New York, 1966.

1997 BRUCE, Kathleen. *Virginia Iron Manufacture in the Slave Era*. New York, 1931.

1998 CAPPON, Lester J. "Trend of the Southern Iron Industry under the Plantation System." *J Econ Bus Hist*, II (1930), 353-381.

1999 CLARK, Victor S. *History of Manufactures in the United States, 1607-1860*. 3 vols. Rev. ed. Washington, D.C., 1929.

2000 COLE, Arthur H. *The American Wool Manufacture*. 2 vols. Cambridge, Mass., 1926.

2001 COLEMAN, Peter J. "Rhode Island Cotton Manufacturing: A Study in Conservatism." *R I Hist*, XXIII (1964), 65-80.

2002 COMMONS, John R., et al., eds. *A Documentary History of American Industrial Society*. 10 vols. 1909-1911. New intr., New York, 1958.

2003 COXE, Tench. *A Statement of the Arts and Manufactures of the United States of America for the Year 1810*. Philadelphia, 1814. (Photographic facsimile by A. Cornman, Jr., New York, n.d.)

2004 COYNE, F. E. *The Development of the Cooperage Industry in the United States, 1620-1940*. Chicago, 1940.

2005 CUMMINGS, Richard O. *The American Ice Harvests: A Historical Study in Technology, 1800-1918*. Berkeley, Cal., 1949.

2006 DAVIS, Lance Edwin. "Stock Ownership in the Early New England Textile Industry." *Bus Hist Rev*, XXXII (1958), 204-222.

2007 DEYRUP, Felicia Johnson. "Arms Makers of the Connecticut Valley . . . 1798-1870." *Smith Col Stud Hist*, 1948.

2008 FLEXNER, James T. *Steamboat Come True: American Inventors in Action*. New York, 1944.

2009 FRANCIS, W. H. *History of the Hatting Trade in Danbury Connecticut from Its Commencement in 1780*. Danbury, Conn., 1860.

2010 FULLER, Grace P. "An Introduction to the History of Connecticut as a Manufacturing State." *Smith Col Stud Hist*, 1915.

2011 GOTTESMAN, Rita Susswein, ed. *The Arts and Crafts in New York, 1777-1799: Advertisements and News Items from New York City Newspapers*. New York, 1954. *1800-1804*. New York, 1965.

2012 GRIFFIN, Richard W. "An Origin of the Industrial Revolution in Maryland: The Textile Industry, 1789-1826." *Md Hist Mag*, LXI (1966), 24-36.

2013 GRIFFIN, Richard W. "The Origins of the Industrial Revolution in Georgia: Cotton Textiles, 1810-1865." *Ga Hist Q*, XLII (1958), 355-375.

2014 HAMMOND, Seth. "The Ante-Bellum Kentucky Cotton Industry, 1790-1860." *Cotton Hist Rev*, I (1960), 47-55.

2015 HANNAY, Agnes. "A Chronicle of Industry on the Mill River." *Smith Col Stud Hist*, 1936.

2016 HAZARD, Blanche E. *The Organization of the Boot and Shoe Industry in Massachusetts before 1875*. Cambridge, Mass., 1921.

2017 KUHLMANN, Charles B. *The Development of the Flour-Milling Industry in the United States*. Boston, 1929.

2018 LEYLAND, H. T. "Early Years of the Hope Cotton Manufacturing Company." *R I Hist*, XXV (1966), 25-32.

2019 LINCOLN, Jonathan T. "The Beginnings of the Machine Age in New England: David Wilkinson of Pawtucket." *N Eng Q*, VI (1933), 716-732.

2020 LOVETT, Robert W. "The Beverly Cotton Manufactory: Or Some New Light on an Early Cotton Mill (1789-1798)." *Bull Bus Hist Soc*, XXVI (1952), 218-237.

2021 McCORISON, Marcus A. "Vermont Papermaking, 1784-1820." *Vt Hist*, XXXI (1963), 209-245.

2022 McGOULDRICK, Paul F. *New England Textiles in the Nineteenth Century*. Cambridge, Mass., 1968.

2023 MEIER, Hugo A. "Technology and Democracy, 1800-1860." *Miss Val Hist Rev*, XLIII (1957), 618-640.

2024 MIRSKEY, Jeannette, and Allan NEVINS. *The World of Eli Whitney*. New York, 1952.†

2025 MONTGOMERY, Florence M. " 'Fortunes to be Acquired'—Textiles in 18th-Century Rhode Island." *R I Hist*, XXXI (1972), 53-63.

2026 MORRISON, John H. *History of New York Ship Yards*. See 1981.

2027 MURPHY, John Joseph. "Entrepreneurship in the Establishment of the American Clock Industry." *J Econ Hist*, XXVI (1966), 169-186.

2028 PRED, Allan. "Manufacturing in the American Mercantile City: 1800-1840." *Ann Assn Am Geog*, LVI (1966), 307-338.

2029 PURSELL, Carroll W., Jr. "Thomas Digges and William Pearce: An Example of the Transit of Technology." *Wm Mar Q*, XXI, 3d ser. (1964), 551-560.

2030 RICKARD, Thomas Arthur. *A History of American Mining*. New York and London, 1932.

2031 TRYON, Rolla Milton. *Household Manufactures in the United States, 1640-1860*. 1917. New York, 1966.

2032 VAN WAGENEN, Jared, Jr. *The Golden Age of Homespun*. Ithaca, N.Y., 1953.

2033 WARE, Caroline F. *The Early New England Cotton Manufacture: A Study in Industrial Beginnings*. Boston, 1931.

2034 WEEKS, Lyman H. *A History of Paper Manufacturing in the United States, 1690-1916*. New York, 1916.

2035 WITTLINGER, Carlton O. "The Small Arms Industry of Lancaster County, 1710-1840." *Pa Hist*, XXIV (1957), 121-136.

2036 WOODBURY, Robert S. "The Legend of Eli Whitney and Interchangeable Parts." *Tech Cult*, I (1960), 235-253.

Entrepreneurs and Business Spokesmen

2037 ALBERTS, Robert C. *The Golden Voyage: The Life and Times of William Bingham, 1752-1804*. Boston, 1969.

2038 BAGNALL, William R. *Samuel Slater and the Early Development of the Cotton Manufacture in the United States*. Middletown, Conn., 1890.

2039 BOYD, Thomas A. *Poor John Fitch: Inventor of the Steamboat*. New York, 1935.

2040 BRUCHEY, Stuart Weems. *Robert Oliver, Merchant of Baltimore, 1783-1819*. Baltimore, Md., 1956.

2041 BUHLER, Kathryn C. *Paul Revere, Goldsmith, 1735-1818*. Boston, 1956.

2042 DAVISON, Robert A. *Isaac Hicks: New York Merchant and Quaker, 1767-1820*. Cambridge, Mass., 1964.

2043 DICKINSON, H. W. *Robert Fulton, Engineer and Artist: His Life and Works*. London, 1913.

2044 FORBES, John Douglas. *Israel Thorndike, Federalist Financier*. New York, 1953.

2045 GRAY, Edward. *William Gray of Salem, Merchant: A Biographical Sketch*. Boston, 1914.

2046 GREEN, Constance McLaughlin. *Eli Whitney and the Birth of American Technology*. Boston, 1956.†

2047 HEDGES, James B. *The Browns of Providence Plantations*. 2 vols. Cambridge, Mass., 1952-1968.

2048 HIDY, Ralph W. *The House of Baring in American Trade and Finance: English Merchant Bankers at Work, 1763-1861*. Cambridge, Mass., 1949.

2049 HUTCHESON, Harold. *Tench Coxe: A Study in American Economic Development*. 1938. New York, 1969.

2050 KONKLE, Burton Alva. *Thomas Willing and the First American Financial System*. London, 1937.

2051 LABAREE, Benjamin W. *Patriots and Partisans: The Merchants of Newburyport, 1764-1815*. Cambridge, Mass., 1962.

2052 McMASTER, John B. *The Life and Times of Stephen Girard*. 2 vols. Philadelphia, 1918.

2053 PHILLIPS, James Duncan. "The Life and Times of Richard Derby, Merchant of Salem." *Essex Inst Hist Coll*, LXV (1929), 243-289.

2054 PORTER, Kenneth Wiggins, ed. *The Jacksons and the Lees: Two Generations of Massachusetts Merchants 1765-1844*. 2 vols. Cambridge, Mass., 1937.

2055 PORTER, Kenneth Wiggins. *John Jacob Astor, Business Man*. Ed. N. S. B. Gras. 2 vols. Cambridge, Mass., 1931.

2056 REDLICH, Fritz. *History of American Business Leaders: A Series of Studies*. 3 vols. Ann Arbor, Mich., 1940-1951.

2057 ROWE, Kenneth Weyer. *Mathew Carey: A Study in American Economic Development*. Baltimore, Md., 1933.

2058 SEABURG, Carl, and Stanley PATTERSON. *Merchant Prince of Boston: Colonel T. H. Perkins, 1764-1854*. Cambridge, Mass., 1971.

2059 WALTERS, Philip G., and Raymond WALTERS, Jr. "The American Career of David Parish." *J Econ Hist*, IV (1944), 149-166.

2060 WESTCOTT, Thompson. *The Life of John Fitch, the Inventor of the Steamboat*. Philadelphia, 1857.

2061 WHITE, Philip L. *The Beekmans in New York in Politics and Commerce, 1647-1877*. New York, 1956.

2062 WILDES, Harry E. *Lonely Midas: The Study of Stephen Girard*. New York, 1943.

VI. Religion

1. General

Interpretive and General Studies

2063 AHLSTROM, Sydney E. *A Religious History of the American People*. New Haven, Conn., 1972.

2064 BILLINGTON, Ray A. *The Protestant Crusade, 1800-1860: A Study of the Origins of American Nativism*. New York, 1938.†

2065 BODO, John R. *The Protestant Clergy and Public Issues, 1812-1848*. Princeton, N.J., 1954.

2066 BOLLER, Paul F., Jr. *George Washington and Religion*. Dallas, Tex., 1963.

2067 BRENT, Robert A. "The Jeffersonian Outlook on Religion." *S Q*, V (1967), 417-432.

2068 BURR, Nelson. *Critical Bibliography of Religion in America*. 2 vols. Princeton, N.J., 1961.

2069 CLEBSCH, William A. *From Sacred to Profane America: The Role of Religion in American History*. New York, 1968.

2070 CURRAN, Francis X. *Major Trends in American Church History*. New York, 1946.

2071 D'ELIA, Donald J. "The Republican Theology of Benjamin Rush." *Pa Hist*, XXXIII (1966), 187-203.

2072 GAUSTAD, Edwin S. *Historical Atlas of Religion in America*. New York, 1962.

2073 HOPKINS, Samuel. *A Treatise on the Millennium*. 1793. New York, 1972.

2074 HUDSON, Winthrop S. *Religion in America*. New York, 1965.

2075 HUMPHREY, Edward F. *Nationalism and Religion in America, 1774-1789*. See 1275.

2076 KLEIN, Herbert S. "Anglicization, Catholicism and the Negro Slave." *Comp Stud Soc Hist*, VIII (1966), 295-327. Comment Elsa V. Goveia. *Ibid.*, pp. 328-330.

2077 KOCH, G. Adolf. *Republican Religion: The American Revolution and the Cult of Reason*. New York, 1933.

2078 LOETSCHER, Lefferts A. "The Problem of Christian Unity in Early Nineteenth-Century America." *Church Hist*, XXXII (1963), 3-16.

2079 MIYAKAWA, T. Scott. *Protestants and Pioneers: Individualism and Conformity on the American Frontier*. See 1284.

2080 MORAIS, Herbert M. *Deism in Eighteenth Century America*. New York, 1934.

2081 NICHOLS, Roy F. *Religion and American Democracy*. Baton Rouge, La., 1959.

2082 NIEBUHR, Richard H. *The Social Sources of Denominationalism.†* New York, 1957.

2083 SANDEEN, Ernest R. *The Roots of Fundamentalism: British and American Millenarianism, 1800-1930*. Chicago, 1970.

2084 SMITH, H. Shelton. *Changing Conceptions of Original Sin: A Study in American Theology since 1750*. New York, 1955.

2085 SMITH, James W., and A. Leland JAMISON. *Religion in American Life*. 2 vols. Princeton, N.J., 1961.

2086 SMITH, Timothy L. "Congregation, State, and Denomination: The Framing of the American Religious Structure." *Wm Mar Q*, XXV, 3d ser. (1968), 155-176.

2087 SWEET, William Walter. *Religion in the Development of American Culture, 1765-1840*. New York, 1952.

2088 WEATHERFORD, Willis D. *American Churches and the Negro: An Historical Study from Early Slave Days to the Present*. Boston, 1957.

Church and State

2089 BEAVER, R. Pierce. *Church, State, and the American Indian: Two and a Half Centuries of Partnership in Missions Between Churches and Government*. See 1533.

2090 BOLLER, Paul F., Jr. "George Washington and Religious Liberty." *Wm Mar Q*, XVII, 3d ser. (1960), 486-506.

2091 COBB, Sanford H. *TheRise of Religious Liberty in America*. New York, 1902.

2092 CUSHING, John D. "Notes on Disestablishment in Massachusetts, 1780-1833." *Wm Mar Q*, XXVI, 3d ser. (1969), 169-190.

2093 ECKENRODE, Hamilton J. *Separation of Church and State in Virginia: A Study in the Development of the Revolution*. Richmond, Va., 1910.

2094 ESTEP, William R. "New England Dissent, 1630-1833: A Review Article." *Church Hist*, XLI (1972), 246-252.

2095 FORD, David B. *New England's Struggle for Religious Liberty*. Philadelphia, 1896.

2096 GOBBEL, Luther L. *Church-State Relationships in Education in North Carolina since 1776*. Durham, N.C., 1938.

2097 GRAHAM, John J. "The Development of the Separation of Church and State in the United States." *Rec Am Cath Hist Soc Phil*, L (1939), 81-87; LI (1940), 1-64, 85-172.

2098 GREENE, Evarts B. *Religion and the State: The Making and Testing of an American Tradition*. New York, 1941.

2099 GREENE, M. Louise. *The Development of Religious Liberty in Connecticut*. Boston, 1905.

2100 HANEY, Thomas O. *Their Rights and Liberties: The Beginnings of Religious and Political Freedom in Maryland*. Westminster, Md., 1959.

2101 HEALEY, Robert M. *Jefferson on Religion in Public Education*. New Haven, Conn., 1962.

2102 KINNEY, Charles B., Jr. *Church and State: The Struggle for Separation in New Hampshire, 1630-1900*. New York, 1955.

2103 McLOUGHLIN, William G. *New England Dissent, 1630-1833: The Baptist and the Separation of Church and State*. 2 vols. Cambridge, Mass., 1971.

2104 MEYER, Jacob C. *Church and State in Massachusetts from 1740 to 1833: A Chapter in the History of Individual Freedom*. Cleveland, Ohio, 1930.

2105 O'NEILL, James Milton. *Religion and Education under the Constitution*. New York, 1949.

2106 PRATT, John W. *Religion, Politics, and Divinity: The Church-State Theme in New York History*. Ithaca, N.Y., 1967.

2107 SANDLER, S. Gerald. "Lockean Ideas in Thomas Jefferson's 'Bill for Establishing Religious Freedom.' " *J Hist Ideas*, XXI (1960), 110-116.

2108 STOKES, Anson P. *Church and State in the United States*. 3 vols. New York, 1950.

2109 STRICKLAND, Reba C. *Religion and the State in Georgia in the Eighteenth Century*. New York, 1939.

Evangelicalism and Missions

2110 BARCLAY, Wade Crawford. *History of Methodist Missions*. New York, 1949.

2111 BERKHOFER, Robert F., Jr. *Salvation and the Savage: An Analysis of Protestant Missions and American Indian Response, 1787-1862*. See 1558.

2112 BROWN, James H. "Presbyterian Social Influence in Early Ohio." *J Presby Hist Soc*, XXX (1952), 209-235.

2113 CARTWRIGHT, Peter. *Autobiography, with an Introduction, Bibliography, and Index by Charles L. Wallis*. Nashville, Tenn., 1956.

2114 CLARK, Joseph B. *Leavening the Nation: The Story of American Home Missions*. New York, 1903.

2115 CLEVELAND, Catherine C. *The Great Revival in the West, 1797-1805*. Chicago, 1916.

2116 CONNOR, Elizabeth. *Methodist Trail Blazer: Philip Gatch 1751-1834: His Life in Maryland, Virginia and Ohio*. Cincinnati, Ohio, 1970.

2117 CROSS, Whitney R. *The Burned-Over District: The Social and Intellectual History of Enthusiastic Religion in Western New York, 1800-1850*. Ithaca, N.Y., 1950.†

2118 ELSBREE, Oliver W. *The Rise of the Missionary Spirit in America 1790-1815*. Williamsport, Pa., 1928.

2119 FOSTER, Charles I. *An Errand of Mercy: The Evangelical United Front, 1790-1837*. Chapel Hill, N.C., 1960.

2120 GABRIEL, R. H. "Evangelical Religion and Popular Romanticism in the Early Nineteenth Century." *Church Hist*, XIX (1950), 34-47.

2121 GOEN. C. C. *Revivalism and Separatism in New England, 1740-1800: Strict Congregationalists and Separate Baptists in the Great Awakening*. Hamden, Conn., 1969.

2122 GOODYKOONTZ, Colin B. *Home Missions on the American Frontier*. Caldwell, Idaho, 1939.

2123 HOUCHENS, Miriam. "The Great Revival of 1800." *Reg Ky Hist Soc*, LXIX (1971), 216-234.

2124 JOHNSON, Charles A. *The Frontier Camp Meeting: Religion's Harvest Time*. Dallas, Tex., 1955.

2125 KELLER, Charles R. *The Second Great Awakening in Connecticut*. New Haven, Conn., 1942.

2126 McLOUGHLIN, William G. *Isaac Backus and the American Pietistic Tradition*. Boston, 1967.

2127 MATHEWS, Donald G. "The Second Great Awakening as an Organizing Process, 1780-1830: An Hypothesis." *Am Q*, XXI (1969), 23-43.

2128 MEAD, Sidney. "The Rise of the Evangelical Conception of the Ministry in America: 1607-1850." *The Ministry in Historical Perspective*. Eds. Richard Niebuhr et al. New York, 1956.

2129 MOODY, V. Alton. "Early Religious Efforts in the Lower Mississippi Valley." *Miss Val Hist Rev*, XXII (1935), 161-176.

2130 MOORE, Margaret D. "Protestantism in the Mississippi Territory." *J Miss Hist*, XXIX (1967), 358-370.

2131 NOTTINGHAM, Elizabeth K. *Methodism and the Frontier: Indiana Proving Ground*. New York, 1941.

2132 POSEY, Walter B. *Frontier Mission: A History of Religion West of the Southern Appalachians to 1861*. Lexington, Ky., 1966.

2133 POSEY, Walter B. *Religious Strife on the Southern Frontier*. Baton Rouge, La., 1965.

2134 SILVEUS, Marian. "Churches and Social Control on the Western Pennsylvania Frontier." *W Pa Hist Mag*, XIX (1936), 123-164.

2135 SONNE, Niels H. *Liberal Kentucky, 1780-1828*. New York, 1939.

2136 STOKES, Durward T. "North Carolina and the Great Revival of 1800." *N C Hist Rev*, XLIII (1966), 401-412.

2137 SWEET, William W. *Revivalism in America: Its Origin, Growth and Decline*. New York, 1944.†

2138 THEOBALD, Stephen L. "Catholic Missionary Work among Colored People of the United States (1776-1866)." *Rec Am Cath Hist Soc Phil*, XXXV (1924-1925), 325-356.

2139 THOMPSON, Henry P. *Into All Lands: The History of the Society for the Propagation of the Gospel in Foreign Parts, 1701-1950*. London, 1951.

2140 WEISBERGER, Bernard A. *They Gathered at the River: The Story of the Great Revivalists and Their Impact upon Religion in America*. Boston, 1958.†

2. Protestant Churches

2141 ALBRIGHT, Raymond W. *A History of the Protestant Episcopal Church*. New York, 1964.

2142 ANDREWS, Edward D. *The People Called Shakers: A Search for the Perfect Society*. New York, 1953.

2143 APTHEKER, Herbert. "The Quakers and Negro Slavery." *J Neg Hist*, XXV (1940), 331-362.

2144 ATKINS, Gaius, and Frederick L. FAGLEY. *History of American Congregationalism*. Boston, 1942.

2145 BARCLAY, Wade Crawford. *Early American Methodism, 1769-1844*. New York, 1950.

2146 BAUMAN, Richard. *For the Reputation of Truth: Politics, Religion, and Conflict among Pennsylvania Quakers, 1750-1860*. Baltimore, Md., 1971.

2147 BRINTON, Howard H. *Friends for 300 Years: The History and Beliefs of the Society of Friends since George Fox Started the Quaker Movement*. New York, 1952.†

2148 BRYDON, George Maclaren. *Virginia's Mother Church and the Political Conditions Under Which It Grew.* Vol. II: *The Story of the Anglican Church and the Development of Religion in Virginia, 1727-1814.* Philadelphia, 1952.

2149 BUELL, Lawrence. "The Unitarian Movement and the Art of Preaching in 19th Century America." *Am Q,* XXIV (1972), 166-190.

2150 CORWIN, Samuel T. *History of the Dutch Reformed Church in the United States.* New York, 1895.

2151 COX, John, Jr. *Quakerism in the City of New York, 1657-1930.* New York, 1930.

2152 DRAKE, Thomas E. *Quakers and Slavery in America.* 1950. Gloucester, Mass., 1965.

2153 JAMES, Sydney V. *A People among Peoples: Quaker Benevolence in Eighteenth-Century America.* Cambridge, Mass., 1963.

2154 LINDLEY, Harlow. "The Quakers in the Old Northwest." *Proc Miss Val Hist Assn,* V (1911-1912), 60-72.

2155 LOVELAND, Clara O. *The Critical Years: The Reconstitution of the Anglican Church in the United States of America: 1780-1789.* Greenwich, Conn., 1956.

2156 MATHEWS, Donald G. *Slavery and Methodism: A Chapter in American Morality, 1780-1845.* Princeton, N.J., 1965.

2157 POSEY, Walter B. "The Protestant Episcopal Church: An American Adaptation." *J S Hist,* XXV (1959), 3-30.

2158 ROBBINS, Caroline. "Honest Heretic: Joseph Priestley in America, 1794-1804." *Proc Am Phil Soc,* CVI (1962), 60-76.

2159 SCHMAUK, Theodore E. *A History of the Lutheran Church in Pennsylvania (1638-1820).* Philadelphia, 1903.

2160 TAUSSIG, Harold E. "Deism in Philadelphia during the Age of Franklin." *Pa Hist,* XXXVII (1970), 217-236.

2161 THOMPSON, Cameron. "John Locke and New England Transcendentalism." *N Eng Q,* XXXV (1962), 435-457.

2162 THOMPSON, Ernest T. *Presbyterians in the South.* Vol. I: *1607-1861.* Richmond, Va., 1963.

2163 THOMPSON, Mack. *Moses Brown, Reluctant Reformer.* Chapel Hill, N.C., 1962.

2164 TOLLES, Frederick B. *Quakers and the Atlantic Culture.* New York, 1960.

2165 TORBET, Robert G. *A History of the Baptists.* Philadelphia, 1950.

2166 WEEKS, Stephen B. *Southern Quakers and Slavery: A Study in Institutional History.* Baltimore, Md., 1896.

2167 WENTZ, Abdel R. *A Basic History of Lutheranism in America.* Philadelphia, 1955.

2168 WRIGHT, Conrad. *The Beginnings of Unitarianism in America.* Boston, 1955.

3. Catholic Church

2169 BAUMGARTNER, Apollinaris W. *Catholic Journalism: A Study of Its Development in the United States, 1789-1930.* New York, 1931.

2170 ELLIS, John T. *American Catholicism.* 2d ed. Chicago, 1969.†

2171 McAVOY, Thomas T. *A History of the Catholic Church in the United States.* Notre Dame, Ind., 1969.

2172 MAYNARD, Theodore. *The Story of American Catholicism.* New York, 1954.†

2173 MELVILLE, Annabelle M. *John Carroll of Baltimore: Founder of the American Catholic Hierarchy.* New York, 1955.

2174 NUESSE, Celestine J. *The Social Thought of American Catholics, 1634-1829.* Westminster, Md., 1945.

2175 RAY, Sister Mary Augustina. *American Opinion of Roman Catholicism in the Eighteenth Century.* New York, 1936.

2176 RIPLEY, Arthur J. *Catholicism in New England to 1788.* Washington, D.C., 1936.

4. Jews

2177 CHYET, Stanley F. "The Political Rights of the Jews in the United States: 1776-1840." *Am Jew Archiv*, X (1958), 14-75.

2178 FEIN, Isaac M. *The Making of an American Jewish Community: The History of Baltimore Jewry from 1773 to 1920.* Philadelphia, 1970.

2179 FONER, Philip S. *The Jews in American History, 1654-1865.* New York, 1946.

2180 FRIEDMAN, Lee M. *Early American Jews.* Cambridge, Mass., 1934.

2181 GRINSTEIN, Hyman B. *The Rise of the Jewish Community of New York, 1654-1860.* Philadelphia, 1945.

2182 HANDLIN, Oscar. *Adventure in Freedom: Three Hundred Years of Jewish Life in America.* New York, 1954.

2183 KORN, Bertram W. "Jews and Negro Slavery in the Old South, 1789-1865." *Pub Am Jew Hist Soc*, L (1961), 151-201.

2184 LEBESON, Anite L. *Jewish Pioneers in America, 1492-1848.* New York, 1931.

2185 MARCUS, Jacob Rader. *Early American Jewry.* 2 vols. Philadelphia, 1951-1953.

2186 MORRIS, Richard B. "Civil Liberties and the Jewish Tradition in Early America." *Pub Am Jew Hist Soc*, XLVI (1956), 20-39.

2187 POOL, David de Sola. *Portraits Etched in Stone: Early Jewish Settlers, 1682-1831*. New York, 1952.

2188 PROCTOR, Samuel. "Jewish Life in New Orleans, 1718-1860." *La Hist Q*, XL (1957), 110-132.

2189 SCHAPPES, Morris U. "Anti-Semitism and Reaction, 1795-1800." *Pub Am Jew Hist Soc*, XXXVIII (1949), 109-138.

2190 WOLF, Edwin, and Maxwell WHITEMAN. *History of the Jews in Philadelphia from Colonial Times to the Age of Jackson*. New York, 1956.

VII. Society and Social Problems

1. Blacks and Slavery

General

2191 ALEXANDER, William T. *History of the Colored Race in America, Containing also Their Ancient and Modern Life in Africa*. New York, 1968.

2192 BALLAGH, James C. *A History of Slavery in Virginia*. Baltimore, Md., 1902.

2193 BASSETT, John Spencer. *Slavery in the State of North Carolina*. Baltimore, Md., 1899.

2194 BRACKETT, Jeffrey R. *The Negro in Maryland: A Study of the Institution of Slavery*. Baltimore, Md., 1899.

2195 BRACKETT, Jeffrey R. "The Status of the Slave, 1775-1789." *Essays in the Constitutional History of the United States in the Formative Period, 1775-1789*. Ed. J. Franklin Jameson. See 298.

2196 CASSELL, Frank A. "Slaves of the Chesapeake Bay Area and the War of 1812." *J Neg Hist*, LVII (1972), 144-155.

2197 CATTERALL, Helen T., ed. *Judicial Cases Concerning American Slavery and the Negro*. 5 vols. Washington, D.C., 1926-1937.

2198 COOLEY, Henry S. *A Study of Slavery in New Jersey*. Baltimore, Md., 1896.

2199 FLANDERS, Ralph Betts. *Plantation Slavery in Georgia*. Chapel Hill, N.C. and Cos Cob, Conn., 1967.

2200 FRANKLIN, John Hope. *From Slavery to Freedom: A History of Negro Americans*. 3d ed. New York, 1967.†

2201 HARRIS, N. Dwight. *The History of Negro Servitude in Illinois, and of the Slavery Agitation in that State 1719-1864*. Chicago, 1904.

2202 HOFSTADTER, Richard. "U. B. Phillips and the Plantation Legend." *J Neg Hist*, XXIX (1944), 109-124.

2203 HOLLANDER, Barnett. *Slavery in America: Its Legal History*. London, 1962.

2204 IRELAND, Ralph R. "Slavery on Long Island: A Study of Economic Motivation." *J L I Hist*, VI (1966), 1-12.

2205 McCOLLEY, Robert. *Slavery and Jeffersonian Virginia*. Urbana, Ill., 1964.

2206 McDOUGLE, Ivan E. *Slavery in Kentucky, 1792-1865*. Washington, D.C., 1918.

2207 McMANUS, Edgar. *Negro Slavery in New York*. Syracuse, N.Y., 1966.

2208 MOONEY, Chase C. *Slavery in Tennessee*. Bloomington, Ind., 1957.

2209 MUNROE, John A. "The Negro in Delaware." *S Atl Q*, LVI (1957), 428-444.

2210 PHILLIPS, Ulrich B. "The Origin and Growth of Southern Black Belts." *Am Hist Rev*, XI (1906), 798-816.

2211 POSTELL, William D. *The Health of Slaves on Southern Plantations*. Baton Rouge, La., 1951.

2212 ROBINSON, Donald L. *Slavery in the Structure of American Politics 1765-1820*. New York, 1971.

2213 SELLERS, James B. *Slavery in Alabama*. University, Ala., 1950.

2214 SHEELER, J. Reuben. "The Negro on the Virginia Frontier." *J Neg Hist*, XLIII (1958), 279-297.

2215 STEINER, Bernard C. *History of Slavery in Connecticut*. Baltimore, Md., 1893.

2216 SYDNOR, Charles S. *Slavery in Mississippi*. New York, 1933.†

2217 TATE, Thad W. *The Negro in Eighteenth-Century Williamsburg*. Williamsburg, Va., 1964.†

2218 TREXLER, Harrison A. *Slavery in Missouri, 1804-1865*. Baltimore, Md., 1914.

2219 TURNER, Edward R. *The Negro in Pennsylvania: Slavery-Servitude-Freedom, 1639-1861*. Washington, D.C., 1911.

2220 WILLIAMS, Edwin L., Jr. "Negro Slavery in Florida." *Fla Hist Q*, XXVIII (1949-1950), 93-110, 182-204.

2221 WILSON, Joseph Thomas. *The Black Phalanx*. See 906.

Interpretive Studies

2222 DAVIS, David B. *The Problem of Slavery in Western Culture*. Ithaca, N.Y., 1966.†

2223 DEGLER, Carl N. *Neither Black nor White: Slavery and Race Relations in Brazil and the United States*. New York, 1971.†

2224 DEGLER, Carl N. "Slavery in Brazil and the United States: An Essay in Comparative History." *Am Hist Rev*, LXXV (1970), 1004-1028.

2225 ELKINS, Stanley M., and Eric McKITRICK. "Institutions and the Law of Slavery: The Dynamics of Unopposed Capitalism." *Am Q*, IX (1957), 3-21. "Slavery in Capitalist and Non-Capitalist Cultures." *Ibid.*, pp. 159-179.

2226 ELKINS, Stanley M. *Slavery: A Problem in American Institutional and Intellectual Life*. 2d ed. Chicago, 1968.†

2227 GENOVESE, Eugene D. "Race and Class in Southern History: An Appraisal of the Work of Ulrich Bonnell Phillips." *Ag Hist*, XLI (1967), 345-358. Comments David M. Potter, Kenneth M. Stampp, and Stanley M. Elkins. *Ibid.*, pp. 359-371.

2228 GENOVESE, Eugene D. "Rebelliousness and Docility in the Negro Slave: A Critique of Elkins' Thesis." *C W Hist*, XIII (1967), 293-314.

2229 GENOVESE, Eugene D. *The World the Slaveholders Made: Two Essays in Interpretation*. New York, 1969.

2230 HARRIS, Marvin. *Patterns of Race in the Americas*. New York, 1964.†

2231 JORDAN, Winthrop. *White over Black: American Attitudes toward the Negro, 1550-1812*. Chapel Hill, N.C., 1968.†

2232 KLEIN, Herbert S. *Slavery in the Americas: A Comparative Study of Cuba and Virginia*. Chicago, 1967.

2233 MORGAN, Edmund S. "Slavery and Freedom: The American Paradox." *J Amer Hist*, LIX (1972), 5-29.

2234 SEWELL, Richard H. "Slavery in the Americas: An Essay Review." *Wis Mag Hist*, LI (1968), 238-243.

2235 STAMPP, Kenneth M. "The Historian and Southern Negro Slavery." *Am Hist Rev*, LVII (1952), 613-624.

2236 STAMPP, Kenneth M. *The Peculiar Institution: Slavery in the Ante-Bellum South*. New York, 1956.†

2237 TANNENBAUM, Frank. *Slave and Citizen: The Negro in the Americas*. New York, 1947.†

2238 WAX, Darold D. "Whither the Comparative History of Slavery?" *Va Mag Hist Biog*, LXXX (1972), 85-93.

Free and Urban Blacks

2239 BLOCH, Herman D. "The New York Negro's Battle for Political Rights, 1775-1865." *Int Rev Soc Hist*, IX (1964), 65-81.

2240 EVERETT, Donald E. "Emigres and Militiamen: Free Persons of Color in New Orleans, 1803-1815." *J Neg Hist*, XXXVIII (1953), 377-402.

2241 FRANKLIN, John Hope. *The Free Negro in North Carolina, 1790-1860*. Chapel Hill, N.C., 1943.

2242 FRAZIER, Edward Franklin. *The Free Negro Family: A Study of Family Origins before the Civil War*. Nashville, Tenn., 1932.

2243 HIRSCH, Lee H., Jr. "The Negro and New York, 1783-1865." *J Neg Hist*, XVI (1931), 382-473.

2244 LANGLEY, Harold D. "The Negro in the Navy and Merchant Service, 1798-1860." See 1095.

2245 LINDSAY, Arnett G. "The Economic Condition of the Negroes of New York Prior to 1861." *J Neg Hist*, VI (1921), 190-199.

2246 LITWACK, Leon F. "The Federal Government and the Free Negro, 1790-1860." *J Neg Hist*, XLIII (1958), 261-278.

2247 LITWACK, Leon F. *North of Slavery: The Negro in the Free States, 1790-1860*. Chicago, 1961.†

2248 McCONNELL, Roland C. *Negro Troops of Antebellum Louisiana: A History of the Batallion of Free Men of Color*. Baton Rouge, La., 1968.

2249 PERLMAN, Daniel. "Organizations of the Free Negro in New York City, 1800-1860." *J Neg Hist*, LVI (1971), 181-197.

2250 ROBINSON, Henry S. "Some Aspects of the Free Negro Population of Washington, D.C., 1800-1862." *Md Hist Mag*, LXIV (1969), 43-64.

2251 RUSSELL, John H. *The Free Negro in Virginia, 1619-1865*. Baltimore, Md., 1913.

2252 WADE, Richard C. "The Negro in Cincinnati, 1800-1830." *J Neg Hist*, XXXIX (1954), 43-57.

2253 WILSON, Charles J. "The Negro in Early Ohio." *Ohio Arch Hist Q*, XXXIX (1930), 717-768.

2254 WRIGHT, James M. *The Free Negro in Maryland, 1634-1860*. New York, 1921.

Culture and Religion

2255 BARDOLPH, Richard. "The Distinguished Negro in America, 1770-1936." *Am Hist Rev*, LX (1955), 527-547.

2256 BOND, Horace Mann. *The Education of the Negro in the American Social Order*. New York, 1934.

2257 BOTKIN, Benjamin. *Lay My Burden Down: A Folk History of Slavery*. Chicago, 1968.†

2258 BULLOCK, Henry Allen. *A History of Negro Education in the South: From 1619 to the Present*. Cambridge, Mass., 1967.†

2259 CURTIN, Philip D., ed. *Africa Remembered: Narratives by West Africans from the Era of the Slave Trade*. Madison, Wis., 1967.†

2260 Du BOIS, W. E. B. *Black Folk Then and Now: An Essay in the History and Sociology of the Negro Race*. New York, 1939.

2261 Du BOIS, W. E. B., ed. *The Negro Church*. Atlanta, Ga., 1903.

2262 EARNEST, Joseph B. *The Religious Development of the Negro in Virginia*. Charlottesville, Va., 1914.

2263 FONER, Philip S., ed. *The Voice of Black America: Major Speeches by Negroes in the United States, 1797-1971*. New York, 1972.

2264 FRAZIER, Edward Franklin. *The American Negro–His History and Literature–The Free Negro Family*. New York, 1968.

2265 FRAZIER, Edward Franklin. *The Negro Church in America*. Liverpool, England, 1964.†

2266 FRAZIER, Edward Franklin. *The Negro Family in the United States*. Rev. ed. New York, 1942.†

2267 HAYNES, Leonard L., Jr. *The Negro Community within American Protestantism, 1619-1844*. Boston, 1954.

2268 HEARTMAN, Charles Frederick, ed. *Phyllis Wheatley, Poems and Letters*. New York, 1915.

2269 HUNTER, Frances L. "Slave Society on the Southern Plantation." *J Neg Hist*, VII (1922), 1-10.

2270 JACKSON, Luther P. "Religious Development of the Negro in Virginia from 1760 to 1860." *J Neg Hist*, XVI (1931), 168-239.

2271 JOHNSTON, Ruby F. *The Development of Negro Religion*. New York, 1954.

2272 LOGAN, Rayford W. "Memoirs of a Monticello Slave." *Wm Mar Q*, VIII, 3d ser. (1951), 561-582.

2273 MEIER, August. "The Emergence of Negro Nationalism: A Study in Ideologies, from the American Revolution to the First World War." *Mid W J*, IV (1951-1952), 96-104.

2274 PORTER, Dorothy, ed. *Early Negro Writing, 1760-1837*. Boston, 1971.

2275 SHERER, Robert G., Jr. "Negro Churches in Rhode Island before 1860." *R I Hist*, XXV (1966), 9-24.

2276 THEOBALD, Stephen L. "Catholic Missionary Work among the Colored People of the United States (1776-1866)." See 2138.

2277 WILSON, Gold F. "The Religion of the Negro Slave: His Attitude toward Life and Death." *J Neg Hist*, VIII (1923), 41-71.

2278 WOODSON, Carter G. *The Education of the Negro Prior to 1861: A History of the Education of Colored People of the United States from the Beginning of Slavery to the Civil War*. Rev. ed. New York, 1928.

2279 WOODSON, Carter G. *The History of the Negro Church*. 2d ed. Washington, D.C., 1945.

2280 WOODSON, Carter G., ed. *The Mind of the Negro as Reflected in Letters Written during the Crisis, 1800-1860*. Washington, D.C., 1926.

Race Relations and Attitudes

2281 BAILOR, Keith M. "John Taylor of Caroline: Continuity, Change, and Discontinuity in Virginia's Sentiments toward Slavery, 1790-1820." *Va Mag Hist Biog*, LXXV (1967), 290-304.

2282 BERRY, Mary Frances. *Black Resistance/White Law: A History of Constitutional Racism in America*. New York, 1971.

2283 BINDER, Frederick M. *The Color Problem in Early National America as Viewed by John Adams, Jefferson and Jackson.* New York, 1968.

2284 BOLLER, Paul F., Jr. "Washington, the Quakers, and Slavery," *J Neg Hist*, XLVI (1961), 83-88.

2285 CLARK, Ernest J., Jr. "Aspects of the North Carolina Slave Code, 1715-1860." *N C Hist Rev*, XXXIX (1962), 148-164.

2286 COHEN, William. "Thomas Jefferson and the Problem of Slavery." *J Amer Hist*, LVI (1969), 503-526.

2287 CUTLER, James Elbert. *Lynch-Law: An Investigation into the History of Lynching in the United States.* New York, 1905.

2288 DANIEL, W. Harrison. "Virginia Baptists and the Negro in the Early Republic." *Va Mag Hist Biog*, LXXX (1972), 60-69.

2289 D'ELIA, Donald J. "Dr. Benjamin Rush and the Negro." *J Hist Ideas*, XXX (1969), 413-422.

2290 FRANKLIN, John Hope. *The Militant South, 1800-1861.* See 1269.

2291 FREEHLING, William W. "The Founding Fathers and Slavery." *Am Hist Rev*, LXXVII (1972), 81-93.

2292 GRAHAM, Pearl M. "Thomas Jefferson and Sally Hemings." *J Neg Hist*, XLVI (1961), 89-103.

2293 GREEN, Constance McL. *The Secret City: A History of Race Relations in the Nation's Capital.* Princeton, N.J., 1967.

2294 GREENE, John C. "The American Debate on the Negro's Place in Nature, 1780-1815." *J Hist Ideas*, XV (1954), 384-396.

2295 HOWE, John R., Jr. "John Adams' Views on Slavery." *J Neg Hist*, LXIX (1964), 204-210.

2296 JOHNSTON, James Hugo. *Race Relations in Virginia and Miscegenation in the South, 1776-1860.* Amherst, Mass., 1970.

2297 LOFTON, John. "Enslavement of the Southern Mind, 1775-1825." *J Neg Hist*, XLIII (1958), 132-139.

2298 MELLON, Matthew Taylor. *Early American Views on Slavery: From the Letters and Papers of the Founders of the Republic.* 1934. 2d ed. New York, 1969.†

2299 MOORE, Wilbert E. "Slave Law and the Social Structure." *J Neg Hist*, XXVI (1941), 171-202.

2300 MORGAN, Edmund S. "Slavery and Freedom: The American Paradox." See 2233.

2301 REDDICK, L. D. "The Negro Policy of the United States Army, 1775-1945." See 1084.

2302 RUCHAMES, Louis, ed. *Racial Thought in America: From the Puritans to Abraham Lincoln.* Amherst, Mass., 1969.

2303 THURSTIN, Helen M. "The 1802 Constitutional Convention and the Status of the Negro." *Ohio Hist*, LXXXI (1972), 15-37.

2304 WEYL, Nathaniel, and William MARINA. *American Statesmen on Slavery and the Negro.* New York, 1971.

Revolts and Runaways

2305   APTHEKER, Herbert. *American Negro Slave Revolts*. New York, 1943.†

\ 2306   CARROLL, Joseph C. *Slave Insurrections in the United States, 1800-1865*. Boston, 1938.

2307   HALASZ, Nicholas. *The Rattling Chains: Slave Unrest and Revolt in the Ante Bellum South*. New York, 1966.

2308   HEADLEY, Joel Tyler. *The Great Riots of New York, 1712-1873*. 1873. Indianapolis, 1970.†

2309   JOHNSTON, James H. "Participation of White Men in Virginia's Negro Insurrections." *J Neg Hist*, XVI (1931), 158-167.

2310   KILSON, Marion. "Toward Freedom: An Analysis of the Slave Revolts in the United States." *Pylon*, XXV (1964), 175-187.

2311   KIMBALL, William J. "The Gabriel Insurrection of 1800." *Negro Hist Bull*, XXXIV (1971), 153-156.

2312   McDOUGALL, Marian Gleason. *Fugitive Slaves, 1619-1865*. Boston, 1891.

2313   McKIBBEN, Davidson B. "Negro Slave Insurrections in Mississippi, 1800-1865." *J Neg Hist*, XXIV (1949), 73-90.

2314   MULLIN, Gerald W. *Flight and Rebellion: Slave Resistance in Eighteenth-Century Virginia*. New York, 1972.

2315   MURDOCH, Richard K. "The Return of Runaway Slaves, 1790-1794." *Fla Hist Q*, XXXVIII (1959), 96-113.

2316   WISH, Harvey. "American Slave Insurrections before 1861." *J Neg Hist*, XXII (1937), 299-320.

Slave Trade

2317   BRADY, Patrick S. "The Slave Trade and Sectionalism in South Carolina, 1787-1808." See 588.

2318   COLLINS, Winfield H. *The Domestic Slave Trade of the Southern States*. New York, 1904.

2319   CREER, Leland Hargrave. "Spanish-American Slave Trade in the Great Basin, 1800-1853." See 1582.

2320   CURTIN, Philip D. *The Atlantic Slave Trade: A Census*. Madison, Wis., 1969.

2321   CURTIN, Philip D. "Epidemiology and the Slave Trade." *Pol Sci Q*, LXXXIII (1968), 190-216.

2322   DONNAN, Elizabeth. *Documents Illustrative of the History of the Slave Trade to America*. 4 vols. Washington, D.C., 1930-1935.

2323   DONNAN, Elizabeth. "New England Slave Trade after Revolution." *N Eng Q*, III (1930), 251-278.

2324   Du BOIS, W. E. Burghardt. *The Suppression of the African Slave-Trade to the United States of America, 1638-1870*. 1896. New York, 1969.†

2325 DUIGAN, Peter, and Clarence CLENDENEN. *The United States and the African Slave Trade, 1619-1862*. Stanford, Cal., 1963.

2326 KLEIN, Herbert S. "North American Competition and the Characteristics of the African Slave Trade to Cuba, 1790-1794." *Wm Mar Q*, XXVIII, 3d ser. (1971), 86-102.

2327 MANNIX, Daniel P., and Malcolm COWLEY. *Black Cargoes: A History of the Atlantic Slave Trade, 1518-1865*. New York, 1962.†

2328 POPE-HENNESSY, James. *Sins of the Fathers: A Study of the Atlantic Slave Traders, 1441-1807*. New York, 1968.†

2329 ROTTENBERG, Simon. "The Business of Slave Trading." *S Atl Q*, LXVI (1967), 409-423.

2330 SHERIDAN, R. B. "The Commercial and Financial Organization of the British Slave Trade, 1750-1807." *Econ Hist Rev*, XI (1958), 249-263.

2331 SPEARS, J. R. *The American Slave Trade: An Account of Its Origin, Growth, and Suppression*. New York, 1901.

2332 WAX, Darold D. "Negro Imports into Pennsylvania, 1720-1807." *Pa Hist*, XXXII (1965), 254-287.

Antislavery

2333 ADAMS, Alice D. *The Neglected Period of Anti-Slavery in America (1808-1831)*. Boston, 1908.

2334 ARBENA, Joseph L. "Politics or Principle? Rufus King and the Opposition to Slavery, 1785-1825." *Essex Inst Hist Coll,* CI (1965), 56-77.

2335 BRUNS, Roger. "Anthony Benezet's Assertion of Negro Equality." *J Neg Hist*, LVI (1971), 230-238.

2336 CALVERT, Monte A. "The Abolitionist Society of Delaware, 1801-1807." *Del Hist*, X (1963), 295-320.

2337 DAVIS, David Brion. "New Sidelights on Early Antislavery Radicalism." *Wm Mar Q*, XXVIII, 3d ser. (1971), 585-594.

2338 KATES, Don B., Jr. "Abolition, Deportation, Integration: Attitudes toward Slavery in the Early Republic." *J Neg Hist*, LIII (1968), 33-47.

2339 LOCKE, Mary S. *Anti-Slavery in America from the Introduction of African Slavery to the Prohibition of the Slave Trade (1619-1808)*. Boston, 1901.

2340 MOSS, Simeon F. "The Persistence of Slavery and Involuntary Servitude in a Free State (1685-1866)." *J Neg Hist*, XXXV (1950), 289-314.

2341 O'BRIEN, S. J., William. "Did the Jennison Case Outlaw Slavery in Massachusetts?" *Wm Mar Q*, XVII, 3d ser. (1960), 219-241.

2342 SHERWOOD, Henry N. "Early Negro Deportation Projects." *Miss Val Hist Rev*, II (1916), 484-508.

2343 SPECTOR, Robert M. "The Quock Walker Cases (1781-1783)—Slavery, Its Abolition, and Negro Citizenship in Early Massachusetts." *J Neg Hist*, LIII (1968), 12-32.

2344 TURNER, Edward R. "The Abolition of Slavery in Pennsylvania." *Pa Mag Hist Biog*, XXXV (1912), 129-142.

2345 WEEKS, Stephen B. "Anti-Slavery Sentiment in the South." *Pub S Hist Assn*, I (1895), 87-130.

2346 ZILVERSMIT, Arthur. *The First Emancipation: The Abolition of Negro Slavery in the North*. Chicago, 1967.

2347 ZILVERSMIT, Arthur. "Quok Walker, Mumbet, and the Abolition of Slavery in Massachusetts." *Wm Mar Q*, XXV, 3d ser. (1968), 614-624.

Economics of the Slave System

2348 BRADFORD, S. Sydney. "The Negro Iron Worker in Ante-Bellum Virginia." *J S Hist*, XXV (1959), 194-206.

2349 CONRAD, Alfred H., and John R. MEYER. "The Economics of Slavery in the Ante-Bellum South." *J Pol Econ*, LXVI (1958), 95-130.

2350 CONRAD, Alfred H., and John R. MEYER. *The Economics of Slavery and Other Studies in Econometrick History*. Chicago, 1964.

2351 CONRAD, Alfred H., Douglas DOWD, Stanley ENGERMAN, Eli GINZBERG, Charles KELSO, John R. MEYER, Harry N. SCHEIBER, and Richard SUTCH. "Slavery as an Obstacle to Economic Growth in the United States: A Panel Discussion." *J Econ Hist*, XXVII (1967), 518-560.

2352 Du BOIS, W. E. B., and Augustus G. DILL. *The Negro American Artisan*. Atlanta, Ga., 1912.

2353 ENGERMAN, Stanley L. "The Effects of Slavery upon the Southern Economy: A Review of the Recent Debate." *Explo Entrep Hist*, IV, 2d ser. (1967), 71-97.

2354 FISCHBAUM, Marvin, and Julius RUBIN, "Slavery and the Economic Development of the American South." *Explo Entrep Hist*, VI, 2d ser. (1968), 116-127.

2355 GENOVESE, Eugene D. "Livestock in the Slave Economy of the Old South—A Revised View." *Ag Hist*, XXXVI (1962), 143-149.

2356 GENOVESE, Eugene D. *The Political Economy of Slavery: Studies in the Economy and Society of the Slave South*. New York, 1965.†

2357 GENOVESE, Eugene. "The Significance of the Slave Plantation for Southern Economic Development." *J S Hist*, XXVII (1962), 422-437.

2358 GOVAN, Thomas P. "Was Plantation Slavery Unprofitable?" *J S Hist*, VIII (1942), 513-535.

2359 GRAY, Lewis C. "Economic Efficiency and Competitive Advantage of Slavery under the Plantation System." *Ag Hist*, IV (1930), 31-47.

2360 LINDEN, Fabian. "Economic Democracy in the Slave South: An Appraisal of Some Recent Views." *J Neg Hist*, XXXI (1946), 140-189.

2361 PHILLIPS, Ulrich B. *American Negro Slavery: A Survey of the Supply, Employment and Control of Negro Labor as Determined by the Plantation Regime*. New York, 1918.†

2362 PHILLIPS, Ulrich B. "The Economic Cost of Slaveholding in the Cotton Belt." *Pol Sci Q*, XX (1905), 257-275.

2363 PHILLIPS, Ulrich B. *Life and Labor in the Old South*. Boston, 1929.

2364 RUSSEL, Robert R. "The General Effects of Slavery upon Southern Economic Progress." *J S Hist*, IV (1938), 34-54.

2365 TAYLOR, Rosser H. *Slaveholding in North Carolina: An Economic View*. Chapel Hill, N.C., 1926.

2366 WOODMAN, Harold D. "The Profitability of Slavery: A Historical Perennial." *J S Hist*, XXIX (1963), 303-325.

2367 YARBROUGH, William Henry. *Economic Aspects of Slavery in Relation to Southern and Southwestern Migration*. See 1666.

2. Humanitarianism and Social Reform

General

2368 BANNER, Lois W. "Religion and Reform in the Early Republic: The Role of Youth." *Am Q*, XXIII (1971), 677-695.

2369 BREMNER, Robert H. *American Philanthropy*. Chicago, 1960.†

2370 COLL, Blanche D. "Perspectives in Public Welfare: Colonial Times to 1860." *Wel Rev*, V (1967), 1-9; VI (1968), 12-22.

2371 D'AGOSTINO, Lorenzo. *The History of Public Welfare in Vermont*. Winooska, Vt., 1948.

2372 GRIFFIN, Clifford S. *Their Brothers' Keepers: Moral Stewardship in the United States, 1800-1865*. New Brunswick, N.J., 1960.

2373 HEALE, M. J. "Humanitarianism in the Early Republic: The Moral Reformers of New York, 1776-1825." *J Am Stud*, II (1968), 161-175.

2374 HOWE, M. A. DeWolfe. *The Humane Society of the Commonwealth of Massachusetts*. Boston, 1918.

2375 JACKMAN, Eugene T. "Efforts Made before 1825 to Ameliorate the Lot of the American Seaman, with Emphasis on His Moral Regeneration." *Am Neptune*, XXIV (1964), 109-118.

2376 KROUT, John A. *The Origins of Prohibition*. New York, 1925.

2377 MELDER, Keith. "Ladies Bountiful: Organized Women's Benevolence in Early 19th Century America." *N Y Hist*, XLVIII (1967), 231-255.

2378 MILLER, Howard S. *The Legal Foundations of American Philanthropy, 1776-1844*. Madison, Wis., 1961.

2379 MOHL, Raymond A. "The Humane Society and Urban Reform in Early New York, 1787-1831." *N Y Hist Soc Q*, LIV (1970), 30-52.

2380 O'BRIEN, Edward J. *Child Welfare Legislation in Maryland, 1634-1936*. Washington, D.C., 1937.

2381 RICE, Edwin W. *The Sunday-School Movement, 1780-1917, and the American Sunday-School Union, 1817-1917*. Philadelphia, 1917.

2382 RISCH, Eran. "Immigrant Aid Societies before 1820." *Pa Mag Hist Biog*, LX (1936), 15-33.

2383 SCHNEIDER, David M. *The History of Public Welfare in New York State, 1609-1866*. Chicago, 1938.

2384 TREUDLEY, Mary B. "The 'Benevolent Fair': A Study of Charitable Organizations among American Women in the First Third of the Nineteenth Century." *Soc Serv Rev*, XIV (1940), 509-522.

2385 WHITENER, Daniel Jay. *Prohibition in North Carolina, 1715-1945*. Chapel Hill, N.C., 1945.

2386 WISNER, Elizabeth. *Social Welfare in the South: From Colonial Times to World War I*. Baton Rouge, La., 1970.

2387 WYLLIE, Irvin G. "The Search for an American Law of Charity, 1776-1844." *Miss Val Hist Rev*, XLVI (1959), 203-221.

Social Problems

Poverty

2388 BENTON, Josiah H. *Warning Out in New England, 1656-1817*. Boston, 1911.

2389 CAPEN, Edward W. *The Historical Development of the Poor Law of Connecticut*. New York, 1905.

2390 CARROLL, Douglas G., Jr., and Blanche D. COLL. "The Baltimore Almshouse: An Early History." *Md Hist Mag*, LXVI (1971), 135-152.

2391 CREECH, Margaret. *Three Centuries of Poor Law Administration: A Study of Legislation in Rhode Island*. Chicago, 1936.

2392 CUTLER, William W., III. "Status Values and the Education of the Poor: The Trustees of the New York Public School Society, 1805-1853." *Am Q*, XXIV (1972), 69-85.

2393 DREWS, Robert S. "A History of the Care of the Sick Poor of the City of Detroit (1703-1855)." *Bull Hist Med*, VII (1939), 759-782.

2394 HEFFNER, William C. *History of Poor Relief Legislation in Pennsylvania, 1682-1913*. Cleona, Pa., 1913.

2395 KELSO, Robert W. *The History of Public Poor Relief in Massachusetts, 1620-1920*. Boston, 1922.

2396 KLEBANER, Benjamin J. "Employment of Paupers at Philadelphia's Almshouse before 1861." *Pa Hist*, XXIV (1957), 137-148.

2397 KLEBANER, Benjamin J. "The Home Relief Controversy in Philadelphia, 1782-1861." *Pa Mag Hist Biog*, LXXVIII (1954), 413-423.

2398 KLEBANER, Benjamin J. "Pauper Auctions: The 'New England Method' of Public Poor Relief." *Essex Inst Hist Coll*, XCI (1955), 195-210.

2399 KLEBANER, Benjamin J. "Public Poor Relief in Charleston, 1800-1860." *S C Hist Mag*, LV (1954), 210-220.

2400 KLEBANER, Benjamin J. "Some Aspects of North Carolina Public Poor Relief, 1700-1860." *N C Hist Rev*, XXXI (1954), 479-493.

2401 MOHL, Raymond A. *Poverty in Early New York, 1783-1825*. New York, 1971.

2402 PENDLETON, O. A. "Poor Relief in Philadelphia, 1790-1840." *Pa Mag Hist Biog*, LXX (1946), 161-172.

2403 STANTON, Martin W. *History of Public Poor Relief in New Jersey, 1609-1934*. New York, 1934.

Crime

2404 BARNES, Harry E. *The Evolution of Penology in Pennsylvania: A Study in American Social History*. Indianapolis, 1927.

2405 BARNES, Harry E. "Origins of Prison Reform in New York State." *Q J N Y Hist Assn*, XIX (1921), 89-99.

2406 BYE, Raymond Taylor. *Capital Punishment in the United States*. Philadelphia, 1919.

2407 DAVIS, David B. "The Movement to Abolish Capital Punishment in America, 1787-1861." *Am Hist Rev*, LXIII (1957), 23-46.

2408 HAYNES, Robert V. "Law Enforcement in Frontier Mississippi." *J Miss Hist*, XXII (1960), 27-42.

2409 LEWIS, Orlando F. *The Development of American Prisons and Prison Customs, 1776-1845, with Special References to Early Institutions in the State of New York*. Albany, N.Y., 1922.

2410 LEWIS, W. David. *From Newgate to Dannemora: The Rise of the Penitentiary in New York, 1796-1848*. Ithaca, N.Y., 1965.

2411 RICHARDSON, James F. *The New York Police: Colonial Times to 1901*. New York, 1970.

2412 TEETERS, Negley K. *They Were in Prison: A History of the Pennsylvania Prison Society, 1787-1937, formerly the Philadelphia Society for Alleviating the Miseries of Public Prisons*. Philadelphia, 1937.

2413 WATSON, David Kemper. *Growth of the Criminal Law of the United States*. House of Representatives, Doc. No. 362, 57th Cong., 1st sess., Washington, D.C., n.d.

Mental Disorder

2414 CATTELL, James M. *Psychology in America*. New York, 1929.

2415 DAIN, Norman. *Concepts of Insanity in the United States, 1789-1865*. New Brunswick, N.J., 1964.

2416 DAIN, Norman. *Disordered Minds: The First Century of Eastern State Hospitals in Williamsburg, Virginia, 1766-1866*. Williamsburg, Va., 1971.

2417 DAIN, Norman, and Eric T. CARLSON. "Social Class and Psychological Medicine in the United States, 1789-1824." *Bull Hist Med*, XXXIII (1959), 454-465.

2418 DEUTSCH, Albert. *The Mentally Ill in America: A History of Their Care and Treatment from Colonial Times*. 2d ed. New York, 1949.

2419 HURD, Henry M., ed. *The Institutional Care of the Insane in the United States and Canada*. 4 vols. Baltimore, Md., 1916-1917.

2420 ROBACK, Abraham Aaron. *History of American Psychology*. New York, 1952.

2421 RUSSELL, William L. *The New York Hospital: A History of the Psychiatric Service, 1771-1936*. New York, 1945.

Medicine and Public Health

2422 ACKERKNECHT, Erwin H. *Malaria in the Upper Mississippi Valley 1760-1900*. See 1428.

2423 BINGER, Carl. *Revolutionary Doctor: Benjamin Rush, 1746-1813*. New York, 1966.

2424 CARRIGAN, Jo Ann. "Impact of Epidemic Yellow Fever on Life in Louisiana." See 1455.

2425 CORNER, George W. "Apprenticed to Aesculapius: The American Medical Student, 1765-1965." *Proc Am Phil Soc*, CIX (1965), 249-258.

2426 COWEN, David L. *Medical Education: The Queen's-Rutgers Experience 1792-1830*. New Brunswick, N.J., 1966.

2427 DALE, Edward E. "Medical Practices in the Frontier." *Ind Mag Hist*, XLIII (1947), 307-328.

2428 D'ELIA, Donald J. "Dr. Benjamin Rush and the American Medical Revolution." *Proc Am Phil Soc,* CX (1966), 227-234.

2429 DUFFY, John. "An Account of the Epidemic Fever that Prevailed in the City of New York from 1791 to 1822." *N Y Hist Soc Q*, L (1966), 333-364.

2430 DUFFY, John. "Eighteenth-Century Carolina Health Condition." *J S Hist,* XVIII (1952), 289-302.

2431 DUFFY, John. *A History of Public Health in New York City, 1625-1866*. New York, 1968.

2432 DUFFY, John. "Hogs, Dogs, and Dirt: Public Health in Early Pittsburgh." *Pa Mag Hist Biog,* LXXXVII (1963), 294-305.

2433 EATON, Leonard K. *New England Hospitals 1790-1833*. Ann Arbor, Mich., 1957.

2434 FLEXNER, James T. *Doctors on Horseback: Pioneers of American Medicine*. New York, 1937.†

2435 HOWARD, William T. *Public Health Administration and the Natural History of Disease in Baltimore, Maryland, 1797-1920*. Washington, D.C., 1924.

2436 JONES, Thomas B. "Calvin Jones, M.D.: A Case Study in the Practice of Early American Medicine." *N C Hist Rev*, XLIX (1972), 56-71.

2437 KETT, Joseph F. *The Formation of the American Medical Profession: The Role of Institutions, 1780-1860.* New Haven, Conn., 1968.

2438 LONG, Esmond R. *A History of American Pathology.* Springfield, Ill., 1962.†

2439 MOORE, Thomas E. Jr., "The Early Years of the Harvard Medical School: Its Founding and Curriculum, 1782-1810." *Bull Hist Med*, XXVII (1953), 530-561.

2440 NORWOOD, William F. *Medical Education in the United States before the Civil War.* Philadelphia, 1944.

2441 O'CONNER, Stella. "The Charity Hospital at New Orleans: An Administrative and Financial History, 1736-1791." *La Hist Q*, XXI (1948), 1-109.

2442 POWELL, John H. *Bring Out Your Dead! The Great Plague of Yellow Fever in 1793.* Philadelphia, 1949.

2443 RANSOM, John E. "The Beginnings of Hospitals in the United States." *Bull Hist Med*, XIII (1943), 514-539.

2444 ROBINSON, G. Canby. "Malaria in Virginia in the Early Nineteenth Century." *Bull Hist Med*, XXXII (1958), 531-536.

2445 SHAFER, Henry Burnell. *The American Medical Profession 1783 to 1850.* New York, 1936.

2446 SHRYOCK, Richard H. *American Medical Research, Past and Present.* New York, 1947.

2447 SHRYOCK, Richard H. "Eighteenth Century Medicine in America." *Proc Am Ant Soc*, LIX (1949), 275-292.

2448 SHRYOCK, Richard H. *The History of Nursing.* Philadelphia, 1959.

2449 SHRYOCK, Richard H. *Medical Licensing in America, 1650-1965.* Baltimore, Md., 1967.

2450 SHRYOCK, Richard H. *Medicine and Society in America, 1660-1860.* New York, 1960.†

2451 SMILLIE, Wilson G. *Public Health: Its Promise for the Future. A Chronicle of the Development of Public Health in the United States, 1607-1914.* New York, 1955.

2452 STEARN, E. Wagner, and Allen E. STEARN. *The Effect of Smallpox on the Destiny of the American Indian.* See 1570.

2453 STOOKEY, Byron. *A History of Colonial Medical Education: In the Province of New York, with its Subsequent Development (1767-1830).* Springfield, Ill., 1962.

2454 THOMS, Herbert. *The Doctors at Yale College 1702-1815 and the Founding of the Medical Institution.* Hamden, Conn., 1960.

2455 WAITE, Frederick C. "The Professional Education of Pioneer Ohio Physicians." *Ohio Arch Hist Q*, XLVIII (1939), 189-197.

2456 WARING, Joseph I. *A History of Medicine in South Carolina, 1670-1825.* Columbia, S.C., 1964.

2457 WILLIAMS, Ralph C. *The United States Public Health Service, 1798-1950*. See 1013.

Women and Women's Rights

2458 BEARD, Mary. *Woman as Force in History: A Study in Traditions and Realities*. New York, 1946.

2459 BENSON, Mary S. *Women in Eighteenth Century America: A Study of Opinion and Social Usage*. New York, 1935.

2460 COTT, Nancy F., ed. *Root of Bitterness: Documents of the Social History of American Women*. New York, 1972.

2461 DEXTER, Elizabeth Anthony. *Career Women of America, 1776-1840*. Francestown, N.H., 1950.

2462 DITZION, Sidney H. *Marriage, Morals, and Sex in America: A History of Ideas*. New York, 1953.

2463 HECKER, Eugene Arthur. *A Short History of Women's Rights from the Days of Augustus to the Present Time with Special Reference to England and the United States*. New York, 1910.

2464 JAMES, Edward T., and Janet W. JAMES, eds. *Notable American Women, 1607-1950: A Biographical Dictionary*. 3 vols. Cambridge, Mass., 1971.

2465 KRADITOR, Aileen S., ed. *Up from the Pedestal: Selected Writings in the History of American Feminism*. Chicago, 1968.†

2466 MACLEAR, Martha. *The History of the Education of Girls in New York and New England, 1800-1870*. Washington, D.C., 1926.

2467 MELDER, Keith. "Ladies Bountiful: Organized Women's Benevolence in Early 19th Century America." See 2377.

2468 RIEGEL, Robert E. "Changing American Attitudes toward Prostitution (1800-1920)." *J Hist Ideas*, XXIX (1968), 437-452.

2469 SMITH, Thelma M. "Feminism in Philadelphia, 1790-1850." *Pa Mag Hist Biog*, LXVIII (1944), 243-268.

2470 STRAUB, Jean S. "Benjamin Rush's Views on Women's Education." *Pa Hist*, XXXIV (1967), 147-157.

2471 TREUDLEY, Mary B. "The 'Benevolent Fair': A Study of Charitable Organizations among American Women in the First Third of the Nineteenth Century." See 2384.

2472 WELTER, Barbara. "Anti-Intellectualism and the American Woman: 1800-1860." *Mid-Am*, XLVIII (1966), 258-270.

2473 WOODY, Thomas. *A History of Women's Education in the United States*. 2 vols. Lancaster, Pa., 1929.

Communitarian Societies

2474 ANDREWS, Edward D. *The People Called Shakers: A Search for the Perfect Society.* See 2142.

2475 ARNDT, Karl J. R. *George Rapp's Harmony Society, 1785-1847.* Philadelphia, 1965.

2476 BESTOR, Arthur Eugene, Jr. *Backwoods Utopias: The Sectarian and Owenite Phases of Communitarian Socialism in America: 1663-1829.* Philadelphia, 1965.

2477 HINDS, William A. *American Communities and Co-operative Colonies.* 2d ed. Chicago, 1908.†

2478 HOLLOWAY, Mark. *Heavens on Earth: Utopian Communities in America, 1680-1880.* New York, 1951.†

2479 KRAUS, Michael. "America and the Utopian Ideal in the Eighteenth Century." *Miss Val Hist Rev,* XXII (1936), 487-504.

2480 WEBBER, Everett. *Escape to Utopia: The Communal Movement in America.* New York, 1959.

Pacifism

2481 BROCK, Peter. *Pacificism in the United States: From the Colonial Era to the First World War.* Princeton, N.J., 1968.† Paperback ed. title *Radical Pacifists in Antebellum America.*

2482 CURTI, Merle. *Peace or War: The American Struggle 1636-1936,* New York, 1936.

2483 GALPIN, W. Freeman. *Pioneering for Peace: A Study of American Peace Efforts to 1846.* Syracuse, N.Y., 1933.

2484 HAMILTON, J. G. de Roulhac. "The Pacifism of Thomas Jefferson." *Va Q Rev,* XXXI (1955), 607-620.

2485 SCHLISSEL, Lillian, ed. *Conscience in America: A Documentary History of Conscientious Objection in America, 1757-1967.* New York, 1968.†

3. The Quality of Life

Manners, Customs, Recreation

2486 ATHERTON, Lewis E. *The Southern Country Store, 1800-1860.* Baton Rouge, La., 1949.

2487 BALTZELL, E. Digby. *Philadelphia Gentlemen: The Making of a National Upper Class.* Glencoe, Ill., 1958.†

2488 BELL, Whitfield J., Jr. "Some Aspects of the Social History of Pennsylvania, 1760-1790." *Pa Mag Hist Biog,* LXII (1939), 281-308.

2489   BLAIR, Walter. *Native American Humor (1800-1900)*. New York, 1931.†

2490   BOATRIGHT, Mody C. *Folk Laughter on the American Frontier*. New York, 1949.†

2491   BROWN, Ralph Hall. *Mirror for Americans: Likeness of the Eastern Seaboard, 1810*. New York, 1943.

2492   CADY, Edwin H. *The Gentleman in America: A Literary Study in American Culture*. Syracuse, N.Y., 1949.

2493   CALHOUN, Daniel H. *Professional Lives in America: Structure and Aspirations, 1750-1850*. See 1256.

2494   CAMPBELL, John C. *The Southern Highlander and His Homeland*. New York, 1921.

2495   CARSON, Gerald. *The Old Country Store*. New York, 1954.†

2496   CARSON, Jane. *Colonial Virginia Cookery*. Williamsburg, Va., 1968.

2497   CLARK, Thomas D. *The Rampaging Frontier: Manners and Humors of Pioneer Days in the South and Middle West*. Indianapolis, 1939.

2498   COLEMAN, John Winston, Jr. *Famous Kentucky Duels: The Story of the Code of Honor in the Bluegrass State*. Frankfort, Ky., 1953.

2499   COLEMAN, J. Winston, Jr. *Stage-Coach Days in the Bluegrass: Being an Account of Stagecoach Travel and Tavern Days in Lexington and Central Kentucky, 1800-1900*. Louisville, Ky., 1935.

2500   COLEMAN, Kenneth. "Social Life in Georgia in the 1780's." *Ga Rev*, IX (1955), 217-227.

2501   CREVECOEUR, Michael G. St. John de. *Letters from an American Farmer*. 1782. New York, 1961.†

2502   CREVECOEUR, Michael G. St. John de. *Sketches of Eighteenth-Century America: More Letters from an American Farmer*. Ed. Henri L. Bourdain, Ralph H. Gabriel, and Stanley T. Williams. New Haven, Conn., 1925.†

2503   CUMMINGS, Richard O. *The American and His Food: A History of Food Habits in the United States*. Rev. ed. Chicago, 1941.

2504   CUTLER, James Elbert. *Lynch-Law: An Investigation into the History of Lynching in the United States*. See 2287.

2505   DALE, Edward D. "Culture on the Frontier." *Neb Hist*, XXVI (1945), 75-90.

2506   DORSON, Richard M. *American Folklore*. Chicago, 1959.†

2507   DULLES, Foster Rhea. *America Learns to Play: A History of Popular Recreation, 1607-1940*. New York, 1940.†

2508   DWIGHT, Timothy. *Travels in New England and New York*. 4 vols. Ed. Barbara Miller Solomon with assistance of Patricia M. King. Cambridge, England, 1969.

2509   EARLE, Alice M. *Two Centuries of Costume in America, MDCXX-MDCCCX*. 2 vols. New York, 1903.

2510   EVANS, Meryle R. "Knickerbocker Hotels and Restaurants, 1800-1850." *N Y Hist Soc Q*, XXXVI (1952), 377-410.

2511 EZELL, John S. *Fortune's Merry Wheel: The Lottery in America.* Cambridge, Mass., 1960.

2512 GAMBLE, Thomas. *Savannah Duels and Duellists, 1733-1877.* Savannah, Ga., 1923.

2513 GOODMAN, Paul. "Ethics and Enterprise: The Values of a Boston Elite, 1800-1860." See 1271.

2514 GOODSPEED, Charles E. *Angling in America: Its Early History and Literature.* Boston, 1939.

2515 HAYNES, Robert V. "Law Enforcement in Frontier Mississippi." See 2408.

2516 HOLLIMAN, Jennie. *American Sports (1785-1835).* Durham, N.C., 1931.

2517 JANSON, Charles William. *The Stranger in America.* 1807. New York, 1935.

2518 LUDLUM, David M. *Early American Hurricanes, 1492-1870. The History of American Weather.* Boston, 1963.†

2519 LUDLUM, David M. *Early American Winters, 1604-1820.* Boston, 1966.

2520 McCLELLAN, Elisabeth. *History of American Costume, 1607-1870.* New York, 1937.

2521 MANCHESTER, Herbert. *Four Centuries of Sport in America, 1490-1890.* New York, 1931.

2522 MODLIN, Charles E. "Aristocracy in the Early Republic." *Early Am Lit*, VI (1972), 252-257.

2523 MOREAU DE SAINT MÉRY, Médéric Louis Elie. *Moreau de St.-Méry's American Journey, 1793-1798.* Garden City, N.Y., 1947.

2524 MORGAN, Helen M., ed. *A Season in New York, 1801: Letters of Harriet and Maria Trumbull.* Pittsburgh, Pa., 1969.

2525 NYE, Russel Blaine. *The Cultural Life of the New Nation: 1776-1830.* New York, 1960.†

2526 QUINCY, Josiah. *Figures of the Past from the Leaves of Old Journals, Illustrated from Old Prints and Photographs.* Ed. M. A. DeWolfe Howe. Boston, 1926.

2527 ROGERS, George C., Jr. *Charleston in the Age of the Pinckneys.* Norman, Okla., 1969.

2528 SCHMIDT, Albert J. "Applying Old World Habits to the New: Life in South Carolina at the Turn of the Eighteenth Century." *Huntington Lib Q*, XXV (1961), 61-68.

2529 SHRYOCK, Richard H. "Cultural Factors in the History of the South." *J S Hist*, V (1939), 333-346.

2530 SIMMONS, Amelia. *American Cookery.* (Facsimile of 1st ed. 1796, with an essay by Mary Tolford Wilson.) New York, 1958.

2531 STEVENS, William Oliver. *Pistols at Ten Paces: The Story of the Code of Honor in America.* Cambridge, Mass., 1940.

2532 TANSILL, Charles C. *The Secret Loves of the Founding Fathers: The Romantic Side of George Washington, Thomas Jefferson, Benjamin Franklin, Gouverneur Morris, and Alexander Hamilton.* New York, 1964.

2533 TYLER, Alice Felt. *Freedom's Ferment: Phases of American Social History from the Colonial Period to the Outbreak of the Civil War.* Minneapolis, Minn., 1944.

2534 WECTER, Dixon. *The Saga of American Society: A Record of Social Aspiration, 1608-1937.* See 1296.

2535 WHARTON, Anne. *Social Life in the Early Republic.* See 571.

2536 WISH, Harvey. *Society and Thought in Early America.* See 1298.

2537 WOODWARD, W. E. *The Way Our People Lived.* New York, 1944.

2538 WRIGHT, Richardson. *Hawkers & Walkers in Early America, Strolling Peddlers, Preachers, Lawyers, Doctors, Players, and Others, from the Beginning to the Civil War.* Philadelphia, 1927.

2539 YODER, Paton. "Private Hospitality in the South, 1775-1850." *Miss Val Hist Rev*, XLVII (1960), 419-433.

Family and Children

2540 CALHOUN, Arthur W. *A Social History of the American Family from Colonial Times to the Present.* 3 vols. Cleveland, Ohio, 1917-1919.

2541 FLEMING, Sanford. *Children and Puritanism: The Place of Children in the Life and Thought of the New England Churches, 1620-1847.* New Haven, Conn., 1933.

2542 FRAZIER, Edward Franklin. *The Free Negro Family: A Study of Family Origins before the Civil War.* See 2242.

2543 FRAZIER, Edward Franklin. *The Negro Family in the United States.* See 2266.

2544 GOODSELL, Willystine. *A History of Marriage and the Family.* Rev. ed. New York, 1934.

2545 HANDLIN, Oscar, and Mary F. HANDLIN. *Facing Life: Youth and Family in American History.* Boston, 1971.

2546 HOMAN, Walter J. *Children and Quakerism: A Study of the Place of Children in the Theory and Practice of the Society of Friends.* Berkeley, Cal., 1939.

2547 JACOBY, George P. *Catholic Child Care in Nineteenth Century New York: With a Correlated Summary of Public and Protestant Child Welfare.* Washington, D.C., 1941.

2548 JOHNSON, Guion G. "Courtship and Marriage Customs in Ante-Bellum North Carolina." *N C Hist Rev*, VIII (1931), 384-402.

2549 KIEFER, Monica M. *American Children through Their Books, 1700-1835.* Philadelphia, 1948.

2550 MORGAN, Edmund S. *Virginians at Home: Family Life in the Eighteenth Century.* Williamsburg, Va., 1952.†

2551 O'BRIEN, Edward J. *Child Welfare Legislation in Maryland, 1634-1936.* See 2380.

2552 WISHY, Bernard. *The Child and the Republic: The Dawn of Modern American Child Nurture.* Philadelphia, 1968.

4. Education

General

2553 BREWER, Clifton H. *A History of Religious Education in the Episcopal Church to 1835.* New Haven, Conn., 1924.

2554 BURNS, James A., and Bernard J. KOHLBRENNER. *A History of Catholic Education in the United States.* New York, 1937.

2555 CONANT, James Bryant. *Thomas Jefferson and the Development of American Public Education.* Berkeley and Los Angeles, 1962.

2556 COON, Charles L., ed. *The Beginnings of Public Education in North Carolina: A Documentary History 1790-1840.* Raleigh, N.C., 1908.

2557 CURTI, Merle. *The Social Ideals of American Educators.* 1935. Rev. ed. Totowa, N.J., 1968.†

2558 EDWARDS, Newton, and Herman G. RICHEY. *The School in the American Social Order: The Dynamics of American Education.* Boston, 1947.

2559 GREENE, Evarts B. "Some Educational Values of the American Revolution." *Proc Am Phil Soc,* LXVIII (1929),185-194.

2560 HANSEN, Allen O. *Liberalism and American Education in the Eighteenth Century.* New York, 1926.

2561 HOBSON, Elsie G. *Educational Legislation and Administration in the State of New York from 1777 to 1850.* Chicago, 1918.

2562 HOFSTADTER, Richard, and Walter P. METZGER. *The Development of Academic Freedom in the United States.* New York, 1955.†

2563 KNIGHT, Edgar W., ed. *A Documentary History of Education in the South before 1860.* 5 vols. Chapel Hill, N.C., 1949-1953.

2564 KURITZ, Hyman. "Benjamin Rush: His Theory of Republican Education." *Hist Educ Q,* VII (1967), 432-451.

2565 MOFFAT, Charles H. "Jefferson's Sectional Motives in Founding the University of Virginia." *W Va Hist,* XII (1950), 61-69.

2566 MOHL, Raymond A. "Education as Social Control in New York City, 1784-1825." *N Y Hist,* LI (1970), 219-237.

2567 MONROE, Paul. *Founding of the American Public School System: A History of Education in the United States, from the Early Settlements to the Close of the Civil War Period.* New York, 1940.

2568 REINHOLD, Meyer. "Opponents of Classical Learning in America during the Revolutionary Period." *Proc Am Phil Soc,* CXII (1968), 221-234.

2569 RUDOLPH, Frederick, ed. *Essays on Education in the Early Republic.* Cambridge, Mass., 1965.

2570 WARFEL, Harry R. *Noah Webster: Schoolmaster to America*. New York, 1936.

Primary and Secondary

2571 CHARMS, Richard de, and Gerald H. MOELLER. "Values Expressed in American Children's Readers, 1800-1950." *J Abnormal Soc Psych*, LXIV (1962), 136-142.

2572 CURRAN, Francis X. *The Churches and the Schools: American Protestantism and Popular Elementary Education*. Chicago, 1954.

2573 DUNN, William K. *What Happened to Religious Education? The Decline of Religious Teaching in the Public Elementary School, 1776-1861*. Baltimore, Md., 1958.

2574 ENGLAND, J. Merton. "The Democratic Faith in American Schoolbooks, 1783-1860." *Am Q*, XV (1963), 191-199.

2575 FELL, Sister Marie Leonore. *The Foundations of Nativism in American Textbooks, 1783-1860*. Washington, D.C., 1941.

2576 GARFINKLE, Norton. "Conservatism in American Textbooks, 1800-1860." *N Y Hist*, XXXV (1954), 49-63.

2577 GOEBEL, Edmund J. *A Study of Catholic Secondary Education during the Colonial Period up to the First Plenary Council of Baltimore, 1852*. New York, 1937.

2578 GRIZZELL, Emit Duncan. *Origin and Development of the High School in New England before 1865*. Philadelphia, 1923.

2579 HOLTZ, Adrian A. *A Study of the Moral and Religious Elements in American Secondary Education up to 1800*. Menasha, Wis., 1917.

2580 KIEFER, Monica M. *American Children through Their Books, 1700-1835*. See 2549.

2581 MIDDLEKAUF, Robert. *Ancients and Axioms: Secondary Education in Eighteenth-Century New England*. New Haven, Conn., 1963.

2582 NIETZ, John A. *Old Textbooks: Spelling, Grammar, Reading, Arithmetic, Geography, American History, Civil Government, Physiology, Penmanship, Art, Music–As Taught in the Common Schools from Colonial Days to 1900*. Pittsburgh, Pa., 1961.

2583 ROSENBACH, Abraham S. W. *Early American Children's Books*. Portland, Me., 1933.

2584 SMITH, Timothy L. "Protestant Schooling and American Nationality, 1800-1850." *J Amer Hist*, LIII (1967), 679-695.

2585 WELTER, Rush. *Popular Education and Democratic Thought in America*. New York, 1962.†

College

2586 BRODERICK, Francis L. "Pulpit, Physics, and Politics: The Curriculum of the College of New Jersey, 1746-1794." *Wm Mar Q*, VI, 3d ser. (1949), 42-68.

2587 BRONSON, Walter C. *The History of Brown University, 1764-1914*. Providence, R.I., 1914.

2588 CARRELL, William D. "American College Professors: 1750-1800." *Hist Educ Q*, VIII (1968), 289-305.

2589 CASSIDY, Francis P. *Catholic College Foundations and Development in the United States (1677-1850)*. Washington, D.C., 1924.

2590 CHEYNEY, Edward P. *History of the University of Pennsylvania, 1740-1940*. Philadelphia, 1940.

2591 COLLINS, Varnum L. *President Witherspoon, 1723-1794*. 2 vols. Princeton, N.J., 1925.

2592 COME, Donald R. "The Influence of Princeton on Hiher ducation in the South before 1825." *Wm Mar Q*, II, 3d ser. (1945), 352-396.

2593 COULTER, Ellis M. *College Life in the Old South*. New York, 1928.

2594 CURTIS, Charles P. "Liquor and Learning in Harvard College, 1766-1924." *N Eng Q*, XXV (1952), 344-353.

2595 DEMAREST, William H. S. *A History of Rutgers College, 1766-1924*. New Brunswick, N.J., 1924.

2596 EASTERBY, James Harold. *A History of the College of Charleston, Founded 1770*. Charleston, S.C., 1935.

2597 GABRIEL, Ralph H. *Religion and Learning at Yale: The Church of Christ in the College and University, 1757-1957*. New Haven, Conn., 1958.

2598 HADDOW, Anna. *Political Science in American Colleges and Universities, 1636-1900*. New York, 1939.

2599 HOFSTADTER, Richard, and C. DeWitt HARDY. *The Development and Scope of Higher Education in the United States*. New York, 1952.

2600 MADSEN, David. *The National University: Enduring Dream of the USA*. Detroit, Mich., 1966.

2601 MIDDLEKAUF, Robert. "A Persistent Tradition: The Classical Curriculum in Eighteenth Century New England." *Wm Mar Q*, XVIII, 3d ser. (1961), 54-67.

2602 MORISON, Samuel Eliot. *Three Centuries of Harvard, 1636-1936*. Cambridge, Mass., 1936.

2603 PAULSTON, Roland G. "French Influence in American Institutions of Higher Learning, 1784-1825." See 1363.

2604 RICHARDSON, Leon B. *History of Dartmouth College*. 2 vols. Hanover, N.H., 1932.

2605 RUDOLPH, Frederick. *The American College and University: A History*. New York, 1962.†

2606 TEWKESBURY, Donald G. *The Founding of American Colleges and Universities before the Civil War*. New York, 1932.

2607 TYLER, Lyon G. *The College of William and Mary in Virginia: Its History and Work*. Richmond, Va., 1907.

2608 WERTENBAKER, Thomas J. *Princeton, 1746-1896*. Princeton, N.J., 1946.

2609 YOUNG, Edward J. "Subjects for Master's Degrees in Harvard College from 1655 to 1791." *Proc Mass Hist Soc*, XVIII (1880-1881), 119-151.

VIII. Science and the Arts

1. Natural Science and Mathematics

2610 BEDINI, Silvie A. *Early American Scientific Instruments and Their Makers*. Washington, D.C., 1964.

2611 BELL, Whitfield J., Jr. "Astronomical Observatories of the American Philosophical Society, 1769-1843." *Proc Am Phil Soc*, CVIII (1964), 7-14.

2612 BELL, Whitfield J., Jr. *Early American Science: Needs and Opportunities for Study*. Chapel Hill, N.C., 1955.

2613 BELL, Whitfield J., Jr. "The Scientific Environment of Philadelphia, 1775-1790." *Proc Am Phil Soc*, XCII (1948), 6-14.

2614 BRASCH, Frederick E. *The Royal Society of London and Its Influence upon Scientific Thought in America*. Washington, D.C., 1931.

2615 COHEN, I. Bernard. "The Beginning of Chemical Instruction in America: A Brief Account of the Teaching of Chemistry at Harvard Prior to 1800." *Chym*, III (1950), 17-44.

2616 COHEN, I. Bernard. "Science and the Revolution." *Tech Rev*, XXVIII (1945), 76-85.

2617 COHEN, I. Bernard. *Some Early Tools of American Science: An Account of the Early Scientific Instruments and Minerological and Biological Collections in Harvard University*. Cambridge, Mass., 1950.

2618 CUTRIGHT, Paul Russell. *Lewis and Clark: Pioneering Naturalists*. Urbana, Ill., 1969.

2619 EARNEST, Ernest. *John and William Bartram, Botanists and Explorers, 1699-1777, 1739-1823*. Philadelphia, 1940.

2620 FÄY, Bernard. "Learned Societies in Europe and America in the Eighteenth Century." *Am Hist Rev*, XXXVII (1932), 255-266.

2621 GEISER, Samuel Wood. *Naturalists of the Frontier*. Dallas, Tex., 1937.

2622 GREENE, John C. "American Science Comes of Age, 1780-1820." *J Amer Hist*, LV (1969), 22-41.

2623 HALL, Courtney R. *Samuel Latham Mitchell: A Scientist in the Early Republic, 1764-1831*. New York, 1934.

2624 HINDLE, Brooke. *David Rittenhouse*. Princeton, N.J., 1964.

2625 HINDLE, Brooke. *The Pursuit of Science in Revolutionary America, 1735-1789*. Chapel Hill, N.C., 1956.†

2626 HINDLE, Brooke. *Technology in Early America: Needs and Opportunities for Study with a Directory of Artifact Collections by Lucius F. Ellsworth*. Chapel Hill, N.C., 1966.†

2627 HINDLE, Brooke. "Witherspoon, Rittenhouse, and Sir Isaac Newton." *Wm Mar Q*, XV, 3d ser. (1958), 365-372.

2628 HORNBERGER, Theodore. *Scientific Thought in American Colleges 1638-1800*. Austin, Tex., 1945.

2629 JELLISON, Richard M. "Scientific Enquiry in Eighteenth Century Virginia." *Hist*, XXV (1963), 292-311.

2630 KERBER, Linda K. "Science in the Early Republic: The Society for the Study of Natural Philosophy." *Wm Mar Q*, XXIX, 3d ser. (1972), 263-280.

2631 KRAUS, Michael. "Scientific Relations between America and Europe in the Eighteenth Century." *Sci Mo*, LV (1942), 259-272.

2632 McKEEHAN, Louis W. *Yale Science: The First Hundred Years, 1701-1801*. New York, 1947.

2633 MARTIN, Edwin T. *Thomas Jefferson: Scientist*. New York, 1952.

2634 MERRILL, George Perkins. *The First Hundred Years of American Geology*. New Haven, Conn., 1924.

2635 OLIVER, J. W. "Science and the Founding Fathers." *Sci Mo*, XLVIII (1939), 256-260.

2636 SMITH, David Eugene, and Jekuthiel GINSBERG. *A History of Mathematics in the United States before 1900*. Chicago, 1934.

2637 SMITH, Edgar Fahs. *Chemistry in Old Philadelphia*. Philadelphia, 1919.

2638 STRUIK, Dirk J. *Yankee Science in the Making*. Boston, 1948.

2639 TERRA, Helmut de. "Alexander von Humboldt's Correspondence with Jefferson, Madison, and Gallatin." *Proc Am Phil Soc*, CIII (1959), 783-806.

2640 WHITFORD, Kathryn, and Philip WHITFORD. "Timothy Dwight's Place in Eighteenth Century American Science." *Proc Am Phil Soc*, CXIV (1970), 60-71.

2641 WILKINSON, Norman B. *E. I. duPont, Botaniste: The Beginning of a Tradition*. Charlottesville, Va., 1972.

2642 WOOLF, Harry. *The Transit of Venus: A Study of Eighteenth-Century Science*. Princeton, N.J., 1959.

2643 YOUNG, Robert Thompson. *Biology in America*. Boston, 1922.

2. *Literature*

2644 BOAS, Ralph Philip, and Katherine BURTON. *Social Backgrounds of American Literature*. Boston, 1937.

2645 BROOKS, Van Wyck. *The World of Washington Irving*. New York, 1945.

2646 BROWN, Esther E. *The French Revolution and the American Man of Letters*. See 1348.

2647 BROWN, Herbert. *The Sentimental Novel in America, 1798-1860*. Durham, N.C., 1940.

2648 CALLOW, James T. *Kindred Spirits: Knickerbocker Writers and American Artists 1807-1855*. Chapel Hill, N.C., 1967.

2649 CHARVAT, William. *Literary Publishing in America, 1790-1850*. Philadelphia, 1959.

2650 CLARK, David Lee. *Charles Brockden Brown: Pioneer Voice of America*. Durham, N.C., 1952.

2651 COWIE, Alexander. *John Trumbull: Connecticut Wit*. Chapel Hill, N.C., 1936.

2652 COWIE, Alexander. *The Rise of the American Novel*. New York, 1948.

2653 DUNLAP, George Arthur. *The City in the American Novel, 1789-1900*. Philadelphia, 1934.

2654 HEMENWAY, Robert. "Fiction in the Age of Jefferson: The Early American Novel as Intellectual Document." *Midcont Am Stud J*, IX (1968), 91-101.

2655 HOWARD, Leon. *The Connecticut Wits*. Chicago, 1943.

2656 HOWARD, Leon. "The Late Eighteenth Century: An Age of Contradiction." *Transitions in American Literary History*. Ed. Harry Hayden Clark, Durham, N.C., 1954.

2657 HUBBELL, Jay B. *The South in American Literature, 1607-1900*. Durham, N.C., 1954.

2658 KRAUS, Michael. "Literary Relations between Europe and America in the Eighteenth Century." *Wm Mar Q*, I, 3d ser. (1944), 210-234.

2659 McILWAIN, Shields. *The Southern Poor White from Lubberland to Tobacco Road*. Norman, Okla., 1939.

2660 MARTIN, John S. "Rhetoric, Society and Literature in the Age of Jefferson." *Midcont Am Stud J*, IX (1968), 77-101.

2661 MARTIN, Terence John. *The Instructed Vision: Scottish Common Philosophy and the Origins of American Fiction*. Bloomington, Ind., 1961.

2662 MOTT, Frank Luther. *Golden Multitudes: The Story of Best Sellers in the United States*. New York, 1947.

2663 NEWLIN, Claude M. *The Life and Writings of Hugh Henry Brackenridge*. Princeton, N.J., 1932.

2664 PARRINGTON, Vernon L. *The Connecticut Wits*. New York, 1926.

2665 PARRINGTON, Vernon Louis. *Main Currents in American Thought: An Interpretation of American Literature from the Beginnings to 1920.* 3 vols. New York, 1927-1930.†

2666 PATTEE, Fred Lewis. *The First Century of American Literature 1770-1870.* New York, 1935.

2667 QUINN, Arthur H. *The Establishment of National Literature.* New York, 1951.

2668 ROTH, George L. "Verse Satire on 'Faction,' 1790-1815." *Wm Mar Q*, XVII, 3d ser. (1960), 473-485.

2669 SIBLEY, Agnes M. *Alexander Pope's Prestige in America, 1725-1835.* New York, 1949.

2670 SILVERMAN, Kenneth. *Timothy Dwight.* New York, 1969.

2671 SIMPSON, Lewis P., ed. *The Federalist Literary Mind: Selections from the Monthly Anthology and Boston Review, 1803-1811, Including Documents Relating to the Boston Athenaeum.* Baton Rouge, La., 1962.

2672 SPENCER, Benjamin T. *The Quest for Nationality.* See 1292.

2673 SPILLER, Robert Ernest, ed. *The American Literary Revolution, 1783-1837.* New York, 1967.

2674 SPILLER, Robert E., et al., eds. *Literary History of the United States.* See 21.

2675 WARFEL, Harry Redclay. *Charles Brockden Brown, American Gothic Novelist.* Gainesville, Fla., 1949.

2676 WELLEK, René. *A History of Modern Criticism, 1750-1950.* 4 vols. New Haven, Conn., 1955-1965.

2677 WHITTLE, Amberys R. "Modern Chivalry: The Frontier as Crucible." *Early Am Lit*, VI (1972), 263-270.

2678 WRIGHT, Lyle H. "A Statistical Survey of American Fiction, 1774-1850." *Huntington Lib Q*, II (1939), 309-318.

3. *Journalism*

2679 AMES, William E. *A History of the National Intelligencer.* Chapel Hill, N.C., 1972.

2680 BAUMGARTNER, Appolinaris W. *Catholic Journalism: A Study of Its Development in the United States, 1789-1930.* See 2169.

2681 BRIGHAM, Clarence S. *History and Bibliography of American Newspapers, 1690-1820.* 2 vols. Worcester, Mass., 1947.

2682 BRIGHAM, Clarence S. *Journals and Journeymen: A Contribution to the History of Early American Newspapers.* Philadelphia, 1950.

2683 ELLIOTT, Robert N., Jr. *The Raleigh Register, 1799-1863.* Chapel Hill, N.C., 1955.†

2684 FORSYTH, David P. *The Business Press in America, 1750-1865.* Philadelphia, 1964.

2685 HAMILTON, Milton W. *The Country Printer, New York State, 1785-1830.* New York, 1936.

2686 HART, Jim. *The Developing Views on the News, Editorial Syndrome, 1500-1800.* Carbondale, Ill., 1970.

2687 LEE, Alfred M. *The Daily Newspaper in America: The Evolution of a Social Instrument.* New York, 1937.

2688 LEHMANN-HAUPT, Hellmut, Lawrence C. WROTH, and Rollo G. SILVER. *The Book in America: A History of the Making and Selling of Books in the United States.* 2d ed. New York, 1951.

2689 LYON, William H. *The Pioneer Editor in Missouri, 1808-1860.* Columbia, Mo., 1965.

2690 McMURTRIE, Douglas C. *A History of Printing in the United States: The Story of the Introduction of the Press and of Its History and Influence during the Pioneer Period in Each State of the Union.* New York, 1936.

2691 MOTT, Frank L. *American Journalism: A History, 1690-1960.* 3d ed. New York, 1962.

2692 MOTT, Frank L. *A History of American Magazines, 1741-1905.* Vol. I: *1741-1850.* New York, 1930.

2693 MOTT, Frank L. *Jefferson and the Press.* Baton Rouge, La., 1943.

2694 POLLARD, James Edward. *The Presidents and the Press.* See 993.

2695 RICHARDSON, Lyon N. *A History of Early American Magazines, 1741-1789.* New York, 1931.

2696 RINK, Evald. *Printing in Delaware 1761-1800.* Wilmington, Del., 1969.

2697 SHIPTON, Clifford Kenyon. *Isaiah Thomas, Printer, Patriot and Philanthropist, 1749-1831.* Rochester, N.Y., 1948.

2698 SILVER, Rollo G. *The American Printer, 1787-1825.* Charlottesville, Va., 1967.

2699 SILVER, Rollo G. *Typefounding in America, 1787-1825.* Charlottesville, Va., 1965.

2700 STEWART, Donald H. *The Opposition Press of the Federalist Period.* See 479.

2701 THOMAS, Isaiah. *History of Printing in America, with a Biography of Printers.* 2 vols. 2d ed. Albany, N.Y., 1874.

2702 WITTKE, Carl F. *The German-Language Press in America.* Lexington, Ky., 1957.

4. The Arts

General

2703 BERMAN, Eleanor Davidson. *Thomas Jefferson among the Arts: An Essay in Early American Esthetics*. New York, 1947.

2704 CANARY, Robert H. *William Dunlap*. New York, 1970.

2705 DICKSON, Harold E. *Arts of the Young Republic: The Age of William Dunlap*. Chapel Hill, N.C., 1968.

2706 GOWANS, Alan. *Images of American Living: Four Centuries of Architecture and Furniture as Cultural Expression*. New York, 1964.

2707 LARKIN, Oliver. *Art and Life in America*. New York, 1949.

2708 MILLER, Lillian B. *Patrons and Patriotism: The Encouragement of Fine Arts in America, 1790-1860*. Chicago, 1966.

2709 New York Museum of Modern Art. *American Folk Art: The Art of the Common Man, 1750-1900*. Ed. Holger Cahill. New York, 1932.

2710 WHITEHILL, Walter Muir. *The Arts in Early American History: Needs and Opportunities for Study, An Essay*. Chapel Hill, N.C., 1965.

Theater

2711 GRIMSTED, David. *Melodrama Unveiled: American Theatre and Culture, 1800-1850*. Chicago, 1968.

2712 HILL, West T., Jr. *The Theatre in Early Kentucky, 1790-1820*. Lexington, Ky., 1971.

2713 JAMES, Reese D. *Cradle of Culture: The Philadelphia Stage, 1800-1810*. Philadelphia, 1957.

2714 LeGARDEUR, René J., Jr. *The First New Orleans Theatre, 1792-1803*. New Orleans, La., 1963.

2715 McNAMARA, Brooks. *The American Playhouse in the Eighteenth Century*. Cambridge, Mass., 1969.

2716 MATES, Julian. *The American Musical Stage before 1800*. New Brunswick, N.J., 1962.

2717 ODELL, George C. D. *Annals of the American Stage*. 15 vols. New York, 1927-1949.

2718 QUINN, Arthur Hobson. *A History of American Drama from the Beginning to the Civil War*. Rev. ed. New York, 1943.

2719 SHOCKLEY, Martin Staples. "The Richmond Theatre, 1780-1790." *Va Mag Hist Biog*, LX (1952), 421-436.

2720 WATSON, Charles S. "Jeffersonian Republicanism in William Ioor's *Independence*, The First Play of South Carolina." *S C Hist Mag*, LXIX (1968), 194-203.

2721 WILLIS, Eola. *The Charleston Stage in the XVIII Century, with Social Settings of the Times*. Columbia, S.C., 1924.

Music

2722 CHASE, Gilbert. *America's Music: From the Piligrims to the Present*. New York, 1955.

2723 COFFIN, Tristram P. *The British Traditional Ballad in North America*. Rev. ed. Philadelphia, 1963.

2724 EBERLEIN, Harold D., and Cortlandt Van Dyke HUBBARD. "Music in the Early Federal Era." *Pa Mag Hist Biog*, LXIX (1945), 103-127.

2725 FOOTE, Henry Wilder. *Three Centuries of American Hymnody*. Cambridge, Mass., 1940.

2726 HASTINGS, George Everett. *The Life and Works of Francis Hopkinson*. 1926. New York, 1968.

2727 HITCHCOCK, H. Wiley. *Music in the United States: A Historical Introduction*. Englewood Cliffs, N.J., 1969.†

2728 HOWARD, John Tasker. *Our American Music: A Comprehensive History from 1620 to the Present*. 4th ed. New York, 1965.

2729 JOHNSON, H. Earle. *Musical Interludes in Boston, 1795-1830*. New York, 1943.

2730 KMEN, Henry A. *Music in New Orleans: The Formative Years, 1791-1841*. Baton Rouge, La., 1967.

2731 LAWS, George Malcolm. *Native American Balladry: A Descriptive Study and a Bibliographical Syllabus*. Philadelphia, 1950.

2732 MacDOUGALL, Hamilton C. *Early New England Psalmody: An Historical Appreciation, 1620-1820*. Brattleboro, Vt., 1940.

2733 SABLOSKY, Irving L. *American Music*. Chicago, 1969.†

2734 SEEGER, Charles. "Music and Class Structure in the United States." *Am Q*, IX (1957), 281-294.

2735 SMITH, Carleton S. "America in 1801-1825: The Musicians and the Music." *Bull NY Publ Lib*, LXVIII (1964), 483-492.

2736 SONNECK, Oscar George Theodore. *Early Concert-Life in America*. New York, 1949.

2737 SONNECK, Oscar George Theodore. *Early Opera in America*. New York, 1915.

2738 SONNECK, Oscar George Theodore. *Francis Hopkinson, the First American Poet-Composer (1737-1791) and James Lyon, Patriot, Preacher, Psalmodist (1735-1794)*. Washington, D.C., 1919.

2739 SPAETH, Sigmund. *A History of Popular Music in America*. New York, 1948.

Painting and Sculpture

2740 BLACK, Mary, and Jean LIPMAN. *American Folk Painting*. New York, 1966.

2741 BRIGGS, Berta N. *Charles Willson Peale, Artist and Patriot*. New York, 1952.

2742 CRAVEN, Wayne. *Sculpture in America: From the Colonial Period to the Present*. New York, 1968.

2743 FLEXNER, James Thomas. *American Painting: The Light of Distant Skies, 1760-1835*. New York, 1954.

2744 FLEXNER, James Thomas. *America's Old Masters: First Artists of the New World*. New York, 1939.†

2745 FLEXNER, James Thomas. *Gilbert Stuart: A Great Life in Brief*. New York, 1955.

2746 GARDNER, Albert Ten Eyck. *Yankee Stonecutters: The First American School of Sculpture 1800-1850*. New York, 1945.

2747 GLASER, Lynn. *Engraved America: Inconography of America through 1800*. Philadelphia, 1970.

2748 GOODRICH, Lloyd. "The Painting of American History: 1775-1900." *Am Q*, III (1951), 283-294.

2749 HAGEN, Oskar. *The Birth of the American Tradition in Art*. New York, 1940.

2750 HARRIS, Neil. *The Artist in American Society: The Formative Years, 1790-1860*. New York, 1966.

2751 ISHAM, Samuel. *The History of American Painting*. New ed. with supp. chaps. by Royal Cortissoz. New York, 1927.

2752 LIPMAN, Jean H., and Alice WINCHESTER. *Primitive Painters in America, 1750-1950: An Anthology*. New York, 1950.

2753 LUDWIG, Allen I. *Graven Images: New England Stonecarving and Its Symbols, 1650-1815*. Middletown, Conn., 1966.

2754 SELLERS, Charles Coleman. *Charles Willson Peale*. 2 vols. Philadelphia, 1947.

2755 SHADWELL, Wendy. *American Printmaking: The First 150 Years*. Washington, D.C., 1969.

2756 TAFT, Lorado. *A History of American Sculpture*. New York, 1930.

Architecture

2757 ANDREWS, Wayne. *Architecture, Ambition and Americans: A History of American Architecture from the Beginning to the Present*. New York, 1955.†

2758 BURCHARD, John, and Albert BUSH-BROWN. *The Architecture of America: A Social and Cultural History*. Boston, 1961.†

2759 CONDIT, Carl W. *American Building: Materials and Techniques from the First Colonial Settlements to the Present*. Chicago, 1968.

146 SCIENCE AND THE ARTS

2760 DORSEY, Stephen P. *Early English Churches in America, 1607-1807*. New York, 1952.

2761 EBERLEIN, Harold D., and Cortlandt HUBBARD. *American Georgian Architecture*. Bloomington, Ind., 1952.

2762 FORMAN, Henry Chandlee. *The Architecture of the Old South: The Medieval Style, 1585-1850*. Cambridge, Mass., 1948.

2763 FRARY, Itana Thayer. *Thomas Jefferson, Architect and Builder*. Intr. Sidney Fiske Kimball. Richmond, Va., 1931.

2764 HAMLIN, Talbot F. *Benjamin Henry Latrobe*. New York, 1955.

2765 JACKSON, Joseph. *The Development of American Architecture, 1783-1830*. Philadelphia, 1926.

2766 KIMBALL, Sidney Fiske. *Domestic Architecture of the American Colonies and of the Early Republic*. New York, 1922.

2767 KIRKER, Harold, and James KIRKER. *Bulfinch's Boston, 1787-1817*. New York, 1964.

2768 MORRISON, Hugh S. *Early American Architecture from the First Colonial Settlements to the National Period*. New York, 1952.

2769 MUMFORD, Lewis. *Sticks and Stones: A Study of American Architecture and Civilization*. 2d rev. ed. New York, 1955.†

2770 NEWCOMB, Rexford. *Architecture of the Old Northwest Territory: A Study of Early Architecture in Ohio, Indiana, Illinois, Michigan, Wisconsin, & Part of Minnesota*. Chicago, 1950.

Decorative Arts

2771 BREWINGTON, M. V. *Shipcarvers of North America*. Barre, Mass., 1962.

2772 DUNLAP, William. *History of the Arts of Design in the United States*. 1834. Reprinted as *A History of the Rise and Progress of the Arts of Design in the United States*. Eds. Frank W. Bayley and Charles E. Goodspeed. Boston, 1918.

2773 FLEMING, E. McClug. "Early American Decorative Arts as Social Documents." *Miss Val Hist Rev*, XLV (1958), 276-284.

2774 LANGDON, William C. *Everyday Things in American Life, 1606-1876*. 2 vols. New York, 1937-1941.

2775 LITTLE, Frances. *Early American Textiles*. New York, 1931.

2776 NAGEL, Charles. *American Furniture, 1650-1850: A Brief Background and an Illustrated History*. New York, 1949.

2777 PICKERING, Ernest. *The Homes of America, as They Have Expressed the Lives of Our People for Three Centuries*. New York, 1951.

2778 ROGERS, Meyric R. *American Interior Design: The Traditions and Development of Domestic Design from Colonial Times to the Present*. New York, 1947.

2779 SENN, T. L. "Farm and Garden: Landscape Architecture and Horticulture in Eighteenth-Century America." *Ag Hist*, XLIII (1969), 149-158.

NOTES

INDEX

INDEX

INDEX

INDEX

INDEX

INDEX

H

INDEX

INDEX

INDEX

M

INDEX

INDEX

S

170

INDEX

Goldentree
Bibliographies
in American
History

Under the series
editorship of
Arthur S. Link

PUBLISHED BY

Harlan
Davidson

A_____ g Corporation

DUE DATE